Canada and the New Constitution

The Unfinished Agenda

Canada and the New Constitution

The Unfinished Agenda

Edited by *STANLEY M. BECK*
and *IVAN BERNIER*

Volume Two

The Institute for Research on Public Policy

L'Institut de recherches politiques

Legal Deposit First Quarter
Bibliothèque nationale du Québec

The Institute for Research on Public Policy / L'Institut de recherches politiques
2149 Mackay Street
Montreal, Quebec H3G 2J2

Design: Robert Burgess Garbutt
Typesetting and Printing: Tri-Graphic Printing (Ottawa) Ltd.

Canadian Cataloguing in Publication Data
Main entry under title:
Canada and the new constitution

Includes some text in French.
ISBN 0-920380-73-5 (set). — ISBN 0-920380-75-1 (v. 1).
— ISBN 0-920380-77-8 (v. 2)

1. Canada — Constitutional law — Amendments —
Addresses, essays, lectures. I. Beck, Stanley M.
II. Bernier, Ivan   III. Institute for Research on
Public Policy

· JL27.C35   342.71'03   C82-090091-5

Acknowledgements

The authors and publishers wish to thank the Minister of Supply and Services Canada for permission to reproduce in this work *The Constitution Act, 1982/La Loi constitutionnelle de 1982.*

Remerciements

Les auteurs et les éditeurs tiennent à remercier le ministre des Approvisionnements et Services Canada pour l'autorisation de reproduire *La Loi constitutionnelle de 1982/The Constitution Act, 1982*.

Contents

Volume One

Contents

Volume Two

Energy and the Canadian Federation: Some Economic Aspects of Optional Constitutions

JOHN F. HELLIWELL
University of British Columbia

Contents

Energy and the Canadian Federation: Some Economic Aspects of Optional Constitutions

Introduction

This paper attempts an economic analysis of the interprovincial distribution of costs and benefits of Canadian crude oil and natural gas, given optional forms of the new Canadian Constitution. Four optional constitutions will be considered. The first analysis will review how energy costs and benefits might be distributed in a federal state with a strong central authority that distributed all its energy-based revenues throughout the country on an equal per capita basis. The remaining three options consist of a federal state with enhanced provincial powers, as conceived by the Ryan proposals[1] that emphasized provincial rights to revenues from provincial natural resources; sovereignty for Quebec; and sovereignty-association for Quebec and Canada. In order to proceed with a quantitative analysis, I shall make some rather arbitrary assumptions about the energy implications of each of the three options that involve a decrease in federal authority.

The Ryan proposals imply little for the energy picture as Quebec has no major resources of oil and gas, and her very substantial hydro-electric resources are, for all practical pur-

3

poses, already completely owned and controlled by the province. The most extreme interpretation of these proposals is that they would involve putting all energy resources into the hands of the provinces, and that all related pricing and trading decisions would be taken in the narrowly defined economic interest of the particular producing province(s). However, the Ryan proposals do include a continuation of the equalization-payments system, and these payments are greatly affected by provincial energy revenues.

Sovereignty for Quebec would entail handling oil and natural gas trade between Quebec and the rest of Canada according to the same pricing and tax provisions that govern energy trade between Canada and the United States. The same arrangement would also exist under sovereignty-association. The energy-related differences between sovereignty and sovereignty-association are, in fact, difficult to guess. One way of hypothesizing such a difference might be to assume that, relative to the United States, Quebec would enjoy preferred access to Canadian oil and gas. Since world-level prices would presumably be charged under both options, the difference between the two arrangements would lie, from Quebec's point of view, in the extra security of supply provided by sovereignty-association. The value of this extra security is difficult to establish, and it is, moreover, rather uncertain that such a special arrangement would be negotiated for Quebec under sovereignty-association. Thus, in the end, our analysis will make a relatively small distinction between the options of sovereignty and sovereignty-association for Quebec.

Techniques and Limitations

In setting up an energy-demand model, we have selected five regions within Canada and four types of energy resources: electricity, coal, crude oil, and natural gas. The production, costs, revenues, and calculation of consumer surpluses are treated in detail only for crude oil and natural gas. This limitation does not pose great problems for the analysis of constitutional changes since, so far, there is little interprovincial trade in thermal coal, and most provinces have independent systems for the generation and distribution of electricity. Thus the inability to calculate the net economic benefits of each province's hydro-electric resources, to take one example, does not much affect the analysis of constitutional change because under three of the options (excepting that of increased federal authority), the net benefits would, in any event, remain in the province where the electricity is generated.

The allocation of consumer surpluses among regions follows quite easily from the regionally based demand model and an accounting procedure that allows for interprovincial transport costs and for especially low prices in energy-producing regions. Since the Prairies are treated as one region in the demand data, and since prices differ in the three Prairie provinces, the allocation among the three is necessarily rather imprecise. The allocation of provincial revenues among the producing provinces is proportionate to the 1976 foreign ownership ratios (amounting to almost 80 per cent) in Canadian oil and gas production. The allocation of the Canadian producer surpluses among provinces raises severe problems. For one thing the distribution of final equity interest by province is not known. Even if this distribution were known, the prices paid for those interests would not be known, and so it would be impossible to tell to what extent economic rents were being obtained by shareholders in each province. In face of these difficulties, the simplest assumption may well be the most defensible: that is, an equal per capita distribution of these equity interests across the country. This assumption undoubtedly understates materially the Alberta per capita ownership, although the results suggest that the net effect on the provincial figures is relatively small.

The issue of energy-supply security or self-sufficiency will be roughly dealt with by calculating the extent to which each of the main regions relies on energy imported from the rest of Canada or from the rest of the world. Total measures for Canada can be calculated, and these differ depending on whether or not Quebec is included as part of Canada. These estimates of foreign and interprovincial dependence naturally differ over time; for this reason, some indication will be given of their past and future trends.

In analysing costs and benefits, should one assume that the optional constitutions have always been in place, or that the new options are to be taken up in 1980 or later? One of the interesting features of the quantitative results is that the accumulated costs and benefits to Quebec were just about in balance in 1980, so that it does not matter which calculation procedure is used. In considering the various constitutional models, it will be assumed that the new régimes started in 1980.

Some Estimated Results under the Existing Constitution

Table 1 shows the distribution by region of the net economic benefits under two different pricing strategies for Canadian crude oil and natural gas. In all of these variants, the existing constitutional powers and tax systems remain unchanged. The results of the 'federal pricing' case involve some guesses about the possible evolution of energy prices under the Liberal government elected in February 1980. The price for domestic crude oil increases by $3.00 per barrel per year towards an ultimate price of $30.00 per barrel (in 1980 Canadian dollars) for conventional crude oil production; natural gas is priced to the users at 85 per cent of British thermal unit (Btu) equivalence (in central Canada) to the delivered price of Canadian conventional crude oil. Moreover it is assumed that domestic users of crude oil will start paying directly to support the cost of the continuing subsidy on oil imports, following the same system as that already in use to support the subsidy on synthetic oil. The 'provincial rights' case involves an average 1980 well-head price of $19.75 per barrel, that is, $5.00 above the price in February 1980, and subsequent annual increases of $10.00 per barrel until equality with world prices is achieved early in 1983. It was assumed that the world price itself would start at about $35.00 (Canadian) per barrel in 1980 and would rise thereafter at the rate of 2 per cent per annum in real terms. Other key assumptions are spelled out in the notes for Table 1.

The top-line figures in each block of Table 1 show the discounted total net values of total economic rents, in billions of end-1980 dollars, accruing to the residents of each province or region. In the second line of each block, these same economic benefits are divided by population and shown as thousands of dollars per capita. The first block of the table shows the probable figures under the policy that the federal government was expected to propose. This policy differed in three important respects from the policy I described in an earlier paper as the 'Federal Liberal' case.[2] The annual 'per barrel' price increases were set at $3 rather than $2; the target for the well-head price of Canadian conventional crude oil was set at $30 (in constant 1980 Canadian dollars) rather than $25; and a phased introduction was planned of a 'per barrel' levy on final consumers of oil products between 1980 and 1985. This levy is large enough to finance entirely, by 1985, the subsidy on imported oil. This last change is by far the most important of the three for improving the federal government's fiscal position.

The second block reflects a phased move toward world prices for Canadian crude oil, with a discount of 5 per cent (relative to Btu equivalence to the world price of crude oil) on natural gas export prices, and 5 per cent (relative to Btu equivalence to the domestic price of crude oil) on natural gas sold for domestic use. This level of discount, it is assumed, will be voluntarily adopted by the producing provinces to obtain a larger market for their natural gas. The results shown in Table 1 are based on the assumption that natural gas exports are, in the 'federal' case, equal to the amounts approved by the National Energy Board and the federal government in late 1979. In the 'provincial rights' case, the levels of natural gas exports from Alberta and British Columbia to the United States are assumed to be larger than those so far approved by the National Energy Board by 7.5 trillion cubic feet (tcf), comprising .5 tcf of additional exports in each year from 1986 to 2000 inclusive.[3]

It is apparent from the Table 1 results for the existing system that even with the gradual movement to an oil price that is less than the world level, the distribution of economic rents among provinces is sharply uneven.[4]

Energy Pricing and Policies in a Federal State with Strong Central Authority

The figures for total Canadian rents per capita in Table 1 can be compared with the province-by-province figures to show the differences between the existing system and what might happen in a federal state with strongly centralized powers. Under such a system, a citizen's province of residence would not affect the amount of net benefits that he or she would receive; at a rough estimate, therefore, we could say that each Canadian would receive net benefits at the national per capita-average level.[5]

What sort of pricing policy would likely be established in a federal state with strongly centralized powers? One might argue that the primary purpose of low prices for crude oil and natural gas in the current Canadian system is to transfer more of the benefits accruing from Alberta to other provinces. Hence, in a strongly centralized state, one might expect to find higher prices imposed to obtain more efficient energy use that, in turn, would produce a larger 'pie' to distribute. However, the figures in

Table 1: Regional Economic Rents[a] from Conventional Crude Oil and Natural Gas under Optional Constitutions

(Present values in millions of end-1980 dollars and in thousands of end-1980 dollars per capita)

		Canada	Atlantic Provinces	Quebec	Ontario	Manitoba	Saskatchewan	Alberta (and NWT)	British Columbia (and Yukon)
1. 'Federal Pricing' Case									
Domestic oil prices up $3/yr to 1990, then move towards $30/barrel in 1980 prices. Natural gas at 85% of Btu parity with domestic oil. Import subsidy gradually becoming self-financing.	(a) Total rents	393	18	56	93	9	20	154	33
	(b) Per capita	16.6	7.9	8.8	10.9	9.3	21.0	80.0	12.5
2. 'Provincial Rights' Case									
Domestic oil prices move up $10 per barrel per year to 100% of world price. Natural gas at 95% of Btu parity. 7.5 tcf additional natural gas exports 1986–2000.	(a) Total rents	381	14	41	58	8	22	204	34
	(b) Per capita	16.1	6.4	6.5	6.8	8.2	22.9	90.4	13.3

Note:
a. All economic rents are present values of all past and future costs and returns, measured at the end of 1980.

Assumptions Applicable to the Results Reported in Tables 1 to 3

1. World oil price equals US$30.00 (C$35.10) per barrel in 1980, rising thereafter at 2% per year in real terms until the end of the century; after the turn of the century, it is constant in real terms. This price is about the middle of the range of OPEC prices at the end of January 1980 if one adds the Energy, Mines and Resources' estimate of US$1.69 for ocean transport and delivery charges to Montreal.

2. In the 'federal pricing' case, the producers of conventional oil receive an average well-head price of $16.25 per barrel (equal to the 1 January price of $14.75 plus 50% of $3) in 1980, $19.25 in 1981, $22.25 in 1982, and so on until 1990. After 1990, the price is adjusted to close 10% of the gap between its (inflation-adjusted) value in the previous year and the 'target price' of $30 per barrel (1980).

   In the 'provincial rights' case, the producers of conventional oil receive an average well-head price of $19.75 per barrel in 1980, $29.75 in 1981, $39.75 in 1982, and the world price in and after 1983.

3. Natural gas for domestic users (at the Toronto city gate) is priced, in the 'federal' case, at 85% of Btu equivalence to domestic crude oil delivered to Toronto, and at 95% in the 'provincial rights' case. Prices elsewhere reflect differences in transport costs and lower prices to users in B.C. and Alberta. Under all the constitutional options, the natural gas prices gradually move towards 100% of Btu parity as the time approaches when Canadian demands are expected to exceed supply from non-frontier sources.

4. Natural gas for export sale is priced at 95% of Btu equivalence to world crude oil, less costs of delivering natural gas from the Canadian border to Chicago. This price is calculated to stand at C$5.54 per million cubic feet (mcf) or US$4.74/mcf in 1980, and to rise thereafter at 2% per year in real terms. This 1980 price is 6% more than the US$4.47/mcf price that came into effect on 17 February 1980.

5. The general rate of inflation was assumed to be 7.5% in 1980 and 6% thereafter. Real Gross National Expenditure was assumed to grow at 4.2% annually from 1979 to 1990 and at 3.2% thereafter.

6. The nominal discount rate used is equal to the assumed rate of general inflation from 1980 onward, plus 7.44%. (The actual rate is used prior to 1980.) The latter figure, which is a calculated average real alternative supply price of capital to Canadian business, is also used as the after-tax opportunity cost on invested capital when calculating net economic rents to producers. Economic rents to governments are net of an income-tax opportunity cost equal to 3% of capital invested. Total rents to the resource are net of a real capital-rental charge equal to 7.44% + 3% = 10.44% of the undepreciated capital.

7. Production of synthetic crude oil from the Alberta oil sands is set exogenously, and the assumption is made that three more plants will have been added to the present two by the end of the century. These additional plants come on stream at four-year intervals, starting in 1986. In all cases, the price of refined oil products consumed in Canada is adjusted to include (over and above the crude oil prices described below) a 'per barrel' charge known as the 'Syncrude levy'. This is set large enough in each year to cover the difference between the world price and the domestic price on all output from oil-sands plants. Under current arrangements, all output from these plants is guaranteed a market at world prices. The size of the Syncrude levy naturally differs depending on the domestic price of crude oil. Given the assumed 'federal pricing' strategy, it is roughly $2.50 per barrel in 1985; given the 'provincial rights' pricing policy, it is zero in 1985 because the Canadian price reaches the world level by 1983.

8. The division of economic rents among provinces is based on oil and gas consumption for the consumer rents, production for provincial government revenues, and population for the Canadian share of producer rents. The distribution of federal revenues among provinces, in Tables 1 and 3 is based on the average federal tax payments by taxpayers in different provinces. The exogenous weights are used as follows:

	Population (mid-1979)	Production of Crude Oil	Production of Natural Gas	Federal Tax Collections
Atlantic Provinces	.0948	—	—	.0596
Quebec	.2660	—	—	.2360
Ontario	.3590	—	.028	.3867
Manitoba	.0436	.008	—	.0360
Saskatchewan	.0404	.107	.022	.0337
Alberta & N.W.T.	.0867	.855	.820	.1201
British Columbia and Yukon	.1095	.030	.130	.1279

9. Natural gas exports in the 'federal pricing' case include the 3.75 tcf of new exports for 1980 to 1987, approved by the National Energy Board in December 1979. In the 'provincial rights' case the level of natural gas exports is increased an additional .5 tcf per year from 1986 to 2000 inclusive. Thus additional exports are used to (more than) offset the reduction in domestic natural gas sales caused by the rapid move towards world prices for crude oil and natural gas.

Table 1 actually show that average economic rents to Canadians are higher when energy prices are lower, as in the 'federal pricing-policy' case, than when they are higher, as in the 'provincial rights' case. Why is this? It is because about 80 per cent of the equity interest in the oil- and gas-producing firms is foreign owned; therefore, while higher energy prices cut the wasteful use of energy, they also lead to a greater 'leakage' of the benefits outside the country. Naturally the extent to which these factors are offsetting — and hence provide the 'best' pricing strategy in a strongly centralized federation — depends on the efficiency of the tax and royalty systems, the degree of foreign ownership in the oil and gas industry, the impact of energy prices on energy demands, and the degree of import dependence.[6] Table 2, which shows the distribution of economic rents to producers, consumers, and governments under the optional régimes, illustrates more clearly than Table 1 the offsetting effects of foreign ownership and economic waste. Table 2 also makes it easier to compare the analysis in this paper with the conclusions reached in earlier papers.

Given either of the pricing strategies examined in this paper, Quebec residents would be about twice as well off under a more centralized federal system than under the current system. It must be emphasized, however, that a system more centralized with respect to oil and gas revenues would no doubt entail similar centralization for other natural resource revenues, and Quebec has higher than average per capita endowments of metallic minerals, forests, and especially hydro-electricity.

On the other side of the coin, Alberta residents would, on average, receive economic rents less than one quarter as large if the benefits of oil and natural gas were spread equally among all Canadians. However, a more centralized state would involve some redistribution to Alberta of the economic benefits of the hydro-electric energy resources of Quebec.

Energy in a Less Centralized Federation

The second group of figures in Table 1 illustrates the distribution of net benefits if more weight were given to the pricing preferences of the producing provinces, especially Alberta. The model has not been rerun to show what would have happened if a more producer-oriented price had been applied ever since 1973, but rather involves fairly rapid price increases starting in 1980.

Table 2: Net Economic Rents from Conventional Crude Oil and Natural Gas under Optional Constitutions

(Billions of end-1980 Canadian Dollars)

	Total Rent (1)	All Producers (2)	Canadian Consumers (3)	After Waste of (4)	Federal Government (5)	Provincial Government (6)	Total Canadian Rents (7)
1. 'Federal Pricing' Case							
Domestic oil prices up $3/yr to 1990, then move towards $30/barrel in 1980 prices. Gas at 85% of Btu parity.							
Oil	201	23	86	8	15	76	183
Gas	243	24	96	58	29	80	209
Total	444	47	182	64	44	156	392
2. 'Provincial Rights' Case							
Domestic oil prices move up $10 per barrel per year to 100% of world price. Gas at 95% of Btu parity. 7.5 tcf additional gas exports 1986–2000.							
Oil	225	51	36	4	34	104	185
Gas	246	42	35	16	43	109	196
Total	471	93	71	20	77	213	381

Notes:

The assumptions are set out in the Notes to Table 1.

Meaning of columns: Column 7 is the sum of 3, 5, 6, and 21.5% of column 2, where 21.5% was the value estimated in 1976 as the Canadian equity-ownership proportion in non-frontier natural gas and crude oil production.

A less centralized control over resource production and pricing, such as that illustrated in the bottom part of Table 1, seems consistent with the constitutional position paper of the Quebec Liberal Party, 1980.[7] However, the Quebec Liberal position ('the Ryan proposals') also places considerable emphasis on maintaining the federal equalization-payments system: "The constitution should oblige the central government to maintain tax equalization and regional development programs."[8]

Table 3 shows the net impact of the current equalization-payments system, established by the 1977 Fiscal Arrangements Act,[9] as applied to 50 per cent of provincial conventional oil and gas revenues in and after 1980. The current system has been regularly 'doctored' so that Ontario would not join the Atlantic provinces, Manitoba, and Quebec as a 'have-not' province. Only the 'have-not' provinces receive equalization payments, which are financed out of general federal revenues. Thus the main effect of the large oil and gas revenues in Alberta is to give rise to payments from the federal government to the 'have-not' provinces. Note that Quebec gains more — and Ontario residents pay more — equalization payments under the 'provincial rights' case than under the 'federal pricing' case, although these equalization gains to Quebec are only about one third as large as the adverse effects of higher oil prices on Quebec indicated in Table 1. In any event Table 3 shows that the current equalization system is so uneven in its redistribution of oil and natural gas revenues that it is likely to be overhauled. Thus the especially favourable treatment of Quebec under the current equalization-payments system could not safely be regarded as a permanent feature of Canadian fiscal arrangements.

The Alberta position is about 25 per cent better under the 'provincial rights' case than under the 'federal pricing' case. The difference is relatively modest because both the 'federal pricing' and 'provincial rights' price levels are far above the average costs of production, and both cases reflect the same prices prior to 1980. This suggests that although the two cases reflect substantially different constitutional models, they both involve increases of the same extent in Alberta's position relative to that of the rest of Canada. Some major change in equalization or taxation would be required to alter that result, and earlier studies[10] indicate that most of the tax changes that have been discussed would not be large enough to shift the basic pattern very dramatically.

Table 3: The Effects of the Current Equalization-Payments System Applied to Provincial Revenues from Crude Oil and Gas

(Net present values of all future receipts minus payments, measured in billions of 1980 Canadian dollars)

	Federal Government	Atlantic Provinces	Quebec	Ontario	Manitoba	Saskatchewan	Alberta	British Columbia
1. 'Federal Pricing' Case								
Domestic oil prices up $3/yr to 1990, then move towards $30/barrel in 1980 prices. Natural gas at 85% of Btu parity with domestic oil. Import subsidy gradually becoming self-financing.	−21.0	3.7	8.9	−8.1	1.5	−.7	−2.5	−2.7
2. 'Provincial Rights' Case								
Domestic oil prices move up $10 per barrel per year to 100% of world price. Natural gas at 95% of Btu parity. 7.5 tcf additional natural gas exports 1985−2000.	−37.8	5.7	13.8	−12.7	2.3	−1.1	−3.9	−4.2

Notes:
The weights used to allocate receipts and payments are listed in the Notes to Table 1.
The numbers shown under the federal government are the present values of all future equalization payments under the current system with 50% equalization of oil and gas revenues. The present values for each province include, as negative components, the present values of the additional federal taxes levied on their residents to finance the equalization payments.

Sovereignty for Quebec

The simplest definition of pure sovereignty consists of the statement that Quebec residents would get no further economic rents from Western Canadian oil and gas beyond the limited extent to which Quebec residents held shares in producing firms that received some part of the net producer rents. Without some preferred trade access to Canadian oil and gas, Quebec's energy self-sufficiency would drop to the proportion of final energy obtained from hydro-electricity (which in our model is about 25 per cent in 1980) and would rise to about 35−40 per cent in 1990 in the world-price 'provincial rights' case shown in Table 1. The present value of all future net monetary losses to Quebec residents would be about $9000 (1980) per capita in the 'provincial rights' case.[11] There would also be none of the oil-induced equalization payments shown in Table 3. It would be appropriate, too, to attach some value to the reduced security of supply, although to estimate the relevant amount is next to impossible.

Sovereignty-Association for Quebec

As I mentioned in my introduction, it is very difficult, in the context of the energy model, to distinguish the implications of sovereignty-association from those of sovereignty. Sovereignty-association would presumably involve for Quebec some form of preferred access to Canadian crude oil and natural gas, with the latter probably becoming more important in the course of time. But within our model calculations there is no straightforward way of attaching a value to this preferred access even if the sovereignty-association documents were more precise about the way in which the relationship would apply to crude oil and natural gas. If Canadian oil and natural gas used in Quebec could be regarded as 'Quebec energy' for the purpose of calculating energy self-sufficiency in that province, then mea- sured self-sufficiency for Quebec would be much higher under the sovereignty-association option than under the sovereignty option.

Viewing sovereignty for Quebec from the standpoint of the rest of Canada, average per capita economic rents would rise by about one third; this increase would reflect the concomitant 25 per cent drop in Canada's population. Similarly Canada's degree of energy self-sufficiency would rise substantially. The only remaining imports would be of American coal to Ontario and offshore crude oil to the Atlantic provinces. Secure Quebec markets for natural gas might be of some value to Alberta.

Conclusion

It is clear that many of the constitutional options that differ distinctively in their political significance have energy implications that are difficult to assess. Even where I have tried to provide some rough measures of the approximate distribution of net economic benefits under optional constitutional arrangements, the calculations can be treated only as very rough guides to the complicated and hard-to-predict political and economic linkages among Canada's regions. Some would argue that such calculations are better not made, in any case, as they may increase, rather than decrease, the difficulties involved in reaching mutually acceptable compromises between West and East, and between Quebec and the rest of Canada. That may be so, although I hope that it is not. In any event the calculations that have been reported in this paper have shown that the 1973–74 and 1979 changes in world energy prices have been so large that they have materially changed the balance of energy benefits under the various constitutional options. The role of Alberta can never again be seen as it was before 1973. The large size and uneven distribution of Canada's energy resources have been major causes of provincial demands for constitutional change. Energy resources, whether the oil of Alberta and Hibernia or the hydro-electricity of Quebec and Labrador, also provide, by their very richness, one of the key impediments to agreement about the ways in which economic powers and revenues are shared within the federation.

Notes

1. Constitutional Committee of the Quebec Liberal Party, *A New Canadian Federation* (Montreal, 1980). (Referred to as 'the Ryan proposals'.)

2. J.F. Helliwell, "The Distribution of Energy Revenues Within Canada: Functional or Factional Federalism?" PNRE Resources Paper #48 (Vancouver: University of British Columbia, Department of Economics, February 1980).

3. The issues involved in natural gas exports are described in J.F. Helliwell, "Trade Policies for Natural Gas and Electricity," in Ontario Economic Council, *Energy Policies for the 1980s: An Economic Analysis* (Toronto, 1980), vol. II, pp. 1–39.

4. In an earlier paper (see note 2), I examined one of the pressures that those disparities are likely to create for Confederation and illustrated the inadequacies of the current system of equalization payments (the effects of which are not included in Table 1 figures) for righting these imbalances. The special position of Quebec in the current equalization-payments system is further discussed on pp. 11–14.

5. The actual situation would probably be more complicated than this conclusion suggests. For example, as long as a substantial proportion of the benefits would pass to consumers by means of lower-than-world-level prices, some fiscal devices would be required to pass equivalent amounts to Canadians without access to domestic natural gas. This would be especially so for Eastern Quebec, the Atlantic provinces, and various parts of other provinces.

6. J.F. Helliwell *et al.*, "The Interaction of Tax Policy and Energy Policy," in *Report of Proceedings of the Thirty-first Tax Conference* (Toronto: Canadian Tax Foundation, 1979). Also PNRE Resources #47. (Vancouver: University of British Columbia, Department of Economics.)

7. The 'Ryan proposals', especially pp. 95–96.

8. *Ibid.*, p. 75.

9. Thomas J. Courchene, *Refinancing the Canadian Federation: A Survey of the 1977 Fiscal Arrangements Act* (Montreal: C.D. Howe Institute, 1979).

10. For example, Helliwell, "The Interaction of Tax Policy and Energy Policy."

11. These numbers can be read directly from Table 1 because simulation results not shown here suggest that until 1980 the federal tax reductions to the oil industry indirectly paid for by Quebec taxpayers have matched almost exactly the 1980 value of the import subsidies received between 1974 and 1979.

The Author

JOHN F. HELLIWELL is Professor of Economics at the University of British Columbia. He holds the degrees of B. Comm. from that university and D. Phil. from Oxford University. Professor Helliwell taught economics at Oxford from 1964 to 1967; since then he has taught at U.B.C. and has held visiting research and teaching positions in Australia, New Zealand, France, Sweden, and the United States. He specializes in empirical studies of macroeconomics, international economics, and natural resources, especially energy. Professor Helliwell held the post of Managing Editor of the *Canadian Journal of Economics* from 1979 to 1982. He is a Fellow of the Royal Society of Canada.

Petroleum and Natural Gas and Constitutional Change

ALASTAIR R. LUCAS
University of Calgary

IAN McDOUGALL
Osgoode Hall Law School
York University

Contents

Petroleum and Natural Gas and Constitutional Change

Introduction

The paper that follows consists of three major sections. The first outlines the present constitutional framework as it relates to the petroleum and natural gas industry. The traditional areas of jurisdiction of both the provincial and federal governments are considered in light of the British North America (BNA) Act and custom. The second portion of the paper discusses the federal perspective with respect to oil and gas management and generally advances a brief for increased central control over the exploitation of these resources. The final portion examines the prospects for varying the existing formal constitutional division of jurisdiction in a fashion that results in increased, rather than reduced, provincial control. Some of the earlier efforts in this direction are also considered here.

The Basic Constitutional Division of Jurisdiction

Present regulatory controls that apply to the petroleum and natural gas industry are as much the product of the unique history of the industry as they are the result of a strictly followed division of jurisdictional competence under the BNA Act. In respect to the formal constitutional legalities, there is little doubt about the 'ownership' of natural resources. Section 109[1] of the

BNA Act confirmed that ownership over natural resources would remain vested in the original provinces party to the new Confederation of 1867. This control over indigenous resources was later extended to the Provinces of Alberta, Saskatchewan, and British Columbia. Thus any limitations that may exist on provincial control can only be those that derive from the division of legislative power between the federal and provincial governments. There can be no serious debate about which jurisdiction has 'ownership' *qua* 'ownership'.

While there is little doubt about the ownership question, it is a mistake to proffer ownership as the answer, in principle, to the so-called 'resources struggle' that now goes on between the provinces and the central government. Far from quelling debate, the very term 'ownership' can be seen on examination to raise more questions than it answers. Just as private ownership of property rarely facilitates unlimited powers of retention or disposition, so provincial 'ownership' cannot be divorced conceptually from the correlative federal power to regulate in a number of areas that will have a substantial effect on the resource sectors. It is, in other words, necessary to qualify the term 'ownership' in order to appreciate fully its constitutional significance to the provinces. Most of the property held in the provinces is owned by private individuals rather than the Crown in right of a particular province. Where this is so, the province merely enjoys a legislative capacity to control, limit, and perhaps even eliminate the rights of ownership vested in private individuals. Nor, as we shall shortly see, is this legislative power exclusive. Thus the statement that provinces have control over property can usually be taken to mean no more than that provincial legislation is the common source of resource control rather than the exclusive source. The major exception to all of this relates to Crown reserves; this subject will be explored more fully in the paragraphs that follow.

The provisions of the BNA Act that govern provincial legislative authority over primary resources include sections 92(5),[2] 92(13),[3] and 92(16).[4] Section 92(5) is central to the management and sale of public lands that belong to the province and is of pivotal importance today. In the Province of Alberta approximately eighty per cent of petroleum and natural gas is produced from public lands. While these lands lie within the exclusive legislative control of the province, they also belong in a proprietary sense to the Crown in right of Alberta. Thus Alberta acts with the dual capacity of a proprietor and a legislator, exercising provincial power whenever oil and gas production occurs within the province. As a proprietor, the province has 'disposed'[5] of its property interest in the produced petroleum and natural gas through the principles of ordinary contract when a lease is made. Yet these agreements have also been made subject to a legislative framework passed under the authority of section 92(5), which generally governs petroleum and natural gas production and thus appears to preserve for the province a measure of continuing discretion over the conditions that govern oil and gas production.

Sections 109 and 117 of the BNA Act coupled with Resources Transfer Agreements have been viewed by the producing provinces as effectively 'entrenching' the property interests of the Crown in right of the province. In advancing this view the provinces are asserting a principle of interjurisdictional immunity in respect to Crown land that would effectively bar almost all federal regulatory power.[6]

Section 92(13) contains the general provincial jurisdiction over property and civil rights. It is this head of jurisdiction that has been used as the traditional support for the oil-producing provinces' enactment of generic regulatory controls that affect most phases of the petroleum and gas industry, whether the production is from Crown or private lands. The exercise of provincial authority in this field is ultimately constrained by the federal government's jurisdiction over interprovincial and international trade and commerce. But there is, by virtue of section 92(16), apparent jurisdiction over matters of local or private significance; this jurisdiction would seem clearly to apply in relation to petroleum and gas both produced and consumed within a single province.

The paragraphs above present the broadest jurisdictional constraints that affect the producing provinces. By way of contrast, the central government's technical jurisdiction over the oil and gas industry arises as an extension of its general power with respect to the regulation of trade and commerce pursuant to section 91(2),[7] its power of taxation with respect to section 91(3),[8] its general jurisdiction under section 92(10)(a)[9] with respect to "Works and Undertakings" connecting a given province with any other or extending beyond its own limits, its declaratory power under section 92(10)(c)[10] with respect to "Works" that are considered to be for the "general Advantage of Canada," and perhaps most important, the central government's residual jurisdiction under the opening paragraph of section 91, with respect to laws for the "Peace, Order and good Government of Canada."[11] While the precise scope of each of these heads of power may involve a substantial amount of judicial controversy, the point would nonetheless seem apparent that the federal government has indisputably pre-eminent control over the terms and conditions under which oil and gas can flow out of the province of production to the national and international markets.

Oil and Gas Management: The Federal Perspective

The Historical Sharing of Jurisdiction

The early history of the petroleum and gas industry was not notably marred by a great deal of constitutional conflict. If anything can be said, it would seem that both the federal and provincial governments shared a concern that the development of the industry should be encouraged. Indeed the health of the industry became a preoccupation that appears to have displaced the giving of much serious attention to the potential for subsequent jurisdictional conflict.[12]

Canada's experience with the petroleum and gas industry began far earlier than in most contemporary producing countries. About the turn of the century, there was a minor flurry (by today's standards) of activity in Southwestern Ontario. Indeed the continent's first oil discovery was in Canada; the first refining process was developed by a Nova Scotian; and the first commercial gas strikes were made in Essex and Haldimand Counties in the Province of Ontario.[13]

Much of our early natural gas production was exported to the United States, a fact that later led to premature shortages and field abandonments. The hardships connected with this experience, coupled with the later and perhaps equally difficult problems over the sharing with the United States of power generation from the Niagara River, led Canada to impose harsh legislative restrictions against the future exportation of oil, natural gas, and electrical power.[14]

A number of factors combined to modify this otherwise rigid prohibition. Before the widespread development of oil and gas activity, the Albertan economy depended mainly on agricultural output and the stability of agricultural markets. Throughout this period federal support was of substantial importance and, indeed, equalization payments continued to be made to Alberta until 1973. More economic diversification in the Western regions was thus desirable from the point of view of the federal government and the Western provinces alike. For this reason the early discoveries in the Turner Valley and at Leduc animated hopes, both nationally and provincially, that the economic growth rate of Western Canada might well be about to experience a classic 'take-off'.[15]

During the early phases of the petroleum and gas exploratory play in Western Canada, there was concern that the industry's growth might be hamstrung by the relative immaturity of the small and distant domestic market. Alberta in particular was concerned to see that the initial markets for its petroleum and gas were growth oriented and capable of sustaining an orderly acceleration of production capability. The American markets were larger than Canada's and closer. Initially, at least, it seemed apparent that Western crude would not be able to compete with the relatively cheaper offshore imports that were being used by the urban industrial markets of Southwestern Ontario and Montreal.

A range of factors moved the federal view of the desirability of petroleum and gas exports into line with that of the Western provinces. The main consideration appears to have related to continental defence. Canada had entered North American Air Defence Command (NORAD) and with the United States shared a common concern that the continent as a whole have land-based sources of energy supply available in the event of offshore naval hostilities or political instabilities in those countries from which petroleum was being imported. The Suez crisis of 1957 and the earlier Korean war heightened the level of federal concern on this point.

Thus the mid-1950s saw both the federal government and the Western provinces agreeing that Western petroleum and natural gas production should enter sizeable export markets in addition to domestic markets. In addition both levels of government were concerned that pricing decisions should be made with a view to the need to increase export-market sales. Finally, both levels of government were anxious to stimulate private investment in the industry and were thus prepared to make generous allowances for the industry in the federal taxation structure and through the establishment of generous provincial royalty rates.

This early partnership of the provinces, the federal government, and the industry was advanced, first, by federal support for the Trans-Canada pipeline project that opened up the natural gas-market regions of Toronto and Montreal, and later by the 1961 National Oil Policy. The federal government in effect guaranteed a domestic outlet for Western oil and gas, despite the fact that Western crude and natural gas were not competitive with alternative offshore petroleum imports. Central to the National Oil Policy, in particular, was the principle of so-called 'self-sufficiency'; under this principle Western Canadian oil production was artificially brought up to — and, indeed, at one point exceeded — the total national demand. The difference between national production and domestic consumption was arbitrarily labelled 'surplus' and exported to the United States.

By way of summary it should be stressed that a number of significant common interests underlay the early co-operation between the federal government and the oil- and gas-producing provinces. First, both levels of government wanted to increase the pace of economic activity in the Western part of the country. The petroleum and gas industry was a potentially significant employer and could ultimately prove to be an important source of both federal and provincial revenue, and a valuable source of foreign exchange if Canada's export potential should live up to industry estimates. While other matters such as defence and the diversification of the domestic energy supply were more or less exclusively the concern of the federal government, they happily coincided with Western ambitions for production. The evaluations by both levels of government of the long-term potential of the country as a petroleum producer were maintained at very high levels by the seemingly unbridled optimism from within the ranks of the 'experts' of the oil and gas industry. Thus neither the producing provinces, particularly Alberta, nor the federal government saw a need for the aggressive protection of domestic consumers against future cost increases or potential shortages. Rather, history indicates that both levels of government believed that Canada's principle difficulties lay in finding ever larger markets for domestic oil and gas production in the name of creating the necessary incentives for private industry to prove our country's purportedly vast potential as a 'world-scale' producer. Any controversy about the appropriate division of economic rent between the federal and provincial levels of government was put aside in favour of providing the maximum stimulus to the private sector. Ill-considered taxation or royalty burdens that might impair the development of the industry and the industry's markets were more substantial concerns than the possibility of forfeiting significant economic returns. Thus, during this early era, friction over the revenue sharing between the provinces and the federal government was a rare occurrence.

During the period before the early 1970s, Canada experienced no constitutional controversies: the provincial and federal governments shared control over the petroleum and gas industry. The federal government, as a result of its power over trade and commerce, had assumed regulatory control over the pipeline infrastructure that connected Alberta, British Columbia, and Saskatchewan with American and Eastern Canadian markets.[16] Indeed, in many respects, Ottawa acted as a marketing agent for the producing provinces by actively promoting the growth of export and domestic markets. This function was encouraged by both the producers and the producing provinces. Ultimately, in 1959, the National Energy Board (NEB) assumed over-all federal jurisdiction.[17] The NEB itself sprang from the primary recommendation of the Borden Royal Commission Inquiry[18] that had been established to sort out a series of industry-related controversies; these included the financing of the Trans-Canada pipeline project and concerns about the volumes, terms, and pricing arrangements relating to the export of natural gas to the United States.[19]

The Emergence of Constitutional Conflict

The relative harmony between the different levels of Canadian government came to an abrupt end partly as a result of the actions of the Organization of Petroleum Exporting Countries' (OPEC) First Ministers in 1973.[20] It would be too much of a simplification to assume that OPEC was alone responsible for Canada's increased domestic intergovernmental tensions. Indeed, prior to the October War in the Middle East, there had been a number of indications that control over petroleum and natural gas would soon become a growing source of friction. In 1972 Alberta commissioned a comprehensive review of royalty structures applying to its natural gas and an exhaustive survey of field-gas prices throughout the province.[21] The province's underlying purpose was simply to increase the amount of revenue that was paid into the provincial treasury from the industry.

It was also a busy year for the federal regulators. In 1972 the NEB published an analysis outlining what it described as "potential limitations" on Canada's petroleum supplies.[22] The analysis was, in fact, by today's standards, overly optimistic. But in 1972 it represented a dramatic reversal of thought about Canada's potential as a petroleum producer over the longer term. For the first time limitations on domestic supplies were acknowledged, and the possibility of adverse production-cost trends was identified as a concern.

In short the decisions of OPEC in late 1973 undoubtedly caused Canada to come to terms with potential issues relating to petroleum supply and price rather more quickly than the country would otherwise have done. Nonetheless, the present controversy over petroleum and natural gas has been shaped by actual, rather than artificial, limitations on both domestic and international supply. We shall discuss this subject in the paragraphs that follow.

Regulatory Tensions with the Producing Provinces: A Federalist Viewpoint

A number of tensions of constitutional importance have evolved between the producing provinces and the federal government over the interval between 1973 and 1981. First is the issue of which level of government should be entitled to establish the market price for domestically produced oil. The producing provinces, while not initially advocates of the domestic adoption of the price set by the OPEC cartel, nonetheless have pressed the view that pricing is properly a provincial prerogative by virtue of their jurisdiction over provincial public property, over "property and civil rights in the province" and, in general, over matters of a local nature. More recently Alberta has conceded federal pricing authority.[23]

The producing provinces have continued to assert their power as proprietors of production from Crown reserves. Alberta, for example, has maintained a system under which Crown oil and gas must be marketed through the Alberta Petroleum Marketing Commission. It can be argued that this includes the province's exclusive power to set prices and to sell at those prices. But from the outset the debate has been a token one since all levels of government have agreed on the need for ultimate development of a negotiated domestic price structure.

On essentially the same constitutional premise, the producing provinces have consistently argued their entitlement to the bulk of resource rents either by virtue of their status as proprietors or as a result of their jurisdiction to levy taxes against freehold operators. In this regard the federal imposition of the Petroleum Export Tax was originally viewed by the producers as an "expropriation of provincial property." On the basis of the Ottawa-Alberta oil-pricing agreement, the federal government has reduced the rate on this tax to zero.

Alberta has resisted Ottawa's attempts to establish priorities for new energy-resource developments. The recent provincial regulatory strictures on new tar-sands development are a good illustration. Despite express federal policy favouring more tar-sands plants, the Alberta Cabinet has refused to allow the necessary regulatory approvals to be issued. One can only assume that this refusal, in part, reflects concern that provincial revenue ambitions for conventional petroleum and natural gas production might otherwise be thwarted. That is to say, the stronger the threat of future shortages, the greater the pressure (and therefore Alberta's leverage) to control current pricing, and, ultimately, the larger the potential profit available to Alberta from present conventional production and future sources of supply of all types, including synthetics. In this regard the connection between the jurisdiction to regulate production and the capacity to control the value of a limited resource is an obvious and central fact of life that is recognized by all participants in the debate, most especially by the producing provinces.

Moreover Alberta and British Columbia have taken the position that a strong provincial role is appropriate in relation to decisions concerning the balance of service between the American export market and the quantities of gas and petroleum held in reserve to supply future Canadian market needs. The NEB approval of natural gas exports, given in 1979, represented the culmination of a great deal of debate on this subject. In this instance the possibility of new gas exports was first raised during the discussions between the then Vice-President Mondale and the Premier of Alberta. The initial round of talks reportedly indicated that Alberta would consider increasing gas flows in exchange for American tariff concessions in the market areas of agricultural and petrochemical products. It would be an understatement to suggest that the jurisdiction of the federal government made the substance of these negotiations presumptuous.

Indeed, at the time, the NEB's most recent published report had declared that there was no gas available for export, and there was general debate that included a number of federal departments about the dangers inherent in the development of a potentially redundant petrochemical industrial base in the Province of Alberta. It is noteworthy, however, that the NEB's export criteria were ultimately adjusted, that an export was facilitated that conformed roughly to the terms considered in the Mondale-Lougheed talks, and that the pace of petrochemical development in Alberta has continued despite the likely effect on future feedstocks for Ontario's counterpart industry.

As a practical issue the provincial view has largely prevailed with respect to petroleum and gas policies since 1973, despite the federal assumption of the power to determine domestic prices unilaterally, if necessary, and notwithstanding the federal Petroleum Export Tax and the Import Compensation Program. The domestic producing provinces, like the international producers of oil, exercise a whip hand by virtue of their threat to regulate production destined for interprovincial markets; this threat has had a major effect on all phases of energy-related arrangements between the federal and provincial governments.

In Alberta particularly, the jurisdictional conflict has been enlarged by a degree of legislative detail. At issue here are the provisions of the Petroleum Marketing Act[24] and the revisions to the Mines and Minerals Act.[25] Under the former provisions the province has assumed the power to set prices "in the public interest of Alberta" through the Alberta Petroleum Marketing Commission (APMC)[26] and in the interim to order the storage of Crown petroleum. The APMC is also empowered, where necessary, to direct pipeline and storage owners to operate their facilities according to its wishes. The Mines and Minerals Act revisions have authorized the provincial Cabinet to curtail production of Crown oil. Taken together, it is clear that Alberta does, in fact, intend to give substance to the theory that its jurisdiction over petroleum and gas will prevail both politically and judicially.

Canada's energy position in 1982 is fundamentally different from its position a decade ago. The new National Energy Program reflects these changes, although the precise shape of our present policy is at this time somewhat undefined.

The most pressing priorities for Canadian energy planners will be determined to a significant degree by events outside the country. Despite the recent contention that we should aim at achieving oil self-sufficiency by 1990, there is virtually no authority that seriously anticipates a reversal of current production declines. At most Canada can attempt a rear-guard action to counter imminent declines in petroleum supplies from both domestic and foreign sources by means of massive conservation and energy substitution, making particular use of natural gas and electrical power.

It will become increasingly important to deal with the fact that the so-called 'energy problem' is not strictly, or even largely, a matter of the quantity of oil available at any given moment. The connection between the cost of supplies and their ultimate value to the economy at large is inescapable. It is of little use to be blessed with massive quantities of petroleum or natural gas that will cost more than people can afford to pay. Indeed the cost of remaining low-cost reserves may yet have to be regulated to offset the cost of premium supplies that might become technically available in the future, but will otherwise remain too expensive to develop. Price blending between low- and high-cost sources of supply may well become in the future a more substantial preoccupation of energy regulation than moving toward a so-called 'world-commodity oil price' with the alleged object of encouraging consumer conservation and of increasing private investment in areas of frontier or synthetic potential. Central policies that depend on steady price hikes may yet result in conservation at the expense of the well-being of the economy and the people. While no one doubts that less energy is used in a recession or depression than in an economically healthy climate, the cure under the former circumstances is clearly worse than the disease itself.

In short Canada will undoubtedly be forced in the future into ever more detailed management of and participation in the energy sector. Concern over costs will increase the pressure for more intimate controls over marketing at an interprovincial level. Even greater worries over supply security and the need to achieve fuel substitution that will reduce oil dependence will also urge a heightened federal presence in the marketing field. The extremely large capital demands of this sector may also produce a greater need to establish the priority of future projects carefully; and here again the federal government may prove to be uniquely qualified to assume the task. Finally, there is the possibility of distress conditions overtaking the constitutional niceties and forcing the most extensive kind of federal regulation. Canada's energy problems are rooted in circumstances that are distinct from those of most other modern Western industrial economies. First, Canada is both a significant producer and a significant consumer of oil and gas. Secondly much of our consumption is directly attributable to harsh climatic conditions and the relatively long distances with which the economy must contend. Canadians, in short, depend as much on the energy demand-and-supply balance for our very survival as we do for our ability to generate wealth and employment.

To say the least, it is at this stage evident that the existing formal constitutional arrangement will necessarily alter in future, if not only to reflect new federal and provincial regulatory ambitions, then at least to reflect the present *de facto* division of regulatory competence between the federal and provincial governments. It is to this topic that we shall now turn.

Constitutional Options

Classical Federalism: Rearrangement of Powers

The oil- and gas-producing provinces have pushed hard in the recent rounds of federal-provincial constitutional discussions for changes in the existing division of powers to strengthen provincial ownership and control of natural resources. Support for this general objective of confirming provincial control over resource development and ensuring that federal policies are and remain compatible with provincial resource strategies is not confined to the producer provinces. At the Premiers' Conference in Regina in August 1978, all ten provinces expressed support for "the confirmation and strengthening of provincial powers with respect to resources."[27] This unanimity on the need for clear constitutional recognition of jurisdiction over development and management of resources, based on provincial ownership, was confirmed by the provincial Premiers at the Federal-Provincial Conference of First Ministers on the Constitution in September 1980.

It is clear, however, that any significant redistribution of powers over resources requires, not only clarification of the existing powers over provincial resource ownership and management, but also modification of certain of the exclusive federal heads of legislative authority.[28] From a provincial standpoint change means abolishing or substantially reducing the scope of these federal powers. To extend the existing provincial power to levy direct taxes so that it would include the power to impose indirect taxes would, in practice, cut into existing federal taxing powers because of the limited taxation-revenue 'pie'.

It is when discussion moves from strengthening provincial powers over natural resources to limiting concomitant federal powers that unanimity among provinces evaporates. Negotiations between federal and provincial First Ministers show clearly that the critical resources issues concern limitation of federal powers, primarily in the areas of trade and commerce and taxation.

Until quite recently it appeared that the federal government might be prepared to make enough concessions to satisfy even the major oil- and gas-producing provinces. For example Bill C−60, the proposed Constitutional Amendment Act of 1978, contained a provision that would have required the federal government to consult with provinces prior to any invocation of the declaratory power.[29] This proposal, however, constituted a federal retreat from earlier Prime Ministerial statements that the declaratory power could be abolished. It also fell short of proposals by some provinces that the power be used only with the concurrence of the province or provinces concerned.[30]

The First Ministers' Conference on the Constitution held in October 1978 established a Continuing Committee of Ministers on the Constitution (CCMC) that was charged with responsibility for achieving consensus on various constitutional issues. A report, including draft proposals, entitled "Resource Ownership and Interprovincial Trade," was submitted to the First Ministers in February 1979. The draft, which became known as the ' "Best Efforts" Draft',[31] addressed the three fundamental issues: resource ownership and management, trade and commerce, and taxation. Included were proposals that would empower provinces to take the following action:

- Exclusively to make laws in relation to exploration, development, conservation, and management of non-renewable natural resources.
- To legislate concerning the export of natural resources from the province, provided that such laws are not discriminatory in terms of prices or supplies. These provincial export laws would prevail over federal trade-and-commerce laws in the event of conflict, except in the case of federal laws concerning international trade and commerce and federal laws for

regulation of trade and commerce within Canada and necessary to serve a "compelling national interest."

- To enact laws to impose direct or indirect taxes on resources,
including primary energy-resource products such as upgraded heavy crude oil. However, such taxes could not
differentiate between resources exported from the province
and those not exported.

These changes would considerably strengthen provincial
powers to manage oil and gas resources. Such amendments to
the BNA Act would reverse the two leading constitutional cases
on resources, both of which were decided in favour of the
federal government by the Supreme Court of Canada. Results
favourable to the Province of Saskatchewan would have been
produced on the taxation issues in both the *CIGOL*[32] and *Central
Canada Potash*[33] cases. Similarly the province would have prevailed in the trade-and-commerce issues in the absence of
federal laws that could be shown to be necessary in order to
serve a compelling national interest.[34] No such directly conflicting federal laws were in place.

The "Best Efforts" Draft proposals received general acceptance in 1979.[35] By the summer of 1980, however, the federal
position had changed. Ottawa now asserted that powers over the
economy must be firmly linked to natural resources issues. The
federal government also rejected the draft provisions that would
have given the provinces primary authority over the export of
resource production. In particular a direct federal paramountcy
provision was substituted for the "Best Efforts" Draft provision
for provincial paramountcy, subject to the exceptions based on
"international trade" and "compelling national interest."[36]
When these revised proposals were placed before the Constitutional Conference of September 1980 by the Prime Minister,[37]
they were described by Premier Lougheed of Alberta as
"nominal and insignificant" and rejected by nine of ten provinces.[38]

Initially the Constitutional Bill, 1981, the federal government's constitutional package, contained no provisions concerning natural resources. Most of the provinces protested this
omission. But the present federal intention is, in any event, that
the proposed constitutional reforms be implemented without
provincial concurrence.

Subsequently, following an exchange of letters between Prime
Minister Trudeau and Mr. Broadbent, the leader of the New

Democratic Party, an amendment relating to resources was added.[39] With one significant exception, this amendment is broadly similar to the "Best Efforts" Draft proposal. The provincial authority to make laws relating to the export to other parts of Canada of primary non-renewable resource products is qualified by a clear and concise federal paramountcy provision.

The course of federal-provincial 'negotiations' and particularly the fate of the "Best Efforts" Draft shows that there are a number of fundamental problems involved in proposals to modify the existing division of powers as a means of settling issues related to energy-resource management and development. First, certain key limits of jurisdiction over existing resources are uncertain. Secondly existing legislation and resource-management practices in producer provinces may be difficult to change as a matter of practice. Thirdly the federal government has recently taken a tough position on proposed broadening of provincial powers over natural resources. Finally, extended provincial resource powers are likely to create a *de facto* special status for producer provinces.

The uncertain status of resources
Federal power to set conditions for the export of natural resources is relatively clear,[40] but there is little agreement on several key issues concerning the current law governing division of powers over resources. First, the scope of the emergency aspect of the peace, order, and good government power as a basis for direct federal management and sale of provincial oil and gas is far from clear. From the Supreme Court's holding that control of inflation is an appropriate subject for emergency authority, we can infer that national energy supply and allocation may also be designated appropriate subjects for federal emergency regulation.[41] We know that while a federal declaration of national emergency is not conclusive, any party challenging this judgement bears a relatively heavy responsibility.[42] But it is not clear whether or not, for example, NEB forecasts of short-term regional fuel-oil shortages would form a sufficient basis for federal assumption of complete management of oil and gas and their production control. Implementation of temporary mandatory allocation or rationing, such as that under the Energy Supplies Emergency Act,[43] would be more consistent with the nature of this kind of 'emergency' and therefore, arguably, more clearly referable to the emergency power.[44]

Nor is it clear that the peace, order, and good government power operates in the same way in relation to provincial resources and public property as it does in relation to heads of otherwise exclusively provincial legislative power enumerated in section 92 of the BNA Act. The source of the peace, order, and good government power lies in the opening words and concluding clause of section 91. This suggests that this ultimate federal power was intended by the BNA Act's draftsmen to operate only against section-92 powers and not against distributive provisions relating to public property that appear elsewhere in the Act. Thus it is arguable that section 109 and related provisions in Part VIII operate to 'entrench' provincial ownership of public property.

Such care to guarantee provincial ownership is consistent with the understanding at Confederation that provincial property would be the foundation of provincial government operation. From this premise it follows that provinces are limited to levying direct taxes. Similarly care was taken, when new provinces entered Confederation after 1867, to guarantee them this natural resource base. This revenue base was granted somewhat grudgingly to the Prairie provinces after years of delay. But once granted by the Resources Transfer Agreements, provincial resource ownership was clearly confirmed by the 1930 BNA Act Amendments.

It can be argued that the "Best Efforts" Draft would clarify the extent of provincial ownership powers, particularly in relation to export laws for provincial resources. But the original "Best Efforts" Draft, the federal revision, and section 57 of the Constitution Bill, 1981 all beg the question of the relationship between provincial powers based on ownership and the federal peace, order, and good government power. Provincial ownership powers are strengthened by the specific reference in section 57 to provincial regulation of the rate of primary production.[45] However, the resources amendments do not completely clarify the extent to which provincial ownership laws could impose conditions that indirectly affect export of oil and gas resources.[46]

The original draft with its "compelling national interest" exception[47] would have codified an interpretive formula for resource-export issues that is closely analogous to some judicial formulations of the broader peace, order, and good government power.[48] Many of the analytical problems discussed above that currently plague the emergency formulation of the general power[49] would become associated with issues relating to the export of oil and gas.

Both the revised "Best Efforts" Draft and section 57 of the Constitution Bill, 1981 bring in the uncertain jurisprudence on the paramountcy doctrine. Development of a conceptual test to determine when paramountcy comes into play has been the most vexing problem. The current "operating incompatibility"[50] criterion is highly sensitive to circumstances so that particular decisions provide little prospective guidance.

Similarly it is not clear whether a declaration of works as "Works . . . for the general Advantage of Canada," in section 92(10)(c), can operate as an expropriation of the oil and gas in the ground that the declared works are designed to produce. Clause (c) refers only to "Works," not "Works and Undertakings." The other clauses of section 92(10) suggest intended limitation to physical works such as transportation facilities. The context suggests regulatory authority rather than direct resource ownership.

It is also far from certain whether, in given circumstances, provincial levies or charges must be designated as indirect taxes (and therefore outside provincial direct taxation powers)[51] or as infringing the trade-and-commerce power. The extent of this uncertainty can be appreciated by comparing the majority judgment of Martland J. and the dissenting judgment of Dickson J. in the *CIGOL* case.[52]

It is not clear, either, how federal taxation powers fit with provincial ownership jurisdiction. An argument can be made that interjurisdictional principles of tax immunity may limit federal powers to tax provincial oil and gas, even by way of export tax, if those reserves are directly developed and sold by the Crown in right of a province.[53] The Alberta government contracted in the summer of 1980 for the drilling of three gas wells near the Montana border. It made arrangements to produce the wells and sell the gas directly to purchasers in Montana, thus setting up the factual basis for a judicial reference to test the limits of federal jurisdiction to regulate and to tax exports of provincially owned natural gas.

In an unanimous decision issued 20 March 1981, the Alberta Court of Appeal held that the Federal Natural Gas and Gas Liquids Tax does not apply to the provincial natural gas described in the Reference.[54] The tax, which is a major component of the National Energy Program, is not directed primarily to export gas. Nor do the Reference facts reflect the

current organization of Alberta's natural gas industry since by
far the most gas is produced under Crown leases by private
producers who would not be immune from the tax. However,
the case does establish a limit to federal taxing powers. It also
tends to confirm the idea of entrenched status for provincial
public property and resources.

Existing provincial resource legislation
A second problem arises from the fact that oil- and gas-
producing provinces have a full and detailed legislative
framework for management and regulation of these resources.
This legislative framework carries the weight of history and
reflects developments in government and in the industry over
the period of exploration and production in each particular
province. It also reflects understandings and accommodations
reached by government and industry from time to time.
Moreover oil and gas interests are conveyed by documents that
are contractual in nature, particularly at the development and
production stages. This lends a relative certainty, or at least
predictability, to the 'rules of the game' under which oil and gas
resources are developed and produced.

For political and administrative reasons, this enabling legislation may be difficult to change so that it reflects variations in the
constitutional division of powers to legislate concerning resources. The oil industry has placed considerable emphasis on
this need for good relations with government and relative
certainty in the 'rules of the game'.

There may also be legal constraints on abrupt provincial
changes in resource tenures. It has been argued, for example,
that the standard Crown oil and gas lease currently used in
Alberta may be legally immune to unilateral revision by
government through legislative means.[55] The argument holds
that in entering into a lease, the parties adopted the contract
mode to govern their relations, notwithstanding the "compliance with laws" clause that purports to authorize the province
to make unilateral changes. There are certain basic or core
terms of this contract, such as the grant of an interest in land,
that are so fundamental to the relationship that they cannot be
unilaterally changed by the government acting under the
"compliance with laws" clause. It has also been pointed out that
the "compliance with laws" clause is part of the covenants and
conditions of the lease, and not part of the basic conveying
provisions. The result is that while the government can attempt

to change leases in its legislative capacity, it may be prevented from asserting that the constitutional basis for such legislation is founded on provincial resource ownership. This legislation may be considered as regulating resources, most of which are exported from the province and consequently *ultra vires* for the regulation of trade and commerce.

It is also possible that the granting clause of Crown oil and gas leases conveys a full interest in the minerals in place so that, following the leasing of oil and gas resources, the Crown's ability to regulate by laws based on provincial resource ownership is at an end.[56] Precisely what is granted depends on the words of the granting clause in each particular lease. But analysis of Alberta Crown leases suggests that the better view is that at most profits *à prendre*[57] are granted, with significant reversionary property interests remaining in the Crown.[58] Even this form of grant suggests that jurisdiction stemming from Crown ownership ends at the well-head when the substances are produced and converted to chattels.

The federal interest in oil and gas resources

Another major problem becomes apparent from the discussion of the fate of the "Best Efforts" Draft. The federal government's inclination to accept the idea of limitation of federal powers over provincial resources has decreased markedly over the past two years. In fact, since the 1980 winter election, federal resolve to increase its *de facto* regulatory position in relation to energy resources has strengthened considerably.

First there was the retreat from the "Best Efforts" Draft brought about by adopting the position that federal paramountcy over energy-resource export was necessary. Next there was the extremely hard-nosed bargaining posture adopted when it became necessary to negotiate with Alberta concerning renewal or extension of the 1974–75 oil- and natural gas-pricing agreements. Alberta took the position that it would accept nothing less than a pricing package equivalent in "value" to that offered by the Conservative government prior to its abrupt departure from office. As negotiations progressed, details were not disclosed, but it became apparent, when the failure of the talks was announced in late July 1980, that the two sides had never been close. Finally, the natural resources amendment that was included in the Constitution Bill, 1981 retained the federal paramountcy provision.

Basically the problem is revenue sharing. There is general agreement that oil prices must rise. But pressing federal revenue requirements resulting from decreasing tax revenues in a shrinking economy, coupled with a mounting deficit, have caused the federal government to press for an increased share of oil revenues. This federal revenue problem is compounded by the petroleum-import-compensation scheme designed to cushion Eastern Canadians against the substantially higher price of imported crude oil. This program cost the federal government more than $3 billion in 1981. In addition, because the equalization-payment system is based on average provincial revenues, increased oil and gas royalties flowing to producer provinces, particularly Alberta, result in increased payments from the federal treasury to 'have-not' provinces. Alberta figures for 1980 suggest that the federal government received only 14 per cent of every oil and gas dollar, with 52 per cent going to the industry and 34 per cent to the Alberta government.[59] A principle objective of the federal National Energy Program, 1980 was to increase the federal share of oil and gas revenues during the 1980−83 period[60] to approximately 24 per cent.

It has properly been pointed out that while revenue sharing is an important current issue, it is not the ultimate issue.[61] The ultimate issue is economic and political power. A growing federal recognition of the power associated with control of the nation's oil and gas resources is undoubtedly behind the stiffening of federal positions on constitutional revisions that would have the effect of shifting greater authority over natural resources to provincial governments.

Special position for producer provinces
A final problem is that while proposals to strengthen provincial powers over natural resources are general in the sense that they would apply to all provinces, their practical effect is to create a special position for the producing provinces. In fact even the current position accords a kind of special position to producer provinces simply because of the fortuitous location of oil and gas deposits within their boundaries. The vagaries of resource location lend a further ambiguity to the issue in that it is difficult to predict whether future discoveries are likely to distort relative degrees of provincial wealth in yet a different way.

Special Status

It has been pointed out that energy-producing provinces currently enjoy a special position, and that efforts are under way to enhance this position through some form of redistribution of powers. However, this does not constitute special status[62] since it does not and would not involve conferring on one or more provinces constitutional powers different from those accorded other provincial governments. Notwithstanding the prominence of "Western alienation" concerns in recent media reports, no element of special constitutional status in relation to natural resources has been proposed by producer provinces. Considerable care was taken in the "Best Efforts" Draft and in section 57 of the Constitutional Bill, 1981 to include non-discrimination limitations on extended export and taxation powers over provincial resources in order to avoid possible development of *de facto* special status in resource matters. The essential concern is the increased political and economic power that would flow from special status based on natural resources.

Discussion of special status is extremely difficult in the context of natural resources. Not only does confusion arise between *de facto* and *de jure* 'special status' when one is discussing the position of producer provinces, but there is room for argument about which provinces enjoy *de facto* special status. Alberta, for example, has contended that consuming provinces such as Ontario have enjoyed a special position under an oil-pricing agreement[63] that kept prices substantially below world-price levels. This position was maintained by the two-dollar-per-barrel price increase announced by Alberta on 1 August 1980 and by the pricing schedule proposed in the National Energy Program. Any new agreement that does not move prices toward world levels at a relatively rapid rate will maintain this special position that, one can argue, gives consuming provinces a "share" of Western energy resources and resource revenues.

It is difficult to imagine that any special status arrangement designed, for example, to address Quebec's language and cultural concerns would have a significant impact on oil and gas resources. In fact it is difficult to imagine any special status that includes powers primarily concerned with economic or public property matters. Discussion of these issues inevitably leads to consideration of some form of sovereignty for the province or region concerned.

Sovereignty

Sovereignty for a Canadian province or region, as it affects oil and gas, invites comparison with current relations regarding oil and gas between Canada and the United States. For example, sovereign status for Quebec would require combinations of international agreements, domestic regulatory systems, and domestic enabling legislation to deal with such matters as follow:

- Pipeline transit
- Export regulations governing the quantity and price of oil and gas
- Taxation and tariffs
- Strategic concerns
- Foreign ownership and control of oil and gas industries
- State oil and gas enterprise
- Marine tanker transit and oil-pollution risks.

New international agreements on such matters as taxation, defence, and pipeline transit would be necessary. Much Canadian regulatory legislation that deals with aspects of all of the matters listed is already in place. However, implementation through regulations, orders, or decisions on particular applications would be required. Legislative amendments would also be enacted to deal with special issues concerning international relations with Quebec. Certain existing international institutions, such as the International Joint Commission, might be modified, with American concurrence, to function as trilateral mechanisms.

The starting point for negotiations with Quebec would undoubtedly be Canada's existing arrangements with the United States. It seems unlikely that positions could be conciliatory in circumstances following separation. On export issues export-price guidelines of the National Energy Board Act[64] that make such conditions as 'surplus to Canadian needs' and 'just and reasonable in the Canadian public interest' would serve as references. Advantage in export negotiations would appear to lie with Canada since Canadian oil and gas imports are likely to be viewed as more secure than offshore sources, particularly given existing transportation systems. The possibility for significant exports of natural gas to Quebec seems good, given the current surplus situation in Western Canada. However, although Alberta's proposals that natural gas prices be reduced during the early years of gas supply to Quebec in order to encourage energy substitution have been viewed favourably by the NEB,[65] they are not likely to be approved for export to a sovereign Quebec. Canadian subsidization of foreign exports for purposes of market development in the early years of Canadian export to the United States are still a sufficient embarrassment to discourage proposals for incentive prices to Quebec.

There would be difficult negotiations concerning offshore resources that would establish a territorial division for offshore exploration on the East coast. The long-simmering disputes between Quebec and Newfoundland concerning Labrador's boundary and transmission of electricity would be thrown into a new focus. The issues would then have to be resolved in international negotiations against international systems and principles of resolving disputes.[66] The issue could be important in terms of oil and gas, given the presence of promising geological structures in the Labrador-shelf area.

Ideas would undoubtedly surface concerning some type of energy arrangement governing the North American continent. However, the current Canadian mood is against such arrangements with the United States, and it is difficult to see why Canada would adopt a more conciliatory attitude in tripartite continental energy discussions that included Quebec. An essential weakness in Quebec's position would be its lack of status as a significant producer of oil and gas. In fact Quebec could not even expect as favourable a position with Canada, in relation to oil and gas, as the United States now enjoys since Quebec would have far less to offer and would possess far less economic and strategic 'clout' than the United States does now.

Traditionally foreign investment in general and American investment in particular have been welcomed by Canada's Western producer provinces. A similar attitude can already be detected in east coast provinces as they move toward the status of oil and gas producers. It may be expected, therefore, that in a new Canada, following Quebec's separation, Western and Atlantic provinces would favour removal or weakening of foreign ownership controls that the current federal government is in the process of extending and sharpening.[67] In the new power balance resulting from a new population distribution and from Western political and economic power flowing from resource revenues, such proposals may be forced on a reluctant Ontario. The ultimate result could be a form of economic union with the United States, with Quebec remaining on the outside in a less favourable position.

Sovereignty-Association

Sovereignty-association differs conceptually from sovereignty merely in that certain bilateral agreements and institutional arrangements would be developed from negotiation between Canada and a sovereign Quebec. To the extent that these arrangements included free trade and a common tariff, relations pertaining to oil and gas would differ little from their situation in the present régime. The difference would be institutional since it must be assumed that decisions on such matters as interstate pipelines and the import and export of oil and gas could no longer be made by the NEB. Some kind of international regulatory agency would be required, though it is likely that this new body would be closely linked to the domestic regulatory agencies of Canada and Quebec and possibly to that of the United States. It is possible that the venerable International Joint Commission could serve as a model for such an international agency.

In sovereignty-association negotiations Quebec would be hampered by its relative lack of major energy-resource production. Its hydro-electric resources would be significant, but these would be outweighed by the power flowing from Canada's status as a producer and exporter of oil and gas.

Conclusions

Perhaps the central conclusion to be drawn from this discussion is that oil and gas have emerged as energy resources that, in their political and economic significance, transcend national constitutions and even arrangements between nations. As OPEC and the events of 1973 have shown, Canada operates an 'oil economy'. Control of these resources, either through ownership or through regulatory jurisdiction, is a primary source of political power. This is true among provinces within a nation just as it is among nations. The Canada-Alberta oil-pricing negotiations provide a graphic illustration of this fact within Canada.

This suggests that it may be impossible in a constitutional document to deal with oil and gas through the division of law-making powers between central government and producer provinces. The provinces have almost become surrogates for economic power and the political power associated with it.

The main problem is that the central issues are fiscal, not jurisdictional. Fiscal matters cannot be easily handled in constitutional documents because constitutions are expressed in terms of legal rights and powers in relation to defined subject matters, and not in terms of numbers or dollars. It would be possible to prescribe relationships in a new constitution in terms of precise figures for sharing oil and gas revenues. However, such a prescription would not be wise, given the complex and changing nature of the oil and gas industry and the changing relative economic positions of Canada's federal government and her various provinces. Such a revenue-sharing formula, once inserted in the Constitution, could be changed only by formal constitutional amendment.

Similarly the economic and political importance of oil and gas resources makes it unlikely that any special status arrangement will involve powers that relate to these resources. Under Quebec's sovereignty, or even under some form of sovereignty-association, the critical importance of energy resources makes it likely that Canada would adopt a stiff posture on oil and gas matters that would leave a sovereign Quebec relatively little better off than the United States in terms of access to Canadian supplies.

Appendix A
Draft Proposal Discussed by First Ministers at the Federal-Provincial Conference on the Constitution, Ottawa, February 5-6, 1979
Resource Ownership and Interprovincial Trade

(1) (present Section 92)

Resources
(2) In each province, the legislature may exclusively make laws in relation to
   a) exploration for non-renewable natural resources in the province;
   b) development, exploitation, extraction, conservation and management of non-renewable natural resources in the province, including laws in relation

(1) Carries forward existing Section 92.

(2) The draft outlines exclusive provincial legislative jurisdiction over certain natural resources and electric energy within the province. These resources have been defined as non-renewable (e.g. crude oil, copper, iron and nickel), forests and electric energy. This section pertains to *legislative* jurisdiction and in no way impairs established *proprietary*

to the rate of primary production therefrom; and

c) development, exploitation,
   conservation and man-
   agement in the province
   and of sites and facilities in
   the province for the generation of electrical energy,
   including laws in relation
   to the rate of primary production therefrom.

rights of provinces over resources whether these re-
sources are renewable or
non-renewable.

Export from the province of resource

(3) In each province, the legislature may make laws in relation to the export from the
province of the primary production from non-renewable
natural resources and forestry
resources in the province and
the production from facilities
in the province for the generation of electrical energy, but
such laws may not authorize
or provide for prices for production sold for export to
another part of Canada that
are different from prices authorized or provided for production not sold for export
from the province.

(3) Provincial governments are
given concurrent legislative
authority to pass laws governing the export of the re-
sources referred to above
from the province. This legislative capacity is in the sphere
of both interprovincial and
international trade and commerce. Provincial govern-
ments are prohibited from
price discrimination between
resources consumed in the
province and those destined
for consumption in other
provinces. This new provincial legislative capacity applies
to these resources in their raw
state and to them in their
processed state but does not
apply to materials manufactured from them.

Relationship to certain laws of Parliament

(4) Any law enacted by the legislature of a province pursuant
to the authority conferred by
subsection (3) prevails over a
law enacted by Parliament in
relation to the regulation of
trade and commerce except to
the extent that the law so
enacted by Parliament,

a) in the case of a law in
   relation to the regulation
   of trade and commerce

(4) The effect of this provincial
legislative responsibility over
trade and commerce di-
minishes the scope but does
not eliminate the federal government's exclusive authority
over trade and commerce.
The exercise of the provincial
power is subject to two limitations. First, the federal government may legislate for interprovincial trade if there is

within Canada, is necessary to serve a compelling national interest that is not merely an aggregate of local interests; or

b) is a law in relation to the regulation of international trade and commerce.

"compelling national interest". This trigger mechanism may apply to circumstances other than an emergency as established under the peace, order and good government power. Second, federal laws governing international trade prevail over provincial laws in international trade, in effect establishing a concurrent power similar to that for agriculture.

Taxation of resources

(5) In each province, the legislature may make laws in relation to the raising of money by any mode or system of taxation in respect of

a) non-renewable natural resources and forestry resources in the province and the primary production therefrom; and

b) sites and facilities in the province for the generation of electrical energy and the primary production therefrom,

whether or not such production is exported in whole or in part from the province but such laws may not authorize or provide for taxation that differentiates between production exported to another part of Canada and production not exported from the province.

(5) Provincial powers of taxation are increased to include indirect taxes over the resources outlined in this section — whether these resources are destined in part for export outside the province. These taxes are to apply with equal force both in the province and across the rest of the country.

Production from resources

(6) For purposes of this section,

a) production from a non-renewable resource is primary production therefrom if

(6) In determining the scope of provincial legislative powers over resources exported from the province, it became necessary to define the degree to

i) it is in the form in which it exists upon its recovery or severance from its natural state, or

ii) it is a product resulting from processing or refining the resource, and it is not a manufactured product or a product resulting from refining crude oil or refining a synthetic equivalent of crude oil; and

b) production from a forestry resource is primary production therefrom if it consists of sawlogs, poles, lumber, wood chips, sawdust or any other primary wood product, or wood pulp, and is not a product manufactured from wood.

which the resource was processed. It is not intended to extend provincial authority to manufacturing but it is intended to extend it to something beyond its extraction from its natural state. Given the varying resources covered by this section, the wording of this sub-section is thought to place the appropriate limitations on provincial powers.

Existing Powers

(7) Nothing in subsections (2) to (6) derogates from any powers or rights that a legislature or government of a province had immediately before the coming into force of those subsections.

(7) This clause ensures that any existing provincial legislative powers found in s. 92 are not impaired by the new section.

Appendix B

"Revised" Federal proposal, from the Statement by the Prime Minister on Resource Ownership and Interprovincial Trade to the Federal-Provincial Conference of First Ministers on the Constitution, 8-12 September 1980.

The Government of Canada, for its part, responds as follows:

• On *ownership and management*, we have no problem in accepting the principle and are in substantial agreement with the text which has been worked out.

• On *exports of resources*, we agree that provinces should have concurrent power over exports to other parts of Canada, subject to federal paramountcy over interprovincial trade. We do not agree that this concurrent power should extend to provincial exports to other countries.

• On *direct taxation*, we are ready to accept the text which is supported by eight provinces.

• On *primary production*, we are also ready to accept the text which is supported by the great majority of the provinces.

The Government of Canada, in making proposals for changes in this important field, has to bear in mind the enormous importance which resources already play in the economy and the lives of Canadians. As resources become more scarce in the world, they will play an even greater part. We must think more than twice before making changes which could substantially reduce the future capacity of the federal government to carry out its responsibility for Canada as a whole. In the circumstances, I believe that the response I have just indicated, which is positive on a number of important points, warrants serious consideration.

Appendix C

PART VII

AMENDMENT TO THE CONSTITUTION ACT, 1867

Amendment to *Constitution Act, 1867*

57. The *Constitution Act, 1867* (formerly named the *British North America Act, 1867*) is amended by adding thereto, immediately after section 92 thereof, the following heading and section:

"Non-Renewable Natural Resources, Forestry Resources and Electrical Energy

Laws respecting non-renewable natural resources, forestry resources and electrical energy

92A. (1) In each province, the legislature may exclusively make laws in relation to

(*a*) exploration for non-renewable natural resources in the province;

(*b*) development, conservation and management of non-renewable natural resources and forestry resources in the province, including laws in relation to the rate of primary production therefrom; and

(*c*) development, conservation and management of sites and facilities in the province for the generation and production of electrical energy.

Export from provinces of resources

(2) In each province, the legislature may make laws in relation to the export from the province to another part of Canada of the primary production from non-renewable natural resources and forestry resources in the province and the production from facilities in the province for the generation of electrical

energy, but such laws may not authorize or provide for discrimination in prices or in supplies exported to another part of Canada.

(3) Nothing in subsection (2) derogates from the authority of Parliament to enact laws in relation to the matters referred to in that subsection and, where such a law of Parliament and a law of a province conflict, the law of Parliament prevails to the extent of the conflict.

(4) In each province, the legislature may make laws in relation to the raising of money by any mode or system of taxation in respect of
(a) non-renewable natural resources and forestry resources in the province and the primary production therefrom, and
(b) sites and facilities in the province for the generation of electrical energy and the production therefrom,
whether or not such production is exported in whole or in part from the province, but such laws may not authorize or provide for taxation that differentiates between production exported to another part of Canada and production not exported from the province.

(5) The expression "primary production" has the meaning assigned by the Sixth Schedule.

(6) Nothing in subsections (1) to (5) derogates from any powers or rights that a legislature or government of a province had immediately before the coming into force of this section."

58. The said Act is further amended by adding thereto the following Schedule:

"THE SIXTH SCHEDULE

Primary Production from Non-Renewable Natural Resources and Forestry Resources

1. For the purposes of section 92A of this Act,
(a) production from a non-renewable natural resource is primary production therefrom if
(i) it is in the form in which it exists upon its recovery or severance from its natural state, or

(ii) it is a product resulting from processing or refining the resource, and is not a manufactured product or a product resulting from refining crude oil, refining upgraded heavy crude oil, refining gases or liquids derived from coal or refining a synthetic equivalent of crude oil; and

(*b*) production from a forestry resource is primary production therefrom if it consists of sawlogs, poles, lumber, wood chips, sawdust or any other primary wood product, or wood pulp, and is not a product manufactured from wood."

Notes

1.   Section 109 British North America Act, 1867: "All Lands, Mines, Minerals, and Royalties belonging to the several Provinces of Canada, Nova Scotia, and New Brunswick at the Union, and all Sums then due or payable for such Lands, Mines, Minerals, or Royalties, shall belong to the several Provinces of Ontario, Quebec, Nova Scotia, and New Brunswick in which the same are situate or arise, subject to any Trusts existing in respect thereof, and to any interest other than that of the Province in the same." See also British North America Act, 1930, 20–21 Geo V, c. 26 (U.K.) which implemented the Resources Transfer Agreements and thereby placed Alberta, Saskatchewan, and B.C. (as to the Railway Belt and Peace River Block Lands) on the same footing as the other provinces under section 109.

2.   British North America Act, 1867, s. 95(5): "The Management and Sale of the Public Lands belonging to the Province and of the Timber and Wood thereon."

3.   *Ibid.*, s. 92(13): "Property and Civil Rights in the Province."

4.   *Ibid.*, s. 92(16): "Generally all Matters of a merely local or private Nature in the Province."

5.   The question of whether and the extent to which property in the resources is granted or disposed of depends on the terms of each particular lease document. Analysis of eighteen Alberta Crown leases used between 1949 and 1981 suggests that there have been no outright grants of oil and gas in the ground. At most, profits *à prendre* (that is, rights to recover and sell the oil and gas) are granted, with a reversionary property right remaining in the Crown. See A. Gervais, "The Nature of the Interest Granted Under Alberta Crown Petroleum and Natural Gas Leases," (unpublished paper on file at University of Calgary Law Faculty, April 1981). Whether or not the provinces can assert constitutional powers based on resource ownership depends in part on whether the Crown provincial has retained a property interest in leased resources.

6.   See text below, pp. 32–44.

7.   British North America Act, 1867, s. 9(12): "The Regulation of Trade and Commerce." See *C.I.G.O.L.* v. *Attorney-General of Saskatchewan*, (1978) 18 N.R. 107 (S.C.C.); (1977) 6 W.W.R. 607 (S.C.C.)

8.   British North America Act, 1867, s. 91(3): "The raising of Money by any Mode or System of Taxation." See *C.I.G.O.L.* v. *Attorney-General of Saskatchewan*, note 7, above.

9. British North America Act, 1867, s. 92(10): "Local Works and Undertakings other than such as are of the following Classes: (a) Lines of Steam or other Ships, Railways, Canals, Telegraphs, and other Works and Undertakings connecting the Province with any other or others of the Provinces, or extending beyond the Limits of the Province."

10. *Ibid.*, s. 10(c): "Such Works as, although wholly situate within the Province, are before or after their Execution declared by the Parliament of Canada to be for the general Advantage of Canada or for the Advantage of Two or more of the Provinces."

11. *Ibid.*, s. 91 (preamble): Two main "Peace, Order and good Government" theories have been developed by the Courts: (1) "National Emergency." See *Reference Re: Anti-Inflation Act*, [1976] 2 S.C.R. 373. (1976) 68 D.L.R. (3d) 453 (S.C.C.) and (2) "National dimensions." See *Attorney-General of Ontario* v. *Canada Temperance Federation*, 1946 A.C. 193. (1946) 2 D.L.R. 1 (P.C.) and Dale Gibson, "Measuring 'National Dimensions'," *Manitoba Law Journal* 7 (1976): 15−27.

12. See generally John Davis, *Canadian Energy Prospects*, Special Study No. 13 prepared for the Royal Commission on Canada's Economic Prospects (Ottawa: Queen's Printer, 1957).

13. See generally Earle Gray, *The Great Canadian Oil Patch* (Toronto: Maclean-Hunter, 1970).

14. See Exportation of Power and Fluids and Importation of Gas Act, S.C. 1955, c. 14.

15. See W. Rostow, "The Challenges of Economic Growth."

16. See the Pipelines Act, R.S.C. 1952, c. 211.

17. See the National Energy Board Act, S.C. 1959, c. 46.

18. See Canada, Royal Commission on Energy, *First Report* (Ottawa: Queen's Printer, 1959).

19. *Ibid.* The concern particularly related to the contractual arrangements between Westcoast Transmission and El Paso Natural Gas in the United States. Additional attention was focused on Canadian Montana and its sales to its parent, Montana Power.

20. That is to say, the embargo and price hikes.

21. See generally Energy Resources Conservation Board, "Review of Field Pricing of Gas in Alberta," E.R.C.B. Report 73−1−OG, (Calgary, July 1973).

22. See National Energy Board, Engineering Branch, *Preliminary Report — Potential Limitations of Canadian Petroleum Supplies, Oil and Gas* (Ottawa, December 1972).

23. Nationally televised address by Premier Peter Lougheed in response to announcement of the National Energy Program, 30 October 1980.

24. Petroleum Marketing Act, S.A. 1973, c. 96 as amended S.A., 1979, c. 60.

25. Mines and Minerals Act, R.S.A., 1970, c. 238 as amended S.A., 1980, c. 76. See s. 135.1.

26. Section 21(1) covers the sale of the lessee's share of petroleum and the power of the APMC to establish the selling price and buyer. See note 24 above.

27. Quoted in Government of Alberta, *Harmony in Diversity: A New Federalism for Canada* (Edmonton, 1978), p. 6.

28. See text pp. 21−24.

29. Constitutional Amendment Act, 1978, Bill C−60, s. 98.

30. Government of Alberta, *Harmony in Diversity*.

31. The natural resources provisions of the 1979 "Best Efforts" Draft are reproduced as Appendix A.

32. *C.I.G.O.L.* v. *Attorney-General of Saskatchewan*, note 7, above.

33. *Central Canada Potash Co. Ltd.* v. *Government of Saskatchewan*, (1979) 88 D.L.R. (3d) 609 (S.C.C.)

34. Rowland J. Harrison, "Natural Resources and the Constitution: Some Recent Developments and Their Implications for the Future Regulation of the Resource Industries," *Alberta Law Review* 18 (1980), p. 9.

35. At the February 1979 First Ministers' Conference, the federal government and all provinces except Quebec and Alberta accepted the proposals.

36. The 1980 "Revised" federal position is attached as Appendix B.

37. Federal-Provincial Conference of First Ministers on the Constitution, 8–12 September 1980. "Notes for a Statement by the Prime Minister of Canada on Resource Ownership and Interprovincial Trade," (Ottawa, 1980), Document No. 800–141038.

38. "Premier Derides Concessions," *The Calgary Herald*, 9 September 1980, p. A–1.

39. Sections 57 and 58 of the Constitution Bill, 1982 which add s. 92A and Schedule 6 to the Constitution Act, 1867 (the BNA Act) are reproduced as Appendix C.

40. See *C.I.G.O.L.* v. *Attorney-General of Saskatchewan*, note 7, above. But see also *Smylie* v. *The Queen*, (1900) 27 O.A.R. 172 (Ont. C.A.)

41. See the "operations" and "effects" criteria stated by Beetz, J. *Reference Re Anti-Inflation Act*, note 11, above, at 458 (S.C.R.)

42. *Ibid.*, at 425.

43. Energy Supplies Emergency Act, S.C. 1978–79, c. 17.

44. See Herbert Marx, "Notes and Comments: The Energy Crisis and the Emergency Power in Canada," *Dalhousie Law Journal* 2 (1975–76): 446–54.

45. Constitutional Amendment Bill, 1981, s. 57 adding s. 92A(1)(b), see Appendix C. "Best Efforts" Draft, "Resources," s. 2(c), see Appendix A.

46. See *Smylie* v. *The Queen*, note 40, above.

47. "Relationship to Certain Laws of Parliament," s. 4(a), see Appendix A.

48. See analysis of "National Dimensions" in Gibson, "Measuring 'National Dimensions'."

49. See *Reference Re Anti-Inflation Act*, note 11, above.

50. See Peter W. Hogg, *Constitutional Law of Canada* (Toronto: Carswell, 1979), pp. 103–14.

51. *C.I.G.O.L.* v. *Attorney-General of Saskatchewan*, note 7, above. *Central Canada Potash Co. Ltd.* v. *Government of Saskatchewan*, note 33, above.

52. See note 7.

53. Under the British North America Act, 1867, s. 125. See G.V. LaForest, *The Allocation of Taxing Power Under the Canadian Constitution*, 2d ed. (Toronto: Canadian Tax Foundation, 1981), p. 150; and Gerard V. LaForest, *Natural Resources and Public Property Under the Canadian Constitution* (Toronto: University of Toronto Press, 1969), pp. 162–63.

54. Alberta Natural Tax Reference, (1981) 28 A.R. 11 (A.C.A.)

55. D.E. Thring, "Alberta, Oil and the Constitution," *Alberta Law Review* 17 (1979): 78–81.

56. *Ibid.*, p. 76.

57. For example, having the right to drill for and to produce oil and gas, without having full ownership of that oil and gas while it is in the ground.

58.   See Gervais, "The Nature of the Interest Granted Under Alberta . . . Leases."

59.   "Ottawa Wants Almost Triple, Energy Study Says," *The Calgary Herald*, 30 September 1980, p. A−1.

60.   Canada, Department of Energy, Mines and Resources, *The National Energy Program* (Ottawa: Minister of Supply and Services Canada, 1980), pp. 108−12.

61.   Harrison, "Natural Resources and the Constitution," pp. 10−12.

62.   As defined by Professor Hogg. See P.W. Hogg, "Definitions," Memorandum to members of Constitutional Change Project Co-ordinating Committee, 25 June 1979.

63.   The federal-provincial oil-pricing agreement originally implemented 1 April 1974 and the Federal-Alberta Natural Gas Pricing Agreements that date from October 1975.

64.   National Energy Board, R.S.C. 1970, c. N−6, s. 83, as amended R.S.C. 1970, c. 27, s. 2, supp. 1.

65.   National Energy Board, Report to the Governor in Council, Q & M Pipe Lines Ltd., May 1980.

66.   K. Beauchamp, M. Crommelin, and A.R. Thompson, "Jurisdictional Problems in Canada's Offshore," *Alberta Law Review* 11 (1973): 431−69.

67.   See "Canada's New Government Assumes Key Energy Role," *Oil and Gas Journal* 78 (16 June 1980): 27−32.

The Authors

ALASTAIR R. LUCAS is currently the Executive Director of the Canadian Institute of Resources Law at The University of Calgary. He was formerly holder of the Chair of Natural Resources Law in the Faculty of Law at The University of Calgary and continues to hold a professorial appointment within the Faculty. Professor Lucas has served as a policy advisor and consultant to several government departments, Law Reform Commissions, and the Science Council of Canada. He is currently Chairman of the Canadian Arctic Resources Committee, founding member and first National Chairman of the Environmental Law Section of the Canadian Bar Association, a member of the Canadian Environmental Advisory Council, and a representative on the Environment Council of Alberta's Public Advisory Group. He has published extensively in the field of environmental, energy and resources law. Most notably, he is co-author of both the *Canada Energy Law Service* and *Canadian Environmental Law*.

IAN McDOUGALL was educated at Simon Fraser University, Osgoode Hall Law School, and Harvard Law School, where he received degrees in both Law and Economics. He is a member of the Faculty of Osgoode Hall Law School where he has taught constitutional law. He has written extensively on energy and regulatory issues.

Constitutional Change and the Forest Industry

R.A. FASHLER
of the British Columbia Bar

A.R. THOMPSON
Westwater Research Centre,
University of British Columbia

Contents

Constitutional Change and the Forest Industry

Introduction

The forest resource is an imposing feature of life in Canada in both a physical and an economic sense. Forests cover approximately 341 566 700 hectares (844 000 000 acres) of land in Canada; that is, nearly 35 per cent of the entire country. Of this forest land nearly 1 750 000 hectares (430 million acres) is economically productive.[1] A 1978 study tells us that over 14 per cent of value added in all Canadian manufacturing originates in the logging, wood, pulp and paper, and allied industries.[2] The same source reports that: "Although Canada accounts for only 5 per cent of total world wood production and 10 per cent of the industrial roundwood harvest, Canadian forest-product exports are very important in world trade. Canada is the leading exporter of softwood lumber, chemical wood pulp and newsprint."[3] Canada's contribution to total world export of these three wood products is 30 per cent, 40 per cent, and 65 per cent respectively.[4] In 1977 Canadian forest-product exports amounted to $7.9 billion or approximately 18 per cent of the value of *all* Canadian commodity exports.[5] A 1979 article in *Readers Digest*, commissioned by the Canadian Institute of Forestry, concluded: "[The forest industry] earns more foreign exchange than the combined exports of oil, gas and coal; twenty-five per cent more than agricultural products; ten times more than fisheries."[6]

57

In 1976 approximately 288 000 people were employed directly in the forest industry in Canada and earned approximately $4.1 billion.[7] When all backward and forward linkages are considered, Reed and Associates estimate that a total of "900,000 Canadians owe their livelihood to the forest industry."[8] Furthermore the forest industry is an important factor in the economy of *all* provinces, except Prince Edward Island.

Unfortunately all is not well within this extremely important resource sector. Wood, unlike minerals, is a renewable resource that if properly managed can provide employment and revenue indefinitely. Until quite recently, however, harvesting has had more in common with mining than with sound forest management. The 'rotation period' of trees (that is, the time it takes to grow a mature crop suitable for harvesting on a sustained yield basis) averages sixty to eighty years; hence errors made many years ago can have disastrous consequences today. Concerned foresters and economists are now telling us that this is exactly what has happened in Canada. The Canadian Institute of Forestry article mentioned above concluded: "It is hard to believe that Canada of all countries, is facing a shortage of wood . . . Shortages of economically accessible timber, already critical in several mill towns across the country, threaten to become general by the end of the century. . . Quite simply, suitable timber is disapppearing faster than it is growing back. There are plenty of trees out there, but they are often the wrong species, poor in quality, or too far from the mills."[9]

Most, if not all, of this shortage is attributable to a predictable 'falldown' phenomenon that occurs when the industry exhausts supplies of old growth timber and begins to harvest second growth forests on a sustained yield basis. Old growth timber yields substantially higher volumes of wood than second growth timber because the older trees have been growing for a much longer period of time. If something is not done to counter the effect of falldown, the consequences will be severe for the entire Canadian economy; they will hit hardest the many people who will lose their jobs and the communities that will lose their main source of economic activity. F.L.C. Reed and Associates, in a 1978 report prepared for the Canadian Forestry Service,[10] advocates a major program of "intensive forest management" across Canada as the best method for maintaining yields in spite of a natural falldown. A major program of capital investment in the form of silvicultural methods like direct seeding, tree improvement, thinning, and fertilization could, it is estimated, lead to gains of 40 to 100 per cent over natural forests in terms of merchantable timber.[11]

Many analysts would like to see a true national forest policy emerge in Canada so that common goals could be articulated and a well co-ordinated and comprehensive effort could be mounted to protect and enhance the crucial function of this resource in the Canadian economy.[12] It is clear that intensive forest management would fulfil a major function in a national forest policy, but observers have pointed out that there are many other aspects of forest-sector management that require immediate attention.[13] Even apparently unrelated areas like education, manpower, and unemployment insurance have forest-policy implications.

The reader may well be wondering what connection there is between problems in forest management and constitutional arrangements. Some analysts contend that the existing institutional framework in Canada contributes substantially, directly or indirectly, to the problems facing Canada's forest sector today. A 1978 article in the *Journal of Forestry* stated:

> Reed and his associates submit that the most important impediments to forest management are institutional in nature and include tenure, funding, jurisdictional rivalry between provincial and federal governments, and the lack of policy formulation and strategic planning. Further, they suggest that the root of the vacuum in policy and planning is the failure of senior governments to cooperate effectively . . .
>
> In sum, forestry in Canada has suffered from the inadequacy of government organization and the adversary relationship of federal and provincial governments inherited from ambiguities in the BNA legislation.[14]

Apart from this general fragmentation, some specific examples of constitutional problems in the forest sector come to mind.

The British North America (BNA) Act[15] distributed the lion's share of legislative jurisdiction over Canada's forest resources to the provinces, but allocated considerable authority over fisheries to the federal government and thereby created a critical interface with a high potential for controversy. Forest operations at all stages, including falling, storage, transportation, and processing, have negative impacts on fish and their aqueous environment. The potential for conflict became actual in the spring of 1979 in the Queen Charlotte Islands of British Columbia, when the federal Department of Fisheries arrested certain loggers who were operating on the basis of a cutting permit issued by the provincial Ministry of Forests.

Another major source of controversy stems from federal power to tax and spend. It is estimated that in 1977 the federal government earned some $835.6 million from taxes and levies on forest-related incomes and transactions.[16] The segment of federal revenues earned from the forest industry in British Columbia alone was approximately $307.5 million.[17] Yet federal expenditures on forestry in that year were approximately $73.6 million throughout Canada; of that sum, a mere $0.3 million was spent in British Columbia.[18] It should be recalled that intensive forest management requires significant levels of capital investment. Again, in 1977, the Government of British Columbia earned approximately $378.5 million from the resource, while its expenditures were approximately $125.2 million.[19] It does not seem fair for a provincial government to have reinvested almost one third of its earnings from the forest sector, while Ottawa returned less than one thousandth of what it received. There has been some increase in the federal contribution in recent years. When the federal government does invest funds, however, a frequently heard complaint is that the resulting programs, even when jointly undertaken with the provinces, represent an improper incursion into provincial fields of jurisdiction.

The power to control and tax exports leaving a province is another issue that raises constitutional questions for the forest industry. British Columbia is extremely concerned with promoting industrial development and employment within the province. One method of achieving this goal is to impose restrictions on unprocessed timber and wood residue leaving the province.[20] There is probably nothing unconstitutional in requiring that timber cut from provincial Crown land be manufactured in the province,[21] but problems may be created by allowing for exemption from this requirement. The province reserves the right to grant an exemption from the manufacturing requirement and to charge a fee for the exemption. This fee is challengeable constitutionally on the grounds that it is not a direct tax "in order to the raising of a revenue for provincial purposes."[22] Furthermore, if the fee were seen by the courts as fixing the price of a commodity destined primarily for international or interprovincial markets, it would be open to challenge on the ground that it constituted an invasion into federal jurisdiction over trade and commerce.[23]

The federal government owns some forested land within the provinces: that is, Indian lands held in trust for the Native people living there, and national parks. British Columbia does not attempt to control exports from these federal lands or from most privately owned lands. Ottawa exercises its own export controls that parallel provincial regulations and are administered in co-operation with the province.[24] The federal controls apply to timber cut from all land within the provinces that is going to foreign markets.

The provinces have several means of regulating the structure of the forest industry, which has a strong tendency toward concentration into very few hands. Some of these means interfere with the interprovincial flow of capital. In early January 1979, for instance, Premier Bennett of British Columbia personally blocked a bid by Canadian Pacific Investments (C.P.I.) of Montreal to take over control of MacMillan Bloedel, the largest forest company operating in the province. Exactly what leverage the Premier brought to bear on C.P.I. was never made explicit, but rights to Crown timber must have figured prominently in the discussions that took place. Premier Bennett probably threatened to terminate cutting rights in provincial forests.

Further, through a combination of legislation and licence terms, the B.C. government influences the complexion of private industry in the province. Certain forest tenures are made available only to smaller operators, while other tenures, normally granted to larger companies, require the licensees to retain independent contractors to harvest a portion of the timber allocated under the licence. Moreover no Crown tenure may be transferred or assigned without the consent of the Minister of Forests. The sale of a control block of shares in, and the corporate amalgamation of, companies holding Crown tenures are considered to be sales of the forest rights themselves and to require ministerial approval.

Clearly any of the devices mentioned above can be utilized to favour operators based in British Columbia over extraprovincial concerns. However, from a constitutional point of view, little can be said to impugn such uses of provincial power.[25] Section 121 of the BNA Act only guarantees the free interprovincial movement of goods and produce, not that of capital. In the eyes of some observers, however, such tampering with normal interprovincial business makes a mockery of nationhood. Although the use of provincial power to prevent investment by residents of another province in provincially owned resources might constitute an incursion into federal jurisdiction (for example, trade and commerce), it is more likely to be seen merely as provincial management of its own property.

In the late 1970s and more recently, there has been a flurry of activity in relation to the forest resource. Professional foresters, economists, and industry members have expressed strong criticisms and recommendations. Major studies, such as the British Columbia Royal Commission on Forest Resources[26] and the two Reed reports,[27] are focusing these concerns. The federal government has responded by allocating more funds to the resource through the Canadian Forest Service and the Department of Regional Economic Expansion, but the industry continues to experience long-term difficulties.

Jurisdictional issues relating to natural resources are considered by many Canadians to be as significant in terms of Canada's future as the issue of political and cultural autonomy for Quebec. Together these issues are straining the federation to its limits. Should our constitutional distribution of powers be changed in the near future, the impact on the forest industry must be given serious and careful consideration. In the following sections of this paper, we shall speculate on how the adoption of four particular constitutional options might affect the existing pattern of forest-sector management in Canada.

Full Sovereignty for Quebec with No Special Form of Association with Canada

The elements of full sovereignty for Quebec are simple and clear. Quebec would be a sovereign country in full control of all policy tools. Any ties with Canada would be established diplomatically, and each state would be motivated primarily by self-interest. The relationship between Quebec and Canada would be similar to that between Canada and the United States. Being close neighbours with similar economies and concerns, all three states would probably continue to co-operate. However, the Canada-Quebec relationship would differ in two important respects from the Canada–United States relationship. First, the United States has far more bargaining power than Quebec in dealings with Canada, and secondly the American economy is more efficient. Furthermore Canada would probably have more bargaining power in dealings with the United States than would Quebec.

If Quebec should separate, a puzzling issue remains: What would become of the Canadian federation? It is almost impossible to predict how the remaining provinces might react. The federation might become more centralized, although that development would be contrary to the trend of recent years. Alternatively, other provinces or regions might decide to follow Quebec's example of independence or even to merge with the United States.

On the assumption that the structure of federation would continue unaltered, it has been contended that:

> The Western Provinces would gain immensely if Quebec were to separate. Then, the Western and Atlantic Provinces would out-vote Ontario in the House of Commons. Free trade with the United States would become attainable and Ontario might have to allow the other provinces to control the railways . . . The provinces could assert their rights to draw revenue from and to control completely the development and management of their natural resources. If decisions were made solely as dictated by hard-nosed calculations of self-interest, the Western Provinces would secede unless they were offered sufficient bribes to make it profitable to stay in the federation. The bribes would have to be substantial.[28]

It is safe to assume that if Quebec separated from Canada and no form of economic association were established between the two entities, it would be very difficult for Canadian forestry personnel to work in Quebec, and vice versa, during times of excessive availability of manpower.

In Quebec all federal activities and funding relating to post-secondary education, employment training, job placement, and unemployment insurance would cease. Quebec would take over all aspects of these social services. All internal sources of tax revenue would be available to the new country to finance such programs, but federal equalization payments would be lost. If the analysts are correct who tell us that Quebec is a net beneficiary under the existing system of federal spending, then social services in a sovereign Quebec would cost the citizens of that state more, while the cost of such services to Canadians would drop. Of course any changes in efficiency resulting from separation, such as reduction of overlap, would be likely to mitigate these tendencies.

More than likely, employment, education, and unemployment policies within a sovereign Quebec would be more sensitive to the needs of the forest industry in that province.[29] Similarly, by virtue of the political shift within Canada described in the quotation above, federal personnel services would probably also become more closely related to regional economic conditions and needs in the truncated Canada.

By separating, Quebec would gain full control over all natural resources within its borders. All federal lands would be taken over, and Quebec would gain full proprietary and legislative control over intraprovincial fisheries. The extent of Quebec's control over the coastal fishery would depend on its success in negotiating with Canada seabed boundaries in the adjacent offshore areas. With unified control, forest planning and management within the province should be more homogeneous, and bureaucratic overlap should be reduced. Environmental protection measures would be unified, as well, so that regulation of forest operations would avoid the complications that now exist in Canada. On the other hand, Quebec would lose the benefit of federal spending for forest management and research (for example, Canadian Forest Service operations in the province, or Department of Regional Economic Expansion grants), although it would have in its control greater tax revenue with which to make up the difference.

Clearly separation would exclude Quebec from direct participation in any Canadian national forest policy. Of course what is learned from the Canadian experience would be available to the new country and vice versa. There is no reason whatever to suppose that scientific exchanges between the two countries would cease. The achievement of a viable national forest policy in what remained of Canada would probably be made easier by the separation of Quebec. With fewer governments to disagree with one another, a national forest policy should be less difficult to achieve.

Transportation of forest products between Canada and a sovereign and 'dissociated' Quebec, to the extent that it goes on today, would be substantially altered. Products and vehicles crossing national boundaries would probably be subject to trade barriers, special charges, and licence requirements. Rail rates between Quebec and Canada would more than likely be altered. In fact the structure of rail rates within what remains of Canada would also be likely to change — in favour of the Western provinces.[30] To the extent that Canadian producers and Quebec compete in the same Canadian markets for forest products, alterations in Canadian transportation policies would work against a sovereign Quebec. If Canada could bargain for preferred transportation treatment in the United States, a small competitive advantage would be given to Canadian forest products in the American market.

It has been claimed that pulp and paper is Quebec's largest export industry.[31] But it is losing its competitive position in the American market, not to other Canadian producers, but to operators in the southern states.[32] Quebec's problem is obsolescence and lack of new capital investment. It has been suggested that a sovereign Quebec would actually become more competitive in this crucial market because "if Quebec were an independent monetary unit, the external value of its currency could be allowed to decrease sufficiently to offset the deteriorating competitive position of much of Quebec industry, not only in relation to competitors in foreign countries but also to those located in other provinces."[33]

Because the prime markets for their products are outside Canada, the forest sectors in most provinces today are not always sensitive to federal economic policies. They are often affected equally, if not more, by changes in American economic policies. For instance, changes in the American interest rate affect the market for Canadian forest products more than do Canadian interest-rate changes. A major exception to this phenomenon is policy governing the exchange rate of Canadian currency.

The constitutional validity of provincial export controls and manufacturing requirements would cease to be an issue for Quebec if that province separated, although it would continue to be one in British Columbia. On the other hand, separation would allow federal export controls to be applied against forest products leaving Canada for Quebec, and import controls might be applied to Quebec forest products entering Canada.

Sovereignty would give the new Quebec government full fiscal control within its territory. For the first time there would be no constitutional barriers to the new state's full assertion of its financial interest in resource rents and profits. Fiscal policy within a sovereign Quebec would probably be simpler and more attuned to local needs than it is now. Ottawa would lose a major source of tax revenues, and Quebec would lose federal spending in its various forms. Quebec is a net recipient under the existing system of equalization. The Parti québécois contends, however, that other provinces, especially Ontario, have benefited more from the kind of federal spending that encourages economic development.[34] In addition Quebec and most other provinces insist that conditional grants received over the years from the federal government were as much an intrusion as they were a benefit.[35] It is also quite possible that separation would eliminate costs associated with bureaucratic overlap and inefficiency to the extent that some of the lost federal spending would be offset. Further, perhaps, full fiscal control would encourage the Government of Quebec to increase investment in intensive forest management in the province.

Separation would end federal activities in the realm of research and development in Quebec. The Canadian Forest Service's Laurentian Research Centre would be closed. Co-operative research ventures would also be affected by separation, but they would not necessarily cease. To the extent that federal research and development activities were ended in Quebec, there would be more funds available for Ottawa to spend in the other provinces.

A sovereign Quebec would have all the tools necessary for complete control of competition, foreign investment, and corporate practices within the province. On the other hand, Canadian foreign investment laws would apply to Québécois seeking to invest in the remaining provinces. Provincial barriers to investment from outside would be exercised even less sympathetically toward a sovereign Quebec than they are now.

Sovereignty-Association

This constitutional option is really just a particular variety of sovereignty. The Quebec government's white paper tells us that, under sovereignty-association, Quebec would retain all the political, legal, and fiscal independence associated with full separation; as two fully sovereign states, however, Canada and Quebec would agree to adopt certain common institutions and policies that would relate, for the most part, to economic matters.[36] The key elements of association would be a common market and monetary union. Quebec's association with Canada would be governed by a "treaty of community association"; the interpretation and application of this treaty would be determined ultimately by a special court of justice. Of course representatives from Quebec would cease to sit in the Canadian Parliament.

Again, it is difficult to foresee how such an arrangement between Canada and Quebec would affect relationships between the remaining partners in Confederation. It seems inevitable that at least some of the provinces would demand a greater degree of autonomy from the central government. More important, it is unlikely to the highest degree that the remaining provinces would become willing partners in an association that gave Quebec greater decision-making authority than they themselves exercise over key, association-wide, policy areas like tariffs, the central bank, and transportation.

The choice of this particular constitutional option would have an impact on the forest industry similar in many respects to that of full separation. If a treaty of community association similar to that outlined in Quebec's white paper were agreed on, it is unclear exactly how that would affect the ability of Canadian forestry personnel to work in Quebec, and vice versa. Although Canadians and Québécois would be permitted to travel freely across an unpoliced border, regulation of the labour market would be a matter reserved for negotiation in a special agreement.[37] It must be assumed that both partners in the association would bargain for labour mobility only to the extent that their own constituency would benefit. The result would probably be restrictions in mobility related to certain jobs and sectors at certain times.

In theory there is no reason why joint bodies could not be set up to administer manpower and employment programs in the association. In reality Quebec is particularly protective of social service programs and is unlikely to agree to anything of the sort. It can be safely assumed, therefore, that an associated, but sovereign, Quebec would control its own manpower and employment programs in a manner similar to that discussed with respect to full sovereignty — a manner, that is to say, entirely concerned with internal needs and priorities.

Forest planning, management, and regulation in Quebec and the Canadian provinces would probably not be significantly affected by the treaty of association; any impact in this area would flow exclusively from sovereignty, as discussed in the preceding section. An association-wide forest policy is extremely unlikely, but not impossible. Furthermore Quebec would almost certainly choose to regulate environmental and fisheries matters alone, with the possible exception of trans-boundary problems.

Transportation is another area the white paper reserves for special agreement between the two associated countries.[38] Of particular interest is the reference in that paper to possible "joint management of public carriers such as Air Canada and Canadian National."[39] The authors of the white paper were strongly critical of rail transport in the existing federation:

"Only 12% of the Canadian railway network is in Québec; Québec has only 0.9 miles of railway per capita compared to the Canadian average of 2.1 miles; and products entering or leaving Québec are subject to rail rates about 40% higher than the Canadian average."[40] If special transportation agreements are negotiated, one can expect very tough bargaining on Quebec's part.

As Canada already has a common market, it is difficult to see how its continuing to operate with a sovereign Quebec could significantly affect existing trade patterns. Free trade within the common market would not by itself alter the amount of business now done in Canada by the forest industries of Quebec and the other Canadian provinces. As to foreign markets, whether Quebec's posture with respect to international trade policies and agreements would coincide with the interests of the other provinces that export forest products would depend on whether Quebec production was already at or near maximum. If it were, Quebec would probably seek no more than to protect its market share, a position unlikely to receive a sympathetic response in the Western provinces.

A common currency within the association would maintain the convenience and low transaction costs of existing Canadian trade patterns. It would also tie together the financial destinies of the association's partners by means of a common exchange rate. This could have negative implications for Quebec's obsolescing pulp-and-paper-processing facilities. As noted above, it has been contended that a separate currency might be preferable for Quebec because it would enable the province's declining competitiveness on the world market to be offset by monetary devaluation.[41]

Under sovereignty-association Quebec would elect to keep complete sovereignty over fiscal matters. As a result it is likely that total investment in intensive forest management would increase. If this form of investment really is urgently required, the Government of Quebec would have no one to blame but itself for a deficiency.

If this option were implemented, federal in-house research currently conducted in Quebec would cease, at least in its present form. Research is, however, a highly suitable avenue for co-operative effort. Not only do existing joint ventures of this sort stand a good chance of continuing in a régime of sovereignty-association, but it would not be surprising to see new ones begun.

The Quebec government's white paper suggests that capital should move freely within the monetary union, subject only to the entitlement of "each party . . . to proclaim an investment code or to adopt, if need be, particular regulations applicable to certain financial institutions."[42] What is meant by 'each party' in the excerpt quoted above is unclear. Currently each province has a securities code, and the federal government may soon have one, too. When the white paper speaks of 'each party', it is apparently referring to the other provinces as well as to Ottawa. If this is so, then no major problem or change from the present situation would be likely to occur. On the other hand, if 'each party' means only the two sovereign states, Quebec's investment in the provinces would be controlled only by a single federal enactment. Such an eventuality would undoubtedly sit very poorly with the Canadian provinces.

Laws applying to the review of foreign investments would not apply to screen the movement of capital entering Canada from Quebec. The only exceptions to the principle of free movement of capital cited in the white paper refer generally to the regulation of securities and to financial institutions. The protection of provincially based forest companies and their Crown-timber holdings does not fit within either exception. Therefore, in principle, it would appear that protectionist tendencies, such as those practised by British Columbia's government in 1979 in relation to the attempt by C.P.I. of Montreal to take over MacMillan Bloedel, would be contrary to the treaty of association.

Special Status for One or More Provinces

Special status is a concept that has evolved in relation to the Province of Quebec. For obvious reasons that province has always enjoyed a measure of particular status *vis-à-vis* the rest of the country. In the 1960s, however, it was proposed that a major systematic adjustment be made so that the distinctive national aspirations of Quebec could be accommodated more appropriately within the Canadian federation.

In 1968 the thrust of this constitutional option was summarized in four main points as follows:

> First, under this proposal the government of Quebec would assume full responsibility for most if not all federal-provincial programs and would receive from the federal government a fiscal

transfer which would fully compensate the province. The government of Quebec would similarly be compensated for new federal-provincial programs — such as medicare — whether or not the province undertook a program similar to that required in other provinces. Secondly, the government of Quebec would under this approach assume responsibility for certain purely federal programs, principally the family allowance and old age security income maintenance programs, and again would be compensated by means of a fiscal transfer from the federal government. Thirdly, the government of Quebec would be given the right to be consulted in respect of other federal policies, including fiscal, tariff and trade policies, and probably monetary policy. . . Fourthly, the government of Quebec might expect to assume certain aspects of federal jurisdiction, such as the right to conclude international arrangements, at least in fields of provincial jurisdiction and certainly to develop something of an international personality.[43]

The major flaw with this type of arrangement, as with sovereignty-association, is that the provinces not given special status are unlikely to agree to the change unless they are offered at least the option of receiving the same benefits themselves. This attitude is reflected in *British Columbia's Constitutional Proposals*:

British Columbia cannot accept a distribution of powers in which a major feature is the granting of some subject matters to some provinces and the denial of those matters to other provinces. British Columbia believes that a Constitution containing broad special powers to be exercised by only one or a few provinces is alien to the original rationale of Confederation, namely the legal equality in law-making terms of all the provinces. British Columbia believes that this equality should be maintained. If certain provinces then acquire a *de facto* special status by exercising or failing to exercise powers which all provinces have, British Columbia would not complain.[44]

Special status would not directly alter the mobility of the labour force throughout Canada. It is conceivable, however, that the province enjoying special status might attempt to exercise indirectly its right of consultation concerning federal programs that affect mobility, such as unemployment insurance and employment resources. There is also a possibility that the province would assume responsibility for providing such programs within its borders.

Provincial control over management, harvesting, and marketing of the forest resource would not be affected appreciably by adoption of this constitutional option because provincial control is already dominant in these areas. It is uncertain whether Ottawa legally could and, if so, whether it would transfer to the province enjoying special status ownership of Indian reserves and national parks and legislative authority over them. The province in question would probably seek to gain full legislative control over fisheries and environmental protection. If it failed in this objective, it would likely seek to influence federal policies through consultation before any major decisions that affected the province were made in these realms. This constitutional option would not create barriers to the establishment of a national forest policy, especially if the province with special status stood to benefit from the change.

It seems that every province and region, except perhaps Ontario, is dissatisfied with the existing system of rail transport in Canada. Undoubtedly a province that enjoyed special status would seek to exercise its right of consultation in relation to national transportation policy.

Special status would give a province much greater influence in a wide range of areas including trade, monetary, and regional economic policies: "Special status in the field of regional economic policy . . . could come to mean the use . . . of a whole range of special powers for the purpose of influencing its industrial and resource development . . ."[45] Obviously this would be of great potential benefit to the forest sector of the province that enjoyed special status and unfair to the industry in the rest of Canada. Nevertheless, under this constitutional régime, the marketing of forest products would probably not change dramatically. Trade patterns in export markets that absorb most Canadian timber products would not be altered significantly.

The adoption of this constitutional option would have major consequences for fiscal arrangements in the special status province. Most, if not all, the power to tax corporate and personal incomes would be transferred to the province. Further, federal payments to the government of that province would continue or increase, but all spending restrictions would be eliminated. Clearly there would be more than a little difficulty in getting the other provinces to accept such a state of affairs.

If these arrangements were implemented, the special status province would be in control of very powerful fiscal tools that could be tailored to the specific needs of that province. A certain degree of fiscal independence for all provinces makes sense in a country like Canada with such distinct economic areas. The forest industry in particular might stand to gain from provincial fiscal autonomy. We have seen that the revenues derived by Ottawa and the provinces from forest operations seem out of balance with government investment that is needed in the resource. As with the options of full sovereignty and sovereignty-association, special status would present fewer impediments to the striking of a healthy equilibrium between public forest revenues and investments in the province with special status. Of course those provinces not benefiting from special status would still have to contend with existing jurisdictional fragmentation. When special status for Quebec was a topical subject, the question was asked: "Would there arise in the minds of other provincial governments, for example, the question as to whether Quebec was in a position to combine its special fiscal status with the equalization payments, towards which the citizens of the other provinces contributed, to finance competitive tax or expenditure incentives to industry? Put more generally, would intergovernmental arrangements, under which all provinces benefit and contribute equally, persist, or would special fiscal status enjoyed by one provincial government force a readjustment designed to bring into balance the fiscal power and the fiscal responsibilities of all governments?"[46]

A province enjoying special status would still be a part of Canada; hence in-house, federal, research-and-development efforts would likely continue in one form or another.

Since a special status province would still be part of Canada, it would continue, when investing in other parts of Canada, to be both immune to federal foreign investment restrictions and exposed to provincial controls. It seems that as long as a province is exercising a legitimate provincial power, such as the management and sale of publicly owned resources, it can lawfully control extraprovincial investment. A province enjoying special status would have an even larger array of tools for directing investment patterns within its borders.

Renewed Federalism: Rearrangement of Division of Powers and Government Institutions within the Current Federal Structure

Several concrete proposals for a rearrangement of the distribution of powers have been put forward by groups like the

Canadian Bar Association,[47] the Quebec Liberal Party,[48] and the federally appointed Task Force on Canadian Unity.[49] These proposals all share, to a greater or lesser extent, the view that a renewed Canadian federation should consist of strong provincial governments coexisting with a strong central government. We are restricting this analysis to a consideration of a restructured constitution compatible with this 'strong central government — strong regional governments' approach.

Generally such proposals call for the exclusive assignment of areas of clear national concern to the federal government. Such areas would include: control of the Canadian economy through monetary policy, interest rates, tariffs, and trade; enhancement of Canadian identity; redistribution of income; equalization of economic regional disparities; defence; national standards; and the power to make and implement international treaties. Similarly areas of clear provincial concern would be allocated to the provinces: these are social and cultural policy, regional economic development, the well-being of regional communities, extensive control of natural resources and property and civil rights. All constitutional restrictions on provincial taxing power would be removed, except with respect to customs and excise taxes and perhaps other levies that have a significant impact on residents of other provinces. Powers necessary for the cultural integrity and national aspirations of particular regions would be made available to all provinces, with the option of not exercising them. Means of increasing consultation between all governments would be encouraged and institutionalized under this approach. A new interprovincial body (that is, a reconstituted Senate) would be set up to act as a forum for such consultation and, more significant, to give the provinces a power of ratification or rejection with respect to certain federal policies and programs likely to have a palpable impact on the regions of Canada.

For the purpose of predicting the likely content of this option, we intend to rely, for the most part, on the Quebec Liberal Party's *A New Canadian Federation*.[50] The proposals in this document are by far the most detailed of those put forward to date. They also represent what is probably the most provincially oriented approach to the option being considered.

The Quebec Liberal Party's proposals suggest that the provinces should have exclusive jurisdiction over "social insurance," defined to include programs like unemployment insurance, government pension plans, and workers' compensation. *A New*

Canadian Federation also tells us that Ottawa has "no role to play" in the area of education, which is seen as including universities, grants and bursaries, employment training, and the regulation of trades and professions.[51] Under this approach the only tool the federal government would wield in relation to social services and education would be the spending power. But expenditures slated for such purposes would first have to be approved by a new interprovincial body, the Federal Council. The Canadian Bar Association, in making its proposals, did not think it advisable to remove unemployment insurance from exclusive federal jurisdiction, but did recommend placing restraints on the federal spending power.[52]

Both these reports call for the guarantee of free movement of people, goods, and capital, and of the right to work in the province of one's choice. The Quebec Liberals would buttress this right with guarantees against discrimination in the areas of social insurance, health, and social services.[53] Newcomers to a province would therefore be entitled to the same services available to long-time residents.

The recommendations of the Quebec Liberal Party would have a significant impact on the way programs and services affecting forestry personnel are structured. The major change likely to be felt by recipients of government services would probably be the loss of portability of benefits. Individuals would continue to receive benefits like unemployment insurance and employment training, and to be entitled to enjoy similar services throughout the country, but they would be subject to regional differences in such matters as eligibility requirements and benefit scales. The major difference, from a forestry perspective, would be that each province would be better able to harmonize educational, employment-training, and social insurance programs with local economic and industrial policies. It is to be hoped that this change would result in educational and other training programs better suited to the changing requirements of the forest sector: that programs would, for example, be better framed to meet current requirements for providing personnel with skills related to intensive forest management.

Under this approach to federalism, professional foresters, like doctors, engineers, and lawyers, could move freely from one province to another. But all professionals would be required to meet the same professional standards applied to those already practising in the area.[54]

All of the proposals agree that the provinces should retain ownership of resources in their territory and legislative control over resource exploration, exploitation, conservation, and management. Both reports appear to accept the continuation of some federal land ownership within the provinces. Hence it is probably safe to assume that Ottawa would continue to own and manage the forest resources on Indian lands and in national parks, subject to the likelihood that Native management and control of Indian lands will increase because Native organizations are demanding a greater degree of self-determination.

All in all, provincial dominance in the area of forest planning, management, and regulation would be slightly strengthened by this approach to federalism; but several crucial indirect controls over these facets of natural resource exploitation would be left with the federal government. Even the Quebec Liberal Party's position allows for fairly wide federal control over interprovincial and international trade and commerce.[55] The federal government would also continue to exercise wide powers in relation to the national economy. In fact *A New Canadian Federation* recommends that a new constitution should *oblige* Ottawa, in conjunction with the provinces, to develop long-range plans for the general economic development of the whole country: "The constitution should make [the federal government] responsible for the concertation [*sic*] of policies and actions in the natural resources sector and particularly in the field of energy."[56] The Constitutional Committee of the Quebec Liberal Party may have had energy resources in mind when it drafted the passage quoted above, but the sentiment expressed is directly applicable to a national forest policy.

It must be recalled that any major federal programs relating to provincial resources would be subject to provincial approval under the new arrangements. Furthermore the provinces would have more in-put than ever in the development of federal economic policies likely to affect provincial resource management.

Both reports recommend that proprietorship and legislative authority over *inland* fisheries be vested exclusively in the provinces, although the Canadian Bar Association has reservations concerning anadromous species.[57] Adoption of this suggestion would eliminate the controversial division of jurisdiction between provincial forestry authorities and the federal Department of Fisheries and Oceans concerning the regulation of log cutting and transportation. The provinces would have full legislative and administrative control over inland fish. They would no longer have to rely on a delegation of authority from the federal government to protect and manage this resource. Some commentators argue that because the forest resource is more valuable to the provincial economy than to the national economy, a provincial fisheries department would be under pressure to engage in trade-offs detrimental to the fishery. It can also be argued that this sort of resolution of resource-use conflicts would result in a better realization of all resource values.

The Quebec Liberal Party recommends that the central government have full jurisdiction over fisheries[58] and environmental protection in *interprovincial and coastal* waters.[59] These proposals also reserve a function for federal criminal sanctions to be applied whenever and wherever serious forms of pollution pose a threat to health or property.[60] All the same, the provinces would probably continue to exercise some control, through foreshore leases or cutting permits, over operations like booming, storage, and processing that cause pollution in coastal waters.

The Quebec Liberal Party's proposals strive to eliminate jurisdictional overlap in the area of environmental protection and fisheries. All the same, it is difficult to believe that some degree of controversy and confusion would not remain.

Under the proposed federal structure, road transportation would remain within exclusive provincial jurisdiction.[61] Rail transport would continue to be regulated as it is today: that is, Ottawa would have jurisdiction over interprovincial lines, and the provinces would control intraprovincial lines.[62] Increased consultation among all governments concerned might resolve some of the objections that have been expressed over the years in relation to national rail transportation. The Quebec Liberal Party suggests that the federal government should continue to control navigation in all navigable waters within and outside provincial territory.[63] All log booming would, therefore, continue to be subject to federal navigation controls.

The Canadian Bar Association recommends that provincial authority include the power to place quotas on provincial resource exports and to require that a resource be processed in the province.[64] The provinces currently exercise this sort of power, but mainly in relation to the property they own. The Canadian Bar Association advises that there should not be any constitutional limitations preventing provincial export controls from being extended to resources produced from private land.[65] Adoption of this proposal would entrench existing provincial policies requiring timber cut from Crown land to be manufactured before leaving the province and extend them to timber produced from all fee-simple lands within the provinces. However, both the Canadian Bar Association and the Quebec Liberal Party would object to the provincial imposition of export taxes on resources leaving a province.[66] Hence the fee authorized under the British Columbia Forest Act on logs and chips exempt from provincial processing requirements would continue to be of questionable legality.

If this constitutional option were implemented, Ottawa would continue to dominate the field of international and interprovincial trade and commerce. Consequently federal export controls presently applied to unprocessed timber products leaving the country would not lose their jurisdictional basis. Tariffs and trade treaties would also continue to be controlled by the central government, although provincial consultation would be increased.

All the proposals for a renewed federalism recommend that guarantees for unrestricted interprovincial trade be strengthened. Presently section 121 of the BNA Act is applied narrowly so that only fiscal impediments to trade are considered unconstitutional. The Quebec Liberal Party recommends that trade within Canada be genuinely free. However, as the proposals recommend that the provinces have jurisdiction to control exports from their territories, guarantees for free trade relating to natural resources would be restricted to preventing discrimination by importing provinces. The Quebec Liberal Party's proposals suggest: "Free trade between the regions presupposes that the provinces will not erect tariff barriers or any other obstacle to the free circulation of products and services across the country. They will also avoid favouring, in a discriminatory way, their local businesses and producers, to the detriment of those of all other regions of the country."[67] With such a guarantee entrenched in the constitution, all discriminatory government practices would be forbidden. For example, a program initiated by the Government of British Columbia in 1980 would probably be unconstitutional. That government set aside $200 million to be made available to British Columbians seeking mortgage funds, at rates well below 'prime', on the strict condition that all lumber used in the construction for which the loan was made be of provincial origin.

This general approach to constitutional reform would effect important changes in existing fiscal arrangements. In the first place all restrictions on the provincial power of taxation would be lifted, except for those on tariffs and customs duties.[68] Moreover property taxes would be exempt from the otherwise comprehensive federal powers to raise revenue.[69] Because Ottawa would retain the jurisdiction to use fiscal policy to maintain national economic stability and equity, no further limits would be put on its power to raise revenue.[70]

The function of the federal spending power would remain prominent in a renewed federation. In fact the constitution would impose a positive responsibility on Ottawa: "To redistribute wealth, so as to reduce disparities and encourage equality of opportunity between the regions of Canada . . ."[71] All the same, serious limitations would be placed on the exercise of the spending power. According to the Quebec Liberal Party, all federal expenditures for purposes within provincial jurisdiction would be subject to meaningful consultation and ratification in the Federal Council.[72] Furthermore any province would be entitled to opt out of a program ratified by the Council with full compensation.[73] Equalization payments and regional economic expansion programs would both be subject to these controls.

The Quebec Liberal Party also recommends that the pattern of taxing and spending authority be structured according to the principle of 'fiscal responsibility', which requires that the tax revenues of both levels of government correspond to their respective responsibilities.[74] This principle would not be entrenched in the constitution, but would serve as a basis of negotiation now and in the future. Such a principle would provide good leverage for provinces seeking to expand their share of tax revenues from the forest and other resource sectors.

If these fiscal recommendations were, in fact, implemented, the provinces would have only themselves to blame if regional forest sectors did not benefit from the change. In the first place, the provinces would have greater revenues to spend for provincial purposes. Secondly regional fiscal policy should be more in tune with local development priorities, including those of the forest sector. Furthermore federal policies and programs would likely be more sensitive to regional viewpoints because provincial governments would participate more in national decision making.

A New Canadian Federation recommends that jurisdiction over research should follow other areas of constitutional authority:

"The federal government, for example, must be able to direct or finance its own research in matters related to national defence or to monetary or international policies. The same is true for the provinces in matters of housing, *natural resources*,[75] land-use and planning, agriculture and manpower, to name but a few of their jurisdictions."[76] This set of proposals would still allow for future federal research programs in areas within provincial jurisdiction, but the necessary expenditures would be subject to provincial approval. The report allows for the continuation of existing federal research bodies concerned with the social and medical sciences,[77] but no mention is made of resource research or of the National Research Council. Existing federal in-house forest-research operations would therefore have an uncertain future if this constitutional option were adopted. There would remain much room, on the other hand, for co-operative or concerted efforts. These recommendations also suggest that university research be financed and directed primarily by provincial authorities.[78]

The provinces would retain the ability to affect competition in the forest sector incidentally by legislating for the management and sale of forest resources. An incursion into federal jurisdiction might well occur, however, should a provincial government attempt to control access to cutting rights on the basis of a company's market share or province of origin. The proposed constitution would guarantee the free interprovincial circulation of capital, as well as of goods and people.[79] It would appear, therefore, that provincial efforts specifically designed to thwart companies headquartered in other parts of Canada from acquiring cutting rights in a province would be *ultra vires*.

With respect to investment in Canada by foreign nationals, the Quebec Liberal Party proposes that: "Overall foreign investment policy would also be under the federal government's authority, subject to provincial jurisdiction over land-use planning, *natural resources*[80] and industrial development."[81] This arrangement would apparently allow the provinces to maintain barriers against foreigners seeking to acquire provincial resource companies or rights to provincial resources. What Ottawa's role would be with respect to foreign investment in Canadian natural resources is unclear from the statement quoted above, but it would appear to be weaker than it is at present.

Conclusions

This paper falls within that part of a national study of the effects of possible constitutional changes in Canada dealing with energy, natural resources, and environmental protection. The forestry resource was deliberately chosen for study on the basis of an opinion that it exemplifies a Canadian resource sector that is subject to highly decentralized management in a constitutional sense since provincial laws and administration serve a far more important function within the forestry-resource sector than do federal laws and administration.

This opinion is clearly substantiated by the existing pattern of forest management in Canada. What is more significant is that the effects that are seen to flow from any of the future constitutional options for Canada would not alter this provincial focus of management. The reasons for this conclusion are found in the intrinsic nature of the resource itself and emphasize again the truism that in a federation, legislative powers are usually divided so as to leave matters of mainly regional concern to regional Legislatures.

This provincial focus may appear to be disproportionately strong because this paper grew out of a case study that concentrated on the forest industry of British Columbia. The Rocky Mountains define a west coast region in the clearest geographical sense. Watershed effects of pulp and paper mills in British Columbia remain entirely within the region, and even acid rain falls west of the Great Divide. To use an economist's expression, there are few 'spillover effects' from forestry operations that require external regulation.

Even in the processing sector, the mountains and the distances from markets make the shipment of raw logs by road and rail impractical beyond British Columbia's borders. As far as lumber and other manufactured wood products are concerned, all regions of Canada, except the Prairie provinces, are essentially self-sufficient so that a federal presence is not required, as it is with oil and gas resources, to ensure supply to all parts of the country. On the contrary, the woods' industry produces products far in excess of Canadian demands. It might be thought that federal action would be necessary to ensure equitable access to export markets by competing producers from different forest regions of Canada. But even here a federal presence does not seem necessary because the producing forest companies have succeeded, by various means, in rationalizing their penetration of foreign markets in order to avoid harmful competition.

The remaining concerns about the forestry resource are constitutional elements that are generally recognized as appropriate for the national level of government. These are matters of mobility of labour and capital, and allocation of resource revenues between regional and national interests. A major concern at the present time is the need for a national forest policy, but its thrust is to ensure wood supplies for the future — a policy that calls for regional action. The call for federal action is mostly for increased federal spending on forestry research and management that will be carried out at the regional level and for national channels of communication to help co-ordinate regional forestry activities.

The exclusively regional nature of the forest resource suggests that it provides one instance where the pervasive problems of jurisdictional overlap and conflict will not plague the drafters of new constitutions. To a large extent this is a correct characterization, but in the significant area of environmental protection, we find a troublesome exception. This exception exists because, when the original framers of the Constitution allocated jurisdiction over coastal and inland fisheries to the Parliament of Canada, they departed from the truism that regional Legislatures ought to be given jurisdiction over regional matters. Since fish are widely recognized as the biological surrogate for measures of environmental quality in watersheds, federal control over fish places federal authorities in a position of direct conflict with provincial forest managers. After all, woods' operations and pulp and paper mills are the chief sources of water-quality degradation. Thus federal preoccupations go beyond regulating fish gear and catches to regulating fish habitats. Once that step is taken, there is obviously overlap with provincial management of the public lands and, particularly, with provincial management of the forests. Consequently British Columbia and, on the east coast of Canada, Newfoundland take the position that any revision of the Constitution should transfer federal fisheries' jurisdiction to the provinces concerned.

Such a solution of the problem of jurisdictional overlap is attractive for its simplicity and its consistency with the truism of regional control over regional matters. But the problem is deceptively complex. For example the salmon resource is an anadromous species that in major respects is a shared resource between Canada and the United States and, in the deep oceans, between those countries and other fishing nations. In other parts of Canada, the watersheds cross provincial boundaries, presenting the complex jurisdictional issues that are seen in the judgments of the Supreme Court of Canada in the *Interprovincial Co-operatives Ltd. Case*,[82] where Manitoba sought to obtain compensation for the loss suffered by its fishermen because of mercury poisoning originating in the Ontario portion of the shared watershed.

Moreover a constitution should be seen as more than a mechanism for allocating powers of government on principles of efficiency. Freedoms and values may be served by inefficient checks and balances. There are in British Columbia vigorous advocates of a continuing federal control over fisheries, who have no commercial interest in the fisheries whatsoever, but who see the need for a federal check on what might otherwise be a provincial forest policy that would ignore the environmental protection values for which the fish stand as surrogate. From this viewpoint inefficiency caused by overlapping management responsibilities and failure to realize optimum market values are necessary trade-offs for preserving other greater, though less quantifiable, environmental values.

This elaboration of the fishery-forestry conflict on the west coast is intended to make the point that in a federal state, jurisdictional overlap between levels of government and resulting conflict and inefficiency may be positive values in the ultimate balance of nationhood.

Our main conclusion is that the forestry resource is likely to remain almost entirely within the provincial sphere of jurisdiction under any new constitution. Finally, we offer specific elements of this conclusion in relation to specific constitutional options.

Advocates of full sovereignty(without association) for Quebec believe that co-operation for mutual benefit among the partners in Confederation is impossible to achieve. They seek to concentrate power in the Quebec government even if certain positive features of federalism must be given up. A sovereign Quebec could not utilize all the instrumentalities now available to the national government. Certain benefits would be lost completely. For example energy supplies from other provinces would be jeopardized, and protected Canadian markets for provincial products would be lost. Other powers would simply be weakened because of the smaller economic base that would result. Spending programs would be limited to provincial fiscal resources, whereas federal expenditures now draw upon the national tax base. Of course Quebec would probably gain increased efficiency from the elimination of bureaucratic overlap. The forest sector in a sovereign Quebec would not, in our assessment, be seriously affected; nor would the separation of Quebec adversely affect the forest sector in other parts of Canada.

The constitutional options of sovereignty-association and special status both seek to increase regional power and at the same time to retain the benefits of a national economy. Sovereignty-association would concentrate all public property, fiscal resources, and legislative jurisdiction within Quebec exclusively in the hands of the Quebec government. The 'treaty of association' established between the federal government and the Quebec government would give Quebec the benefit of a monetary and customs union with Canada and preferred use of national transportation facilities. Furthermore Quebec would participate as an equal with Ottawa in determining association-wide policies concerning tariffs, a central bank, and transportation.

Special status would keep Quebec within Confederation, but the province would acquire increased legislative jurisdiction and fiscal resources from Ottawa. The province would still continue to receive federal funds, but would be free from conditions governing their spending. Finally, Ottawa would be obliged to consult with Quebec in certain key areas of national policy.

Clearly both sovereignty-association and special status would provide maximum benefit to all sectors of the Quebec economy, including the forest industry. It is equally clear that constitutional arrangements that give one province substantial fiscal or economic powers and rights not made available to the other provinces would be unacceptable to the latter. On the other hand, if special status were limited to cultural and linguistic matters, it is likely that objections would be minor.

Renewed federalism would produce less drastic alterations in the distribution of powers. All provincial governments would benefit from some increases in legislative jurisdiction and fiscal resources. Still, the federal government would retain sufficient legislative and fiscal powers to make its presence strongly felt in national affairs. Just as important as changes in jurisdiction would be the establishment of new political institutions such as a reconstituted Senate, a constitutional court, or a revamped electoral system. All proposals for a renewed federalism would increase the avenues for consultation among governments at the policy-development stage. Furthermore they would require ratification of programs by provincial representatives in those cases where there are strong overlapping interests. Certainly the adoption of this option would benefit regional forest sectors, but not to the extent that Quebec would benefit from sovereignty-association or special status.

The forest sector in each province would not suffer particular hardship under any of these constitutional options. It might reach maximum effectiveness within a particular province enjoying sovereignty-association or special status, but that would be at the expense of the remaining provinces and consequently be politically unacceptable. What little disadvantage the forest sector suffers in each region by reason of divided provincial and federal jurisdictions under the present Constitution is not a reason to divide the country.

Notes

1. I. Place, "Forestry in Canada," *Journal of Forestry* 79 (September 1978): 557–62.

2. F.L.C. Reed and Associates, *Forest Management in Canada and Forest Sector Revenue* (1978), p. 36. (Hereinafter cited as *Forest Sector Revenue*.)

3. *Ibid.*, p. 40.

4. *Ibid.*, p. 41.

5. *Ibid.*, p. 39.

6. *Readers Digest*, August 1979, p. 151.

7. *Forest Sector Revenue*, p. 38.

8. *Ibid.*

9. *Readers Digest*, p. 151.

10. F.L.C. Reed and Associates, Forest Management Institute, *Forest Management in Canada*, study prepared for the Canadian Forestry Service, Environment Canada (1978). (Hereinafter cited as *Forest Management*.)

11. *Ibid.*, p. 122.

12. See generally G. Nagle, "What Is National Forest Policy in Canada?" *The Forestry Chronicle* 54 (December 1978), p. 291; G. Nagle, "A National Forest Policy for Canada?" *Journal of Forestry* 79 (November 1978), p. 718; Canadian Council of Resource and Environment Ministers, *Forestry Imperatives for Canada* (May 1979); *Forest Management*; *Forest Sector Revenue*.

13. *Ibid.*

14. F. Wetton, "Evolution of Forest Policies in Canada," *Journal of Forestry* 79 (September 1978), pp. 565–66.

15. British North America Act, 1867, 30 & 31 Vict. c. 3 (U.K.). (Hereafter cited only within the text.)

16. *Forest Sector Revenue*, p. 27.

17. *Ibid.*

18. *Ibid.*

19. *Ibid.*

20. Forest Act, R.S.B.C. 1979, c. 140, Part 12.

21. See *Smylie* v. *The Queen*, (1900) 27 O.A.R. 172.

22. See *Attorney-General of British Columbia* v. *MacDonald Murphy Lumber Co.*, (1930) 2 D.L.R. 721, (1930) A.C. 357 (P.C.), (1930) 1 W.W.R. 830; *Texada Mines Ltd.* v. *Attorney-General of British Columbia*, [1960] S.C.R. 713, (1960) 32 W.W.R. 37, (1960) 24 D.L.R. (2d) 81 (S.C.C.); *Canadian Industrial Gas and Oil Ltd.* v. *Government of Saskatchewan*, (1978) 80 D.L.R. (3d) p. 449 at p. 482 (S.C.C.)

23. *Canadian Industrial Gas and Oil* v. *Government of Saskatchewan*, note 22 above, pp. 484–89.

24. Export and Import Permits Act, R.S.C. 1970, c. E–17.

25. *Cf. Morgan* v. *Attorney-General for the Province of Prince Edward Island*, [1976] 2 S.C.R. 349.

26. British Columbia, Royal Commission on Forest Resources, *Timber Rights and Forest Policy in British Columbia*, 2 Vols. (Victoria: Queen's Printer, 1976). (Hereinafter cited as *Pearse Report*.)

27. *Forest Sector Revenue* and *Forest Management*.

28. M. Moore, "Fact and Fantasy in the Unity Debate," (December 1978), pp. 6–7.

29. It must be cautioned that it is only an assumption that policies authored by a regional government will be more sensitive or more beneficial to local needs. The very opposite might prove to be true. Be that as it may, this is an assumption that we have made in this paper.

30. Moore, "Fact and Fantasy . . .," pp. 6–7.

31. *Ibid.*, p. 20.

32. *Ibid.*

33. *Ibid.*, p. 30, note 15.

34. Québec, Conseil exécutif, *Québec-Canada: A New Deal* (Quebec: Éditeur officiel, 1979). (Hereinafter cited as *P.Q. Proposals, 1979*.)

35. *Ibid.*, p. 20.

36. *Ibid.*, pp. 47–65.

37. *Ibid.*, p. 59.

38. *Ibid.*, pp. 58–59.

39. *Ibid.*, p. 59.

40. *Ibid.*, p. 26.

41. Moore, "Fact and Fantasy . . .," p. 30, note 15.

42. *P.Q. Proposals, 1979*, p. 58.

43. A. Johnson, "The Dynamics of Federalism in Canada," *Canadian Journal of Political Science* 1 (1968), p. 27.

44. Government of British Columbia, "The Distribution of Legislative Powers," *British Columbia Constitutional Proposals*, Paper No. 8, September 1978, p. 21.

45. Johnson, "The Dynamics of Federalism in Canada," pp. 28–29.

46. *Ibid.*, pp. 30–31.

47. Canadian Bar Association, Committee on the Constitution, *Towards a New Canada* (Toronto, 1978). (Hereinafter cited as *C.B.A. Report, 1978*.)

48.   Constitutional Committee of the Quebec Liberal Party, *A New Canadian Federation* (Montreal, 1980). (Hereinafter cited as *Ryan Proposals, 1980*.)

49.   Task Force on Canadian Unity, *A Future Together* (Ottawa: Minister of Supply and Services Canada, 1979).

50.   *Ryan Proposals, 1980*, pp. 91–92.

51.   *Ibid.*, pp. 77–78, 86.

52.   *C.B.A. Report, 1978*, pp. 75–77, 82.

53.   *Ryan Proposals, 1980*, p. 92.

54.   *Ibid.*, pp. 104–5.

55.   *Ibid.*, p. 102.

56.   *Ibid.*, p. 96.

57.   That is, those species that ascend rivers to spawn. *C.B.A. Report, 1978*, p. 109.

58.   *Ryan Proposals, 1980*, p. 97.

59.   *Ibid.*, p. 116.

60.   *Ibid.*

61.   *Ibid.*, p. 110.

62.   *Ibid.*

63.   *Ibid.*, p. 111.

64.   *C.B.A. Report, 1978*, p. 108.

65.   *Ibid.*

66.   *C.B.A. Report, 1978*, p. 108; *Ryan Proposals, 1980*, p. 102.

67.   *Ryan Proposals, 1980*, p. 105.

68.   *Ibid.*, p. 74.

69.   *Ibid.*

70.   *Ibid.*

71.   *Ibid.*, p. 68.

72.   *Ibid.*, pp. 51–52.

73.   *Ibid.*, p. 68.

74.   *Ibid.*, pp. 73–75.

75.   Emphasis added.

76.   *Ibid.*, p. 78.

77.   *Ibid.*

78.   *Ibid.*, pp. 77–78.

79.   *Ibid.*, p. 105.

80.   Emphasis added.

81.   *Ibid.*, p. 102.

82.   (1975), 53 D.L.R. (3d) 321 (S.C.C.)

The Authors

ROBERT A. FASHLER has taken a degree in Political Science at McGill University and an LL.B. from the University of British Columbia. He was called to the Bar in that province and is currently practising law in Victoria, B.C.

ANDREW THOMPSON is a Professor of Law and the Director of the Westwater Research Centre at the University of British Columbia, where he teaches Natural Resources Law. He is the author of numerous books and articles dealing with petroleum and mining law, environmental law, and resource-management issues.

Les ressources naturelles dans une perspective de changement constitutionnel : le cas du Québec

FRANÇOIS CHEVRETTE
Université de Montréal

Table des matières

Les ressources naturelles dans une perspective de changement constitutionnel : le cas du Québec

Introduction

Nous présenterons dans les pages qui suivent quelques réflexions au sujet des conséquences de certains nouveaux modes de distribution du pouvoir politique sur le secteur des ressources naturelles, nous plaçant dans une perspective primordialement québécoise. Dès le départ, quelques précisions s'imposent.

Si le champ de la présente étude est vaste[1], il se trouve limité par le fait que l'accent sera mis sur une seule province, le Québec. On peut justifier de plusieurs façons cette limitation. Mis à part le fait que le Québec est véritablement à l'origine de la crise constitutionnelle canadienne, il a toujours défendu des positions très décentralisatrices à propos des ressources naturelles, alors même qu'il se trouve, comme on le verra plus loin, dans une position de dépendance accentuée pour plusieurs d'entre elles. Il y a là un étrange paradoxe qui mérite que l'on s'y attarde.

Nos conjectives seront fondées sur quatre options constitutionnelles : le fédéralisme renouvelé, le statut particulier, la souveraineté-association et l'indépendance pure et simple du Québec. Pour tenter d'apprécier, par exemple, l'impact d'un régime de souveraineté-association sur le secteur des ressources, il faut évidemment savoir de quelles ressources le Québec est doté ou dépourvu, quelles sont les ressources qu'il exporte ou importe et quels sont ses partenaires à l'échange. Cependant, les changements constitutionnels, qui s'opèrent habituellement lentement, prennent place à l'intérieur d'une certaine continuité historico-politique. On peut donc, en forçant à peine les choses, voir comme une donnée la position historique et politique du Québec en matière de ressources, aux fins d'une extrapolation sur les possibilités et les conséquences de certaines réformes constitutionnelles. Ainsi, dans un premier temps, nous examinerons les données historico-politiques et physico-économiques avant de passer aux extrapolations de la réforme constitutionnelle.

Les données politiques et économiques

Il est admis que les gouvernements canadiens, tant fédéral que provinciaux, ont à peu près tous adopté, et ce jusqu'à la fin des années 1950, une politique économique non interventionniste et de laisser-faire dans le domaine des mines et même dans l'ensemble du secteur des ressources naturelles[2]. Une situation économique générale de bas prix et de surplus prévalait alors dans ce secteur, ce qui amenait l'autorité publique à adopter une vision optimiste des « richesses » naturelles du Canada et à se comporter, non pas comme un agent de réglementation, mais comme un propriétaire soucieux de voir à l'exploitation de son domaine et d'en faciliter le développement au maximum. Pendant ce temps, il n'y a pas eu d'affrontements politiques et constitutionnels majeurs entre les deux niveaux de gouvernement[3], la constitution donnant le droit de propriété des terres et des ressources aux provinces[4], qui ont donc eu pendant longtemps le haut du pavé en cette matière.

Toutefois, il était à prévoir que, si les politiques gouvernementales passaient un jour de l'abstention à l'intervention et si le gouvernement fédéral, pour des motifs de rareté ou encore de surplus d'une ressource, commençait à régir les ressources naturelles, de sérieux conflits constitutionnels pourraient surgir. Juridiquement, il paraît clair que, grâce notamment à ses pouvoirs commerciaux et fiscaux[5], l'autorité fédérale peut avoir des coudées assez franches dans le contrôle des ressources. En revanche, les provinces, même si elles n'ont compétence que sur le commerce local[6], ont la propriété de celles-ci, et cela leur donne une espèce de légitimité historique et politique pour s'opposer aux interventions fédérales ou pour justifier les leurs. Comme l'écrit un auteur :

> (...) crown ownership is available as an ideological weapon for use against the federal government, against the private sector, or against provincial governments whose political opponents perceive them as being too generous

*to the private sector. Almost any federal intervention in resource policy can
be branded as an attempt to deprive the provinces of their property, while
the mining firms and their numerous friends in provincial capitals can at
times be placed on the defensive by appeals to protect the public domain
against the encroachment of private greed. The Constitution and the
political culture thus ensure that the Canadian version of the almost
universal demand in recent years for community control over mineral
resources is at least as likely to be 'economic provincialism' as 'economic
nationalism'* [7].

Les ressources constituent depuis longtemps une espèce de
symbole politique et constitutionnel pour les provinces. La
position historique du Québec à ce sujet en est peut-être la
meilleure illustration.

La position historique du Québec

Au cours des débats sur la confédération, en 1865, la question
des ressources a été assez largement débattue; mais ceux qui en
ont discuté l'ont fait évidemment dans une politique de propriétaire, mettant l'accent sur la compétence des provinces sur
les terres publiques, la colonisation, les forêts et les redevances à
tirer des concessions d'exploitation minière[8]. La question ne
posait donc pas beaucoup de difficultés constitutionnelles.

Il en est allé ainsi pendant fort longtemps, au point que, même
en 1956, le rapport de la Commission royale d'enquête sur les
problèmes constitutionnels relevait comme seule difficulté
majeure du secteur le fait que le gouvernement fédéral taxait de
façon exagérée les revenus des compagnies exploitantes. Sur
cela, la Commission insistait beaucoup[9]. À coup sûr, cette
taxation était une question importante, et elle le demeure. Mais
ce n'est là qu'une des questions importantes auxquelles on fait
face aujourd'hui. De façon très typique, la Commission notait
aussi que « le territoire et les ressources naturelles sont l'assise
économique de l'autonomie provinciale, le gouvernement de la
Province ayant l'initiative des moyens à prendre pour en assurer
la conservation et l'exploitation rationnelle »[10].

Une politique gouvernementale peu interventionniste et surtout soucieuse de faciliter l'exploitation des ressources en con-
sentant des avantages, fiscaux en particulier, aux entreprises
était peu susceptible de provoquer des conflits entre gouvernements ni, évidemment, entre ceux-ci et les exploitants. C'était
l'époque des « *good relations on all sides* »[11] et, si divergences il y
avait, c'était au niveau de la concurrence fiscale. Or, le Québec a

pratiqué pendant longtemps une politique d'incitation à
l'exploitation, au point qu'on a pu soutenir que la résistance à
l'industrialisation, qui a eu cours un long moment dans une
certaine partie de l'opinion québécoise, ne s'est guère mani-
festée dans le domaine des ressources naturelles[12]. « Nous
n'avons pas peur des capitaux étrangers (...). Je préfère im-
porter des dollars américains plutôt que d'exporter des travailleurs canadiens », déclarait le premier ministre Taschereau en
1927[13]. Les mines, les forêts et les forces hydrauliques ont été au
cœur du développement économique du Québec.

Cependant, le souci de favoriser l'exploitation des ressources
ne s'est pas accompagné ou n'a pu s'accompagner d'un souci
équivalent de favoriser une part de transformation sur place des
produits. Certes ce phénomène n'est pas particulier au Québec
et découle en grande partie de la spécialisation des économies. Il
demeure que, dans le cas du Québec, l'impôt à l'exportation
aurait été un moyen de favoriser une plus large transformation
sur place. Mais, comme cet impôt est de compétence fédérale
exclusive[14], on n'aurait pu y recourir qu'en endossant une
intrusion fédérale dans le domaine des ressources. Cet argument semble avoir joué lorsque, au tournant du siècle, le Québec
s'est refusé à envisager la possibilité d'un impôt à l'exportation
sur le bois de pulpe[15].

À ce sujet, on rapporte qu'en 1910 le Québec, imitant en cela
l'Ontario, a décrété un embargo sur le bois de pulpe coupé sur
les terres de la Couronne et destiné à l'exportation vers les
États-Unis dans le but de favoriser sa transformation sur place.
Un an plus tard, les États-Unis abolissaient la douane sur
l'importation du papier journal, ce qui a rendu possible
l'implantation d'usines américaines de transformation au
Québec[16]. Une telle action du Québec était sans doute
irréprochable au point de vue constitutionnel. En effet, en
période normale, même l'autorité fédérale ne peut forcer une
province à exporter; au surplus, on reconnaît aux provinces une
liberté de manœuvre sur les ressources des terres publiques
qu'elles n'ont pas sur le commerce des produits du domaine
privé[17]. Il est certain toutefois que le Québec ne pourrait taxer,
par exemple, l'exportation d'amiante, à la fois parce qu'on est en
présence de biens du domaine privé, et que cette mesure serait
considérée comme une imposition indirecte et une réglementation commerciale, l'une et l'autre interdite aux provinces. À quoi
l'on peut encore ajouter qu'à la différence du bois de pulpe,
l'amiante est caractérisée par une structure de la demande qui
rend difficile un traitement sur place du produit.

En résumé, le Québec, jusqu'à la fin des années 1950 à tout le moins, a mené une politique que la constitution non seulement ne gênait pas mais appuyait clairement, dans la mesure où elle consacrait le Québec comme le plein propriétaire des ressources, libre de les gérer à sa guise et de développer pour ce faire un tissu de liens commerciaux avec les capitaux étrangers, américains en particulier. Comme on l'a vu, les accrochages fédéraux-québécois étaient mineurs et surtout centrés sur la fiscalité des entreprises. Si le Québec a parfois constaté que la constitution le privait de certains pouvoirs, en particulier du contrôle des exportations, il a paru assez bien s'en accommoder.

Mais la situation a pris une nouvelle tournure depuis le début des années 1960. D'une part s'est posé le problème de la propriété et de la compétence législative sur les ressources au large des côtes, problème relativement bien identifié et qui a été l'occasion pour le Québec de réaffirmer avec beaucoup de vigueur son autorité en la matière. D'autre part s'est posé le problème plus diffus et plus complexe encore de la distribution des ressources entre les régions du pays et du rôle, actuel ou éventuel, du gouvernement fédéral comme arbitre de ces questions. On pense évidemment à la crise pétrolière de 1973 et à la politique fédérale qui en est découlée.

Examinons d'abord le problème des ressources au large des côtes, plus limité et mieux identifié au point de vue juridictionnel[18]. Quand le gouvernement fédéral a demandé l'avis de la Cour suprême sur la question de la propriété et du contrôle des ressources sous-marines au large des côtes de la Colombie-Britannique, le premier ministre du Québec a refusé de reconnaître la juridiction de la cour[19]. Une fois le jugement rendu en faveur de l'autorité fédérale[20], le premier ministre du Québec a refusé de considérer ce jugement applicable au Québec en invoquant le « principe fondamental » de « la propriété exclusive des provinces sur le domaine public et les ressources naturelles »[21]. On peut s'étonner de voir ainsi invoqué un principe constitutionnel à l'encontre d'un jugement qui visait précisément à interpréter la constitution. Mais cela montre bien que le principe a une importance politique telle que, si la constitution ou l'interprétation qu'on en donne viennent à lui porter atteinte, c'est la constitution qu'il faut changer ou la légitimité du tribunal qu'il faut mettre en question. C'est une position analogue qu'a adoptée la Saskatchewan ces dernières années. Deux jugements importants de la Cour suprême l'ayant privée de certains pouvoirs fiscaux et commerciaux sur ses ressources[22], les autorités provinciales ont aussi conclu qu'il fallait envisager de changer la constitution[23].

Voyons maintenant l'attitude du Québec face au rôle du gouvernement fédéral dans la répartition des ressources entre les régions.

Une des premières interventions fédérales significatives à ce chapitre fut l'élaboration et la mise en application de la politique nationale du pétrole entre 1958 et 1973. L'objectif bien connu de cette politique fédérale, qui a été à l'époque une politique de compromis, était de réserver au pétrole de l'Ouest canadien une part du marché du pays, celui à l'ouest de la vallée de l'Outaouais, tout en continuant de permettre à l'Est de s'approvisionner en pétrole étranger à des prix inférieurs, préservant ainsi pour les raffineurs montréalais le bénéfice des prix d'importation.

Ces dernières années, cette politique a été vivement critiquée par le Québec, tant sous le gouvernement Bourassa que sous le gouvernement Lévesque, et l'on a décrit ainsi les effets de la fameuse ligne Borden : stagnation des raffineries montréalaises pendant sept ans, expansion d'une zone de raffinage rivale sur l'axe Sarnia-Toronto, incitation aux compagnies internationales à s'établir à l'est du Québec pour s'éloigner de la fameuse ligne de partage[24].

Même si le Québec n'a pas participé aux travaux et aux audiences de la Commission Borden qui, de 1957 à 1959, avait élaboré cette politique, et même s'il ne semble pas avoir désapprouvé celle-ci à l'époque[25], il serait tout à fait erroné d'y voir l'acceptation d'une forme d'arbitrage par le gouvernement central. Lors de la conférence des premiers ministres, les 22 et 23 janvier 1974, le premier ministre du Québec rappelait la compétence exclusive des provinces sur les ressources naturelles, prônait une collaboration intergouvernementale dans l'établissement des programmes énergétiques et favorisait un rapprochement du prix du pétrole canadien du niveau international. Plus récemment, lors de la conférence des premiers ministres du 12 novembre 1979 sur la politique énergétique, le porte-parole du Québec déclarait : « Le Québec considère que les provinces ont un droit exclusif de propriété sur leurs ressources naturelles. Le Québec ne saurait donc approuver une décision unilatérale du gouvernement fédéral en matière de pétrole ». Il proposait alors une entente négociée sur le prix du pétrole, un rapprochement de celui-ci du prix international ainsi qu'un régime de prêts par les provinces productrices aux

provinces consommatrices visant à ce que les premières partici-
pent au développement énergétique des secondes. Il s'opposait
enfin fermement à l'établissement de taxes fédérales addition-
nelles sur la consommation d'essence, voyant ce geste comme
« une ingérence additionnelle du gouvernement fédéral dans ce
champ de taxation ».

Par ces positions, le Québec cherche surtout, outre un
rapprochement avec les provinces productrices de pétrole et de
gaz face à l'Ontario et à Ottawa, à rester maître du développement de ses propres ressources, hydroélectriques en particulier,
et même de l'ensemble de son développement économique,
quitte à sacrifier parfois une part de ses intérêts immédiats. En
pratique, il lui est quasiment impossible de nier tout rôle au
gouvernement fédéral dans la répartition des ressources entre
les régions; dès lors sa position consiste plutôt à minimiser en
quelque sorte ce rôle.

La rhétorique constitutionnelle constitue évidemment un des
principaux instruments de cette politique, et le Québec n'est pas
la seule province à y avoir recours. Certes, c'est une simplification d'invoquer l'autorité provinciale exclusive sur les ressources, alors que le gouvernement fédéral a compétence sur le
commerce interprovincial et international, la taxation directe et
indirecte, les gazoducs et les oléoducs, les coûts de transport, la
localisation des ports, l'énergie nucléaire, et qu'il exerce déjà son
contrôle sur les exportations d'électricité du Québec par l'intermédiaire de l'Office national de l'énergie. Mais, si ambigu
soit-il, le principe de la propriété provinciale sur les ressources conserve beaucoup d'impact.

Pour le Québec, le principe de l'autorité exclusive des
provinces sur leurs ressources a depuis toujours une importance
telle qu'on peut dire qu'il est en quelque sorte au-dessus de la
constitution. Mais les positions politiques et constitutionnelles
sont une chose, les données physiques et économiques en sont
une autre. Nous ferons donc un bref bilan des ressources du
Québec et des principaux courants commerciaux dont celles-ci
font l'objet.

Un bilan des ressources

Pour ce bilan, nous nous en sommes tenu à quelques observations générales, tout en prenant soin de renvoyer le lecteur aux
études spécialisées les plus pertinentes[26]. Nous examinerons
successivement la situation du Québec dans le secteur
énergétique et dans les secteurs des mines et des forêts.

En matière énergétique, une donnée majeure est la complète dépendance du Québec dans le domaine des hydrocarbures (pétrole, gaz et charbon), aucun gisement important de combustibles fossiles n'ayant été découvert en sol québécois[27]. Le Québec, qui a commencé de s'approvisionner en pétrole de l'Ouest canadien au moment de la crise de l'énergie et grâce à l'oléoduc Sarnia-Montréal, devra sans doute revenir au pétrole d'outre-mer d'ici quelques années à cause de l'épuisement de nos réserves. En revanche, le gaz naturel en provenance de l'Ouest, qui a peu pénétré le marché québécois à ce jour, verra augmenter sa part dans la consommation globale jusque vers les années 1990, où il sera probablement remplacé graduellement par le gaz des îles Arctiques et par les ressources au large de la côte Atlantique[28].

Dans quelle mesure l'électricité, seule forme d'énergie primaire produite en abondance à des coûts inférieurs, peut-elle compenser la forte dépendance du Québec quant aux hydrocarbures? La position du Québec en la matière semble bonne, et, si le pourcentage de l'électricité dans la consommation énergétique globale croît comme prévu, la dépendance du Québec diminuera d'autant[29]. Notons aussi l'importance du bas coût de l'électricité pour les industries consommant beaucoup d'énergie (pâtes et papiers, première transformation des métaux, chimie, aluminium). On doit constater cependant que « il ne faut pas compter sur les exportations d'électricité pour équilibrer les comptes extérieurs du Québec dans le secteur de l'énergie »[30].

Au Canada, l'électricité est un secteur où des entreprises de grande taille se sont implantées dans un cadre essentiellement provincial et l'autorité fédérale n'a pas eu à intervenir, sauf quant au contrôle qu'elle exerce présentement sur les exportations à l'étranger et sur l'établissement des réseaux à cette fin. Vu la faiblesse relative des échanges interprovinciaux d'électricité[31], il se peut que les contrôles fédéraux ne s'accroissent pas beaucoup. Comme on l'a signalé précédemment, on peut prévoir aussi que l'électricité, combinée au développement de certaines énergies nouvelles, permettra au Québec de diminuer sa dépendance du pétrole, à la fois canadien et étranger, produit sur lequel l'autorité centrale a des pouvoirs importants[32]. On peut prévoir en revanche une dépendance accrue du Québec envers le gaz canadien qui, comme le pétrole, fait l'objet d'une réglementation fédérale[33]. Quant à la fission nucléaire, sur laquelle Ottawa a aussi des pouvoirs importants, le Québec ne prévoit pas pour l'instant la nécessité de développements majeurs.

Passons maintenant aux secteurs des mines et des forêts.

Le secteur minier, où la présence fédérale est assez minime, ne compte que pour 2 à 3 % du produit intérieur brut québécois. Ce secteur est à la baisse, et la main-d'œuvre n'y représente que 1 % de la population active. Le secteur n'est pourtant pas négligeable, étant essentiel à certaines régions dont il constitue la seule base d'industrialisation. Par ailleurs, le minerai brut, concentré et semi-transformé, comptait en 1975 pour 37,6 % des exportations totales du Québec. Dans l'ensemble de la production primaire québécoise, le secteur minier est le plus important (43,7 %), en avance sur les forêts, l'agriculture et les pêcheries. Comme il est lui-même en amont de la métallurgie et de la sidérurgie, il « pourrait fort bien devenir la clef d'un développement économique plus poussé. En ce sens, il serait peut-être opportun de le situer au moins près du cœur de ce que pourrait être l'économie québécoise »[34].

Dans le cas des minéraux, « la presque totalité de la production est exportée; cependant, sauf pour l'amiante, les montants en cause ne sont pas très élevés. En revanche, pour le minerai de fer, il y a là une exportation importante du Québec, mais sa place parmi les producteurs mondiaux reste fort modeste »[35].

L'industrie minière québécoise est donc importante; mais peu de ses produits ont un intérêt stratégique évident. Elle est primordialement dirigée vers l'exportation internationale, qui n'est pas diversifiée puisqu'elle est tournée en grande partie vers les États-Unis. Ce qui frappe surtout, c'est la faible transformation sur place des minerais, phénomène qui tient à plusieurs facteurs, parmi lesquels nous retrouvons l'étroitesse du marché ainsi que le très grand contrôle étranger et l'intégration verticale des entreprises, les filiales se chargeant d'approvisionner les maisons-mères américaines en matières premières[36].

Quelques mots enfin sur l'industrie forestière, qui se classe première parmi les industries manufacturières du Québec quant au nombre de travailleurs et aux salaires versés, et deuxième quant à la valeur ajoutée et la valeur des expéditions. Le Québec est premier producteur canadien de papier journal (46 %), de pâte de bois (33 %) et d'autres papiers (38 %), mais il ne produit que 15 % du bois d'œuvre et moins de 10 % du contreplaqué. Cependant, la part du Québec est en régression, même pour les secteurs forts, à cause surtout de la concurrence de la Colombie-Britannique[37]. Les États-Unis étant ici encore le principal partenaire commercial du Québec, ce secteur est donc extrêmement vulnérable à la conjoncture américaine, et le

déplacement de l'activité économique du nord-est vers le
sud-ouest américain pourrait contribuer à limiter la croissance
des exportations québécoises.

Notons enfin que la structure tarifaire canado-américaine
importe beaucoup, mais que les possibilités d'améliorer la
position du Québec sont très limitées. Une hausse des tarifs,
comme on l'a parfois demandée aux États-Unis, serait néfaste à
l'ensemble de la production forestière canadienne, alors qu'une
baisse générale favoriserait les produits finis américains et au
mieux d'autres provinces avant le Québec. De même dans le
secteur minier, comme nous l'avons déjà montré, une baisse des
tarifs favoriserait peu l'industrie primaire du Québec, vu la
faible élasticité d'offre des produits miniers non transformés et
la lenteur d'ajustement de la production, et elle aurait un plus
grand impact sur l'industrie manufacturière ontarienne[38].

Gardant à l'esprit les données qui précèdent, tentons maintenant de faire quelques conjectures sur la politique québécoise
des ressources.

Des conjectures sur le changement constitutionnel et la politique des ressources

Le fédéralisme renouvelé

Même si les pouvoirs fédéraux en matière de ressources
naturelles sont plus considérables qu'on ne le croit souvent,
certains prétendent que la compétence d'Ottawa est insuffisante
et qu'elle devrait être accrue[39]. Toutefois, il nous semble que,
dans le contexte politique actuel, toute réforme constitutionnelle envisageable irait dans le sens non pas nécessairement
d'une diminution marquée des pouvoirs fédéraux mais, à coup
sûr, d'une certaine augmentation des pouvoirs des provinces. Le
thème du contrôle provincial des ressources est en effet si fort,
au Québec et ailleurs, qu'une centralisation accrue paraît
nettement improbable[40]. Du reste, certaines propositions de
réforme avancées à ce jour confirment cette tendance.

L'idée serait en particulier de faire en sorte que les provinces
puissent gérer et mettre en marché leurs ressources plus
librement qu'aujourd'hui. Un avant-projet constitutionnel
d'origine fédérale, discuté lors de la rencontre fédérale-
provinciale des premiers ministres tenue à Ottawa les 5 et 6
février 1979, fournit un exemple intéressant de cette orien-

tation[41]. On y reconnaît une compétence provinciale exclusive sur l'exploitation, la mise en valeur, la conservation et la gestion des ressources, de même que sur leur exportation et leur taxation, à la condition toutefois que la taxe soit applicable à tous les produits primaires, qu'ils soient exportés ou pas. L'avant-projet maintient la compétence fédérale sur le commerce interprovincial et international d'exportation. L'exportation des ressources naturelles et des produits primaires qui en sont issus relève donc de compétence partagée. L'avant-projet fédéral prévoit même qu'en cas de conflit, ce serait les mesures provinciales qui l'emporteraient, sauf en cas de « nécessité d'envergure nationale qui ne représente pas un ensemble d'intérêts locaux » ou dans le domaine du commerce international.

Comme il fallait s'y attendre, certaines provinces en réclament beaucoup plus et, même si de telles revendications proviennent vraisemblablement davantage des provinces de l'Ouest que du Québec, ce dernier y souscrit sans réserve. Dans un document de travail de la réunion des premiers ministres provinciaux tenue à Toronto les 1er et 2 octobre 1976 — document élaboré après de longues consultations entre les provinces —, on prévoyait une compétence provinciale exclusive sur les « terres, mines et minéraux » et sur toute taxation des ressources naturelles, ajoutant que les taxes payées aux provinces devaient être déductibles des revenus des entreprises aux fins de l'application des lois fiscales fédérales. On excluait l'application du pouvoir déclaratoire fédéral aux ressources, et les compétences fédérales, en particulier celle sur le commerce, ne pouvaient être exercées que « sous réserve » de la compétence provinciale sur les ressources et non plus « nonobstant » cette dernière. Le document optait enfin pour un contrôle provincial sur les ressources au large des côtes, l'avant-projet fédéral de février 1979 prônant pour sa part une forme de compétence conjointe ou concurrente.

C'est une proposition semblable qu'a présentée le Québec lors de la négociation constitutionnelle de l'été 1980. Cette proposition prévoit une prépondérance provinciale sur le commerce interprovincial et exclut l'application aux ressources du pouvoir déclaratoire et, dans une certaine mesure, du pouvoir fédéral sur les entreprises et les ouvrages interprovinciaux. Le Québec favorise en matière de ressources les ententes réciproques entre les provinces, et il est clair qu'il veut ainsi se garantir la plus complète autonomie sur ses ressources hydroélectriques.

Toutes ces propositions présentent certaines difficultés juridiques d'ordre technique qu'il n'est pas de notre propos d'analyser ici. Il convient plutôt d'en faire ressortir les conséquences politiques et économiques éventuelles. Il est assez difficile d'admettre, en régime fédéral, un pouvoir provincial prépondérant sur tout commerce interprovincial de ressources naturelles. À ce titre, l'avant-projet fédéral pourrait constituer une solution de compromis, si ce n'était de la difficulté de définir ce qu'est une « nécessité d'envergure nationale ». Comme, en pareil cas, l'avant-projet laisse intacts les pouvoirs fédéraux, les risques de politiques économiques provinciales hautement restrictives ne seraient pas très grands, encore que, pour contrer l'action d'une province, le parlement fédéral devrait légiférer; à l'heure actuelle, l'effet de dissuasion est obtenu par la menace d'un simple recours aux tribunaux, sans parler évidemment des contraintes économiques. On peut soutenir que, en cas de stricte nécessité, un contrôle politique, exercé par le pouvoir fédéral, serait préférable à un contrôle judiciaire, qui se prête souvent assez mal à l'appréciation des politiques commerciales et qui peut être déclenché à n'importe quel moment par un individu ou une entreprise[42]. On s'est beaucoup plaint dans le passé de l'impossibilité pour les provinces d'agir sur leur commerce d'exportation. Ce changement pourrait améliorer les choses. Il ne réglerait cependant pas tout, et, dans la mesure où l'impôt provincial à l'exportation continuerait d'être prohibé, il ne mettrait pas nécessairement fin aux étatisations provinciales que l'on opère dans le but de maîtriser plus aisément le commerce extérieur de certaines entreprises.

Si cette tendance se concrétise, le phénomène des négociations interprovinciales s'intensifiera, ne serait-ce qu'entre les provinces de l'Est, qui devront s'entendre sur un partage du territoire sous-marin. De plus en plus de décisions économiques à impact extraprovincial seront prises en fonction des intérêts de la province concernée, ce qui ne peut qu'entraîner des tensions. Le débat sur les ressources se politisera, éventuellement région contre région, et l'autorité fédérale jouera davantage un rôle d'arbitre que celui d'initiateur.

Le statut particulier

Le régime de statut particulier est caractérisé, à l'intérieur d'un régime fédéral, par l'introduction d'un élément d'asymétrie dans les rapports fédéraux-provinciaux, le titulaire de la compétence sur certaines matières étant d'une part le gouvernement fédéral pour la majorité des provinces et d'autre part la ou les provinces qui jouissent d'un statut particulier[43]. En d'autres termes, les provinces, dans un tel régime, n'auraient pas toutes les mêmes pouvoirs; une ou plusieurs d'entre elles exerceraient certaines compétences qui, pour les autres, appartiendraient à l'autorité fédérale.

Les auteurs canadiens ont surtout mis l'accent sur les difficultés que ce système pourrait engendrer quant à la représentation des provinces ayant un statut particulier au sein des institutions fédérales[44]. On semble s'être assez peu intérrogé, cependant, sur le genre de compétence pouvant se prêter à un régime de statut particulier. À cet égard, on peut soutenir que la compétence sur les ressources naturelles serait peut-être une de celles qui, en contexte canadien, se prêterait le moins à une pareille différence de statut entre les provinces.

Pour qu'un régime de statut particulier soit applicable, il faut que le secteur visé soit suffisamment centralisé pour qu'une décentralisation un tant soit peu significative puisse être opérée au profit de certaines provinces. Bien entendu, on peut atteindre le même résultat si une majorité de provinces délègue au pouvoir central certains pouvoirs, d'autres ne le faisant pas et se retrouvant de ce fait dans une situation de statut particulier. Le secteur des ressources naturelles au Canada est décentralisé à tel point qu'on ne voit pas aisément ce que l'on pourrait donner en plus; on ne voit pas aisément non plus ce qu'une majorité des provinces pourrait consentir à déléguer à l'autorité fédérale. Certes, il n'est pas du tout impensable que les pouvoirs provinciaux sur les ressources soient augmentés, et une révision de la constitution, si elle était opérée, irait vraisemblablement dans ce sens. Il nous semble toutefois qu'à cause de leur nature même, les pouvoirs provinciaux qui pourraient être ainsi accrus pourraient difficilement l'être au bénéfice d'une ou de quelques provinces.

Toutes les provinces ont des ressources, complémentaires ou concurrentes, et on conçoit que le rôle du pouvoir central est, dans une certaine mesure, d'arbitrer leurs désaccords. Il est dès lors difficile d'imaginer qu'une ou plusieurs provinces conservent sur ces ressources des pouvoirs qui seraient exercés par l'autorité fédérale, cette dernière agissant alors à la fois comme arbitre et comme défenseur des provinces sans statut particulier. Il est naturel que les provinces tiennent toutes à peu près au même point à leurs ressources. Cela milite en faveur de l'uniformité de leur statut constitutionnel dans ce secteur[45].

Notons qu'une reconnaissance de la compétence et de la propriété des provinces sur les ressources au large des côtes conduirait à une espèce de statut particulier *de facto*, les provinces non côtières se trouvant complètement privées des bénéfices de ces ressources. Toutefois, dans l'optique de plusieurs provinces, il s'agirait non pas d'un statut particulier mais au contraire d'une mesure d'uniformité, les ressources au large des côtes devant, comme les autres, relever des pouvoirs provinciaux.

L'indépendance du Québec

Dans la rhétorique politique, qu'elle soit favorable ou défavorable à l'indépendance, les ressources naturelles constituent une arme importante, bien qu'à double tranchant. Le Québec est tour à tour présenté comme riche et important exportateur, ou démuni et dépendant du pétrole et du gaz de l'Ouest, qui lui viennent à prix favorable et dont l'acheminement est favorisé par la politique fédérale du transport. Tout compte fait, la sécurité d'approvisionnement en pétrole et en gaz canadiens est probablement de nature à renforcer l'attachement au régime fédéral, d'autant que ce régime n'a pas à ce jour entraîné une régie fédérale importante sur l'électricité, laissant au Québec une grande autonomie sur cette importante ressource. La question énergétique ne paraît donc pas être un atout pour la thèse de l'indépendance. Cela dit, nous tenterons quand même d'apprécier les conséquences de l'indépendance sur la politique des ressources.

Dans le domaine énergétique, il paraît clair que la dépendance du Québec sur l'importation demeurera considérable. Les conséquences de la souveraineté sur le niveau des prix sont cependant difficiles à apprécier. Elles pourraient être assez peu marquées si les prix de l'énergie canadienne atteignaient le niveau des prix internationaux. Le Québec n'y perdrait donc pas en retournant au pétrole importé, auquel il devra de toute façon retourner d'ici quelques années. Par ailleurs, le fait de s'approvisionner à titre d'État indépendant ne devrait pas non plus le défavoriser, puisque la demande canadienne d'énergie internationale ne paraît pas suffisante pour avoir une influence sur l'offre. En revanche, les importations d'énergie par le Québec auraient probablement un impact considérable sur la valeur de

la devise québécoise ainsi que sur l'implantation d'industries
secondaires utilisant du matériel importé. On a déjà mentionné
que les exportations d'électricité québécoise aux États-Unis ne
compenseraient certainement pas le déficit des comptes
extérieurs pour les importations pétrolières et gazières. Il va
sans dire que les conséquences de l'option souveraineté dépen-
draient beaucoup de la façon dont le Québec pourrait réduire
ses importations et éventuellement exploiter de nouvelles
découvertes[46].

Au chapitre des mines et de l'industrie forestière, il s'agit
avant tout de savoir dans quelle mesure l'indépendance pourrait
améliorer l'exportation. Rappelons qu'au Québec, le tiers des
exportations consistent en des matières brutes alors qu'en
Ontario ce chiffre baisse à moins de 10 %. Elles sont peu diversifiées, les plus importantes étant le papier, le minerai,
l'amiante, le cuivre et l'aluminium, et les principaux clients se
chiffrent au nombre de huit ou neuf. Comme ce secteur en
général s'est assez mal comporté ces dernières années et comme
les exportations les plus dynamiques (automobiles, énergie)
n'ont pas profité au Québec, on peut songer à blâmer la
politique commerciale et tarifaire fédérale. Mais on a vu
précédemment les effets limités de la politique tarifaire sur le
commerce des matières premières. Certes, le Québec, s'il avait sa
propre monnaie, pourrait stimuler son commerce d'exportation
en recourant à la dévaluation. On a déjà noté, cependant, que
l'élasticité de l'offre est faible dans le cas des matières premières
et que ces dernières occupent une part importante dans les
livraisons du Québec à l'étranger. Comme les importations
canadiennes sont très diversifiées et que le Canada importe
plusieurs produits de base, il est dans une mauvaise situation
pour participer à la cartélisation de certains de ses produits.
Peut-être un Québec indépendant serait-il mieux placé pour le
faire[47] et pourrait-il négocier des accords sectoriels avec les
États-Unis dans ses domaines forts, par exemple l'aluminium ou
le zinc, bien que, de façon générale, la perspective d'accords
sectoriels dans le domaine industriel ne paraît pas très bonne
aux experts[48] et que l'approche sectorielle canadienne à la
Ronde Tokyo n'ait pas eu beaucoup de succès dans le domaine
minéral.

L'indépendance permettrait-elle au Québec de réaliser une
politique des ressources plus cohérente et plus efficace, et de
parvenir à hausser la productivité et à abaisser les coûts? Bien
sûr le Québec récupérerait tout son territoire et tous ses impôts,

sa fiscalité serait uniforme, et il ne serait pas nécessaire d'entreprendre de nouveau cette concertation pour une « politique minérale nationale » qui n'a pas eu de suite au cours des années 1970. Les chevauchements de programmes disparaîtraient aussi, même si une étude de la question a montré que, dans le domaine des ressources, ils avaient été relativement peu nombreux par rapport à l'ensemble des missions de l'État[49]. Dans tout ce tableau, il semble toutefois que la question la plus importante et la plus problématique demeure celle des approvisionnements en énergie à l'étranger.

La souveraineté-association

Il est évidemment très difficile de faire des conjectures sur ce que contiendrait un traité d'association Canada-Québec sur la politique des ressources de chacun des partenaires. Une union monétaire réduirait l'effet néfaste des importations du Québec sur son économie, et il est vraisemblable que le Québec souhaiterait un accès privilégié aux sources d'énergie canadienne et une certaine sécurité d'approvisionnement. À propos des livraisons du Québec dans le reste du Canada, on a vu que les exportations québécoises de ressources sont surtout dirigées vers l'étranger, et il y a peu de raisons pour que cet état de choses se modifie considérablement. Au reste, dans la plus importante étude réalisée à ce jour sur la souveraineté-association[50], les auteurs ont mis l'accent surtout sur les échanges de produits manufacturés, soutenant que ce secteur est plus sujet aux changements pouvant résulter des modifications aux rapports commerciaux canadiens.

Il s'agit donc de savoir ce que le Québec pourrait offrir en échange d'un certain accès privilégié aux ressources canadiennes. À cet égard, il semble que le Québec pourrait tirer profit à la fois de sa position géographique et de l'importance économique de son marché pour le pétrole et le gaz canadiens. Il serait en effet essentiel pour le reste du Canada d'avoir un droit de passage sur le territoire québécois, pour les besoins du commerce international en général et pour les communications entre les deux parties du territoire canadien. On sait aussi que le marché du gaz, peu développé à ce jour, est en expansion au Québec, qui pourrait offrir ainsi un débouché intéressant pour le gaz albertain et pour les réserves des îles Arctiques.

On peut donc penser qu'il est fort probable qu'un traité d'association Canada-Québec ne serait pas silencieux sur la question des ressources énergétiques.

Conclusion

Concluons simplement en rappelant le caractère bien particulier, au point de vue politique et constitutionnel, de la question des ressources au Canada, et la position paradoxale de certains gouvernements. C'est le cas du Québec, qui a continué de maintenir une position très autonomiste, alors que les changements majeurs intervenus ces dernières années dans le secteur énergétique ont accentué sa dépendance d'autres régions du pays et auraient pu le rendre plus sympathique aux politiques fédérales. Mais c'est aussi le cas jusqu'à un certain point du gouvernement fédéral. Alors même que ce dernier met de plus en plus l'accent sur la liberté des échanges à travers le pays et dénonce les mesures provinciales qui y font obstacle, il est peut-être prêt à concéder aux provinces, dans le secteur des ressources, des pouvoirs qui ne seraient assurément pas toujours exercés dans le sens de cette liberté.

Notes

1. Les ressources naturelles se divisent en ressources renouvelables ou non énergétiques (eau, forêts, pêcheries, hydroélectricité) et en ressources non renouvelables ou énergétiques (pétrole, gaz, charbon, mines).

2. Voir notamment Donald J. Patton, « The Evolution of Canadian Federal Mineral Policies » et Gérard Gaudet, « Forces Underlying the Evolution of Natural Resource Policies in Quebec », dans *Natural Resources in U.S. —Canadian Relations*, vol. 1, *The Evolution of Policies and Issues*, Carl E. Beigie et Alfred O. Hero, Jr., éd., Boulder, Colorado, Westview Press pour le compte de C.D. Howe Research Institute et de la World Peace Foundation, 1980, pp. 203–247 et 247–265.

3. On parle ici d'affrontements politiques et constitutionnels de grande intensité et non pas de simples conflits judiciaires qui eux ont été nombreux entre les deux ordres de gouvernement dans le domaine des ressources. Pour une analyse proprement juridique, voir l'ouvrage de Gérard V. La Forest, *Natural Resources and Public Property Under the Canadian Constitution*, Toronto, University of Toronto Press, 1969.

4. Article 109 de l'A.A.N.B. 1867.

5. Le Parlement a compétence sur le commerce interprovincial et international et sur tout mode de taxation [art. 91(2) et (3) de l'A.A.N.B. 1867]. Sont aussi pertinents le pouvoir fédéral sur les entreprises et les ouvrages interprovinciaux et internationaux [art. 92(10)(a)], le fameux pouvoir déclaratoire fédéral [art. 92(10)(c)] et même le pouvoir général du Parlement de légiférer pour « la paix, l'ordre et le bon gouvernement » du pays (art. 91, paragraphe introductif), ce dernier ne paraissant toutefois pouvoir justifier, selon la jurisprudence récente, des interventions fédérales dans des champs provinciaux qu'en contexte d'urgence.

6. Article 92 (16) de l'A.A.N.B. 1867.

7.   Garth Stevenson, « The Process of Making Mineral Resource Policy in Canada », dans *Natural Resources in U.S. –Canadian Relations*, vol. 1, *The Evolution of Policies and Issues*, Carl E. Beigie et Alfred O. Hero, Jr., éd., Boulder, Colorado, Westview Press pour le compte de C.D. Howe Research Institute et de la World Peace Foundation, 1980, p. 170.

8.   *Débats parlementaires sur la question de la confédération des provinces de l'Amérique britannique du Nord*, Québec, Hunter, Rose et Lemieux, 1865, notamment dans les interventions de l'honorable James Skead (p. 247, sur les forêts), de l'honorable Hector Louis Langevin (p. 379, sur la colonisation) et de Christopher Dunkin (pp. 520 et 1026, sur les revenus miniers). Les interventions sur le principe de la propriété provinciale des terres de la Couronne ont été multiples.

9.   Québec, Commission royale d'enquête sur les problèmes constitutionnels, *Rapport*, Montréal, Province de Québec, 1956, vol. 3, t. 1, p. 372; et vol. 1, pp. 25, 41, 258 – 261, 283.

10.   *Ibid.*, vol. 3, t. 1, p. 365. On y insiste sur l'électricité, les forêts et les mines comme piliers du développement économique du Québec (pp. 331 sqq.).

11.   Wendy MacDonald, *Constitutional Change and the Mineral Industry in Canada*, Kingston, Ont., Institute for Intergovernmental Relations: Centre for Resource Studies, Queen's University, 1980, p. 21.

12.   Gaudet, « Forces Underlying the Evolution . . . », p. 250.

13.   *Ibid.*

14.   Articles 91(3) et 122 de l'A.A.N.B. 1867.

15.   Gaudet, «Forces Underlying the Evolution . . . », p. 260.

16.   *Ibid.*, p. 259, pour le récit de ce conflit.

17.   Il faut comparer, à ce sujet, *Smylie* c. *La Reine* (1900) 27 O.A.R. 172 (C.A. Ont.) et *Attorney-General for British-Columbia* c. *McDonald Murphy Lumber Company, Limited* (1930) A.C. 357; 2 Olmsted 659. Dans le premier cas, une province a pu interdire l'exportation hors du pays de bois coupé sur les terres publiques mais non ouvré dans la province. Dans le second cas, on a jugé invalide tout bois non ouvré dans la province en question. Quant au Québec, voir la *Loi sur l'utilisation des ressources forestières*, L.R.Q. 1977, chap. U – 2, art. 2; et la *Loi sur l'exportation d'énergie électrique*, L.R.Q. 1977, chap. E – 23, art. 1.

18.   La revendication la plus ferme du Québec en matière de ressources au large des côtes a trait au golfe Saint-Laurent. Le Québec a toujours soutenu que le golfe était partie intégrante de son territoire, selon un partage avec les provinces de l'Atlantique basé sur les lignes équidistantes des rives. N'excluant pas complètement un arbitrage fédéral pour le partage territorial entre les provinces concernées, le Quebec privilégie toutefois des ententes entre celles-ci. Le problème des ressources s'insère donc dans le thème politique plus vaste de l'intégrité du territoire; du reste, la Commission d'étude sur l'intégrité du territoire, mise sur pied en 1967 par le gouvernement du Québec, a approuvé la position du gouvernement au sujet du golfe dans son rapport (vol. 7.1, *La frontière dans le Golfe du Saint-Laurent, le rapport des commissaires*, Québec, Éditeur officiel, 1972). La question des frontières septentrionales est d'une autre nature, puisque ce qu'on a déjà envisagé à ce sujet était une extension des frontières provinciales dans la baie James, la baie d'Hudson et le détroit d'Hudson, et non pas la revendication par le Québec de territoires lui appartenant. Sur cette question et sur le récit des pourparlers entre le gouvernement fédéral et le Québec, l'Ontario et le Manitoba, voir notamment la Commission d'étude sur l'intégrité du territoire, vol. 5.1, *Les frontières septentrionales, le rapport des commissaires*, Québec, Éditeur officiel, 1971.

19.   Déclaration du premier ministre Jean Lesage à la conférence fédérale-provinciale du 19 juillet 1965 tenue à Ottawa. Sur la position du Québec, voir

Québec, ministère des Affaires intergouvernementales, *Les positions tradition-nelles du Québec sur le partage des pouvoirs, 1900–1976*, Québec, M.A.I., 1978, pp. 35–38.

20.   *Reference Re: Offshore Mineral Rights of British Columbia*, (1967) R.C.S. 792.

21.   Lettre du premier ministre Jean-Jacques Bertrand au premier ministre Pierre Elliott Trudeau, le 5 février 1969.

22.   *Central Canada Potash Co. Limited et al.* c. *Le gouvernement de la Saskatchewan*, (1979) 1 R.C.S. 42, où fut jugé invalide un plan provincial de commercialisation de la potasse parce qu'il était applicable à des produits exportés; *Canadian Industrial Gas & Oil Ltd.* c. *Le Gouvernement de la Saskatchewan et al.*, (1978) 2 R.C.S. 545, où fut jugé invalide un impôt provincial sur le revenu minier, au motif qu'il s'agissait à la fois d'un impôt indirect et d'une simple réglementation interdite du commerce.

23.   Les déclarations du premier ministre Blakeney sont reproduites dans MacDonald, *Constitutional Change* . . ., pp. 38–39.

24.   J. Gilles Massé, *Les objectifs d'une politique québécoise de l'énergie*, Québec, Éditeur officiel du Québec, 1972, pp. 98–101; M. Massé était le ministre responsable des questions d'énergie dans le gouvernement Bourassa. Des critiques non moins sévères ont été formulées sous le gouvernement Lévesque. Voir, par exemple, Québec, Développement économique, *Bâtir le Québec : énoncé de politique économique, synthèse, orientations et actions*, Québec, Éditeur officiel du Québec, 1979, p. 25.

25.   Ce n'est en pratique qu'en 1970, lors de la célèbre affaire *Caloil*, qu'il l'a remise en question. Voir *Caloil Inc.* c. *Le Procureur général du Canada*, (1971) R.C.S. 543, où fut jugé valide un règlement de l'Office national de l'énergie interdisant de transporter de l'essence à moteur importée à l'ouest d'une ligne divisant la province de l'Ontario.

26.   Nous empruntons beaucoup à l'étude de Pierre-Paul Proulx, Louise Dulude et Yves Rabeau, *Étude des relations commerciales Québec–USA, Québec-Canada : options et impacts, contraintes et potentiels*, préparée pour le compte du ministère des Affaires intergouvernementales du Québec, Québec, Éditeur officiel du Québec, 1979, pp. 430–585. Cette étude contient une bibliographie de taille aux pp. 460 (énergie), 535 (mines) et 585 (forêts). Nous empruntons aussi à l'important rapport de Bernard Bonin et Mario Polèse, avec la collaboration de Jean-K. Samson, *À propos de l'association économique Canada–Québec*, Québec, ÉNAP, 1980. Il s'agit assurément de l'étude la plus sérieuse à ce jour des possibilités d'une telle association économique.

27.   Il existe cependant un certain potentiel de pétrole et de gaz dans le sous-sol québécois. Voir, par exemple, Québec, Direction générale de l'énergie, *La politique québécoise de l'énergie : assurer l'avenir*, Québec, Éditeur officiel du Québec, 1978, p. 56. Quant au charbon, d'un intérêt marginal pour la province, le Québec l'importe en sa totalité, en très grande partie en provenance des États-Unis, tout comme l'Ontario. Les coûts de transport rendent prohibitif l'approvisionnement en charbon canadien.

28.   Même s'il ne faut pas minimiser les difficultés de substitution du gaz au pétrole, le Québec espère doubler d'ici 1990 le taux de consommation du gaz par rapport à la consommation totale d'énergie et le voir passer de 6 à 12 %. Entre 1971 et 1976, la consommation de gaz s'est accrue de 59 %.

29.   L'électricité compte pour 22 % dans le bilan actuel de la consommation énergétique de la province, et la prévision gouvernementale, que d'aucuns jugent trop optimiste, est à l'effet que ce taux sera de 41 % en 1990. On prévoit aussi que la puissance installée de Hydro-Québec doublera ou presque de 1977 à 1985, et on estime qu'une fois complétés les travaux du complexe La Grande, environ 40 % du potentiel hydraulique rentable restera encore non aménagé.

On retrouve ces prévisions et ces estimations dans Québec, Direction générale de l'énergie, *La politique québécoise.* . . .

30.   Proulx, Dulude et Rabeau, *Étude des relations commerciales* . . . , p. 459. Ces auteurs rapportent que les achats québécois d'hydrocarbures au prix mondial auraient été de 2,4 $ milliards en 1976, soit 28 % des importations totales (ce montant a plus que doublé depuis lors), alors que les ventes d'électricité à la Power Authority de l'état de New York (PASNY) entre 1977 et 1981 sont de 123 $ millions (234 $ millions en 1979). Les importations de Churchill Falls sont considérables (28 % de la puissance de Hydro-Québec en 1977, 15 % en 1985, 11 % en 1990) et plus importantes que les exportations vers l'état de New York, le prix de vente dans ce dernier cas étant cependant beaucoup plus élevé. Comme les marchés de l'électricité des diverses provinces canadiennes ne sont pas complémentaires, à cause de la concordance des variations saisonnières, les échanges portent sur les ajustements et les surplus : il n'y a pas de vente d'énergie dite « ferme », et l'on estime que les réseaux d'interconnexion entre le Québec et les provinces voisines sont suffisants et satisfaisants. Les échanges avec les États-Unis sont plus importants, vu la différence de climat et l'absence de barrière tarifaire sur l'électricité. Voir en particulier l'analyse de Jean-Charles de Groote, « Note sur la collaboration en matière d'énergie électrique », dans *Le Québec et ses partenaires économiques canadiens : perspectives d'avenir*, textes préparatoires du Congrès de l'Association des économistes québécois (avril 1979), rassemblés par Michel Boisvert *et al.*, Montréal, Les Éditions Quinze, 1979, pp. 115–133.

31.   Voir la note 30.

32.   Le gouvernement du Québec s'est fixé un objectif de réduction de 20 % de la demande de pétrole brut entre 1975 et 1980. Voir Québec, Direction générale de l'énergie, *La politique québécoise* . . . , p. 66.

33.   Voir les conclusions en ce sens de l'étude de Jean-A. Guérin, « Les échanges énergétiques du Québec avec ses partenaires économiques canadiens », dans *Le Québec et ses partenaires économiques canadiens : perspectives d'avenir*, textes préparatoires du Congrès de l'Association des économistes québécois (avril 1979), rassemblés par Michel Boisvert *et al.*, Montréal, Les Éditions Quinze, 1979, pp. 93–113.

34.   Proulx, Dulude et Rabeau, *Étude des relations commerciales* . . . , p. 465.

35.   Bonin et Polèse, *À propos de l'association économique* . . . , p. 65. Trente-cinq pour cent de la production québécoise d'amiante, soit près de 40 % de la production mondiale, est exportée aux États-Unis, de même que 60 % de la production du fer et de l'acier, soit 40 % des importations américaines. On peut observer une dépendance réciproque semblable pour l'aluminium. Représentant 70,6 % des exportations canadiennes en 1975 — le Canada vient en tête des exportateurs mondiaux — 65,5 % de l'aluminium québécois est exporté aux États-Unis, soit 51,4 % des importations américaines. Sur l'ensemble des produits minéraux exportés du Québec, 38,9 % (en 1973), 53,1 % (en 1974) et 47,3 % (en 1975) l'étaient aux États-Unis. Notons que les réserves québécoises d'amiante et de fer sont considérables; il en va différemment du nickel, du zinc et du cuivre, une dizaine de mines de cuivre ayant fermé leurs portes depuis quelques années. Malgré le manque de bauxite et la multiplication des producteurs, il semble que le Québec, qui dispose d'électricité à bon prix, peut être optimiste au sujet de sa production d'aluminium.

36.   C'est ainsi, par exemple, qu'en 1975 le Québec expédiait, en minerais et concentrés, 79,3 % de son fer. Notons cependant que les possibilités de transformation sur place de l'amiante sont plus limitées qu'on ne le croit généralement et qu'il en va de même pour l'aluminium, les frais de transport appelant une transformation proche des points de consommation.

37.   « La tendance est à la diminution de l'importance relative de ces activités primaires dans le produit intérieur brut que ce soit pour l'agriculture, les forêts, la pêche et les mines et carrières. Par rapport à l'ensemble du Canada, l'importance relative du Québec a baissé pour l'agriculture et les mines, et plus récemment pour l'industrie forestière également » (Bonin et Polèse, *À propos de l'association économique* . . . , p. 30). Le bas prix de l'énergie compense toutefois pour les coûts de transport dus à l'éloignement des sites.

38.   Voir Proulx, Dulude et Rabeau, *Étude des relations commerciales* . . . , pp. 512–513, où les auteurs s'appuient sur une étude de Roma Dauphin, « Les effets des variations du taux de change sur les exportations du Québec », étude effectuée pour le ministère québécois de l'Industrie et du Commerce, Québec, MIC, 1978.

39.   Voir, par exemple, Ian McDougall, « L'énergie et l'avenir du fédéralisme : harmonie nationale ou hégémonie continentale? », dans R.B. Byers et Robert W. Reford, *Le défi canadien : la viabilité de la Confédération*, Toronto, Institut canadien des affaires internationales, 1979, pp. 339–371. L'auteur favorise une forte régie fédérale du secteur énergétique.

40.   Peu après la décision de la Cour suprême dans *Central Canada Potash Co. Limited et al.* c. *Le gouvernement de la Saskatchewan*, (1979) 1 R.C.S. 42, le premier ministre Blakeney écrivait à son homologue fédéral pour protester contre cette décision. Il observait notamment : « Je dois (...) vous avouer honnêtement que le temps est venu pour votre gouvernement de répondre aux aspirations légitimes des provinces de l'Ouest. En continuant de négliger l'Ouest, vous mettrez en péril l'existence même de notre pays » (lettre du 10 octobre 1978).

41.   Voir aussi Canada, La Commission de l'unité canadienne, *Se retrouver : observations et recommandations*, Ottawa, ministre des Approvisionnements et Services Canada, 1979, p. 98. Le rapport du Comité sur la constitution de l'Association du Barreau canadien (*Vers un Canada nouveau*, Montréal, Fondation du Barreau canadien, 1978, p. 118) suggérait d'autoriser les provinces à restreindre l'exportation de produits, à exiger leur transformation sur place et à établir des programmes de contingentement et de stabilisation des prix sur les produits d'exportation. Sur ce point, les propositions constitutionnelles du parti libéral du Québec sont plus évasives. On se contente de souhaiter que les pouvoirs fédéraux sur le commerce ne nuisent pas aux attributions provinciales sur les ressources, et l'on souhaite aussi des actions fédérales concertées avec les provinces. Voir *Une nouvelle fédération canadienne*, document de la Commission constitutionnelle du parti libéral du Québec, Montréal, parti libéral du Québec, 1980, p. 100.

42.   Pour une critique en ce sens, voir Paul C. Weiler, « The Supreme Court of Canada and Canadian Federalism », dans *Law and Social Change*, Jacob Ziegel, éd., Toronto, Osgoode Hall Law School/York University, 1973, p. 39.

43.   Logiquement, on peut dire que le concept de statut particulier vise aussi la situation d'une ou de plusieurs provinces ayant non pas plus mais moins de pouvoirs que la majorité. Si, par exemple, trois provinces déléguaient à Ottawa leur compétence sur les relations de travail, elles auraient un statut particulier par rapport aux sept autres. En pratique, toutefois, on emploie surtout l'expression *statut particulier* pour désigner un statut de plus grande décentralisation.

44.   Voir, par exemple, Pierre Elliott Trudeau, *Le fédéralisme et la société canadienne française*, Montréal, Éditions HMH, 1967, pp. xi et 37; et André Dufour, « Le statut particulier », *La revue du Barreau canadien*, vol. 45 (1967), p. 451. D'autres ont approuvé ou critiqué ce système pour des motifs plus généraux. Voir, par exemple, Jacques Brossard, « Fédéralisme et statut particulier », dans *Problèmes de droit contemporain. Mélanges Louis Baudouin*, Adrian Popovici, éd., Montréal, Les presses de l'université de Montréal, 1974,

p. 425; et A.W. Johnson, « The Dynamics of Federalism in Canada », *Revue canadienne de science politique*, 1 (1968), p. 26.

45. Le professeur Smiley a déjà fait remarquer qu'il y a une grande différence dans le mode de déroulement d'une négociation fédérale-provinciale selon le secteur ou le domaine sur lequel elle porte. On ne négocie pas de la même façon, ajoutait-il, selon qu'il s'agit de se partager quelque chose — un champ fiscal ou des subsides — ou d'harmoniser ses interventions ou sa réglementation, par exemple sur l'énergie, l'environnement, la protection du consommateur ou le transport. Voir Donald V. Smiley, *Canada in Question: Federalism in the Seventies*, 2ᵉ éd., Montréal, McGraw Hill, 1976, p. 64. De façon analogue, on peut avancer qu'il y a des secteurs qui se prêtent mal ou peu à certains modèles de partage des responsabilités politiques.

46. Sur divers points, voir l'étude de R.J. Rahn, « L'énergie et l'indépendance du Québec », dans *Économie et indépendance*, textes du congrès de l'Association des économistes québécois (avril 1977), colligés et présentes par Luc-Normand Tellier, Montréal, Les Éditions Quinze, 1977. Notons que le programme de souveraineté-association du gouvernement du Québec (*La nouvelle entente Québec-Canada*, Québec, Éditeur officiel du Québec, 1979) met l'accent sur les ressources naturelles du Québec, en particulier sur l'hydroélectricité (pp. 95−96) et dénonce violemment l'« intrusion extrêmement dangereuse » (p. 22) d'Ottawa dans le domaine des ressources. Le volet *association* contient cependant peu de choses précises sur les ressources.

47. Cette idée est évoquée dans l'étude de Proulx, Dulude et Rabeau, *Étude des relations commerciales . . .* , pp. 532−634.

48. Bonin et Polèse, *À propos de l'association économique . . .* , pp. 344−345.

49. On renvoie ici à l'étude de Germain Julien et Marcel Proulx, sous la direction de Arthur Tremblay, *Le chevauchement des programmes fédéraux et québécois*, Québec, École nationale d'administration publique, 1978. Sur l'ensemble des problèmes juridiques reliés à l'indépendance, voir Jacques Brossard, *L'accession à la souveraineté et le cas du Québec : conditions et modalités politico-juridiques*, Montréal, Les presses de l'université de Montréal, 1976. Sur la question territoriale en particulier, l'auteur est d'avis que le Québec indépendant aurait droit aux frontières maritimes dont bénéficient les États souverains en droit international (p. 501), mais qu'il lui serait difficile de réclamer un partage de l'Arctique suivant la théorie dite des secteurs (p. 504).

50. Bonin et Polèse, *À propos de l'association économique. . . .*

L'auteur

FRANÇOIS CHEVRETTE est professeur titulaire à la Faculté de droit de l'université de Montréal. Après avoir complété ses études de droit à cette faculté en 1965, il a été admis au Barreau du Québec en 1966 et a poursuivi ensuite des études de droit public et de science politique à l'université de Paris. Il est spécialisé dans le domaine du droit constitutionnel et des libertés fondamentales. Le professeur Chevrette fut aussi conseiller spécial auprès du ministère des Affaires intergouvernementales en 1976−1977.

Environmental Protection and Enhancement under a New Canadian Constitution

DALE GIBSON
University of Manitoba

Contents

Environmental Protection and Enhancement under a New Canadian Constitution

Introduction

The purpose of this paper is to consider appropriate arrangements of constitutional powers as they apply to environmental management in each of four conceivable constitutional futures for Canada:

- A renewed federalism of a type generally similar to that which now prevails
- A new federalism in which there would be room for special status for one or more provinces on certain significant matters
- A situation in which Quebec would be fully independent, with the remaining provinces federally united
- A situation of 'sovereignty-association' between Quebec and a federally united Canada.

The term 'environment' will be used in a somewhat restricted sense throughout this paper to denote an amenity — a more or less healthful and enjoyable living space for humans and other vital creatures — rather than a source of wealth. This is not to ignore the fact that the environment is also the source of all material wealth. Indeed it is the exploitation of this wealth that poses the principal threat to the quality of the living space. By defining 'environment' as 'an amenity', I am merely trying to

115

isolate the 'quality-control' aspect of the problem for special consideration.

The virtue of special consideration may not be immediately evident. Under the existing Canadian Constitution, although certain elements of the environment are accorded specific attention — "fisheries,"[1] "public lands,"[2] "lands, mines, minerals, and royalties,"[3] for example — governmental jurisdiction over the protection and enhancement of environmental quality is not mentioned expressly; it adheres instead to a number of other federal and provincial powers.[4] Since this arrangement has produced what some observers, at least, regard as a generally satisfactory distribution of environmental jurisdiction,[5] one may ask why it would be desirable to list environmental quality control separately in any new constitution. While it would be premature to attempt an answer to that key question at this stage of the paper, it will be assumed for the purpose of the following discussion that 'environmental protection and enhancement' will be a discrete head of governmental jurisdiction under any new constitutional arrangement. After examining the ramifications of such an approach, we shall be in a better position to discuss its advisability.

We shall further assume that the municipal level of government is subsumed by the provincial order. Operationally this assumption is naïve. There are many environmental problems that lend themselves more readily to municipal than to province-wide solutions. Nevertheless, no new constitution that may be made for Canada in the foreseeable future is likely to experiment with tripartite federalism; constitutional powers will continue to be divided dichotomously. It is possible that once the fundamental federal-provincial division of powers has been agreed on, there may be a further provincial-municipal allocation, based either on provincial constitutions or on purely political considerations, but this paper will not address that stage of the problem. Thus any reference to matters suitable for provincial jurisdiction should be understood to include those for which municipal responsibility might be appropriate.

It is somewhat surprising, given the importance of the subject and the energy that has been expended in recent years on studies of constitutional reform, that relatively little attention has been paid to future constitutional arrangements for environmental management. A selection of proposals that have been made is set out in an appendix to this paper.[6]

Although the aim of the paper is to present an objective discussion, it will not be possible to avoid stating personal opinions. So many possibilities are involved that unless some are eliminated by the expression of preferences from time to time, conclusions will be unattainable.

Factors Involved

The most difficult aspect of any attempt to fashion suitable constitutional arrangements for the future is to decide on the criteria of suitability. A number of factors come to mind that might be relevant to the design of constitutional provisions concerning the environment. When examined more closely, some of these factors prove to be of great importance, while others are of little or no significance. This section of the paper will attempt to examine several arguably relevant factors: control techniques, environmental sectors, and territory affected.

Control Techniques

The war against environmental degradation must obviously be waged on many fronts, and to be effective the government or governments concerned must employ a wide range of legal weaponry. Among the more important of these weapons are the following:

- General criminal law (criminal nuisance,[7] and so on)
- Special legislated prohibitions (such as the pollution prohibitions in the federal Fisheries Act,[8] or municipal anti-noise by-laws)
- General schemes to monitor and regulate environmental quality (federal Clean Air Act[9] and Canada Water Act,[10] provincial clean environment legislation, and so on)
- Licensing controls (fishing and hunting quotas, automobile-licensing standards, and so on)
- Zoning
- Private law (the torts of private and public nuisance, for example)
- Positive programs (such as the creation of recreational facilities and the preservation of wilderness enclaves).

It might appear at first glance that it would be possible, when planning for a new constitution, to determine which ones of these control techniques would be more suitable for the central government and which for the provincial governments, and then to distribute constitutional jurisdiction accordingly. Regrettably this is not so. Every government, federal or provincial, that is involved in environmental regulation must be able to employ all, or almost all, these tactics. At present both orders of government can employ all but two of them: general criminal law is the exclusive domain of the Parliament of Canada,[11] and most of the private law field is reserved for the provincial Legislatures.[12] These exceptions are not as important as they might seem since the provinces have the power to enforce their laws by means of prohibitions with penal consequences,[13] and the federal Parliament may create private law remedies if they are necessarily incidental to some legitimate head of federal jurisdiction.[14] In short, in terms of control technique, there is very extensive overlap of federal and provincial powers under the existing Constitution. That is as it should continue to be in the future; satisfactory environmental protection and enhancement require that within their respective spheres of responsibility, all governments should have fully equipped tactical arsenals available.

Control tactics do not, therefore, provide useful criteria for determining an appropriate future allocation of constitutional powers.

Environmental Sectors

Discussions of environmental issues are often organized according to the sector of the environment affected: air, water, or land. It is tempting to speculate that a similar division of governmental responsibilities for the environment might be appropriate, but it requires only brief reflection to conclude that it would not. For one thing, two or more of these sectors are often attacked by a single source of contamination. Air pollution from factory chimneys can produce acid rain which, in turn, poisons the land and water on which it falls. Fertilizers and pesticides spread or sprayed on farm lands can be carried into waterways by spring run-off. Underground storage or disposal of toxic chemicals can endanger ground water. And so on. Division of jurisdiction on the basis of whether air, water, or land is affected would result in needless duplication of control machinery.

Another reason that governmental powers cannot usefully be distributed according to the sector of the environment affected is that in each sector federal control would seem appropriate in some situations and provincial control in others. While the problem of preventing noxious odours from feed lots or garbage dumps from interfering with the enjoyment of neighbouring domestic property is clearly local in nature, it is just as clear that the federal government has a legitimate role to play, at least in large-scale air pollution that creates a risk of international contamination. Although there is no doubt that the water quality of intraprovincial lakes and streams should generally be a provincial responsibility, other governments ought to be involved in the case of interprovincial and international waterways. Even in the case of land, an extraprovincial dimension exists wherever there is a significant threat of contamination to surface or ground water that might eventually flow across provincial boundaries.

The last few examples suggest a criterion that might be at least partially useful in distributing constitutional powers: territoriality. This criterion will be examined next.

Territory Affected

It makes much sense in a federal system to base at least prima facie constitutional jurisdiction over any subject on its territorial ramifications. Federalism is, after all, a system of government that strives to place issues of purely local import within local control and issues with wider impact under central control. By this standard the provinces would be given jurisdiction over environmental matters contained entirely within provincial bounds, and matters having wider impact would be at least partially under federal control. (It is assumed that the airspace above each province is provincial territory, at least in its lower reaches; if it should ever be decided that the airspace is federal territory,[15] and if that decision should be perpetuated in the new constitution, the implications of the territorial principle would be markedly different.) The application of this principle would not be without problems, however. Some of these would indicate that only a modified form of territoriality would be desirable.

In the first place, the federal principle itself is not wholly territorial. The central government has, and will continue to have, control over many enterprises that operate within the territorial limits of the various provinces. Federally owned or regulated transportation and communication systems, for example, though usually connected to facilities outside a given province, have permanent intraprovincial establishments and operations that often have significant environmental impact. Federal Indian reserves and national parks are located in the provinces. Although the notion of federal 'enclaves' immune from provincial laws has been rejected by the Supreme Court of Canada,[16] federally owned and regulated enterprises must be permitted to operate within the provinces, primarily in accordance with federal directives, if federal jurisdiction is to mean anything. This implies that some environmental problems, even though contained entirely within the geographic bounds of a single province, must be regarded as having an extraprovincial dimension merely because of the involvement of a federally owned or regulated enterprise; and these problems must thus be subject to less than exclusive provincial jurisdiction. On the other hand, to exempt such federal operations completely from the burden of provincial environmental laws would grievously impair the ability of the provinces to protect their own environments. I have argued on other occasions that federal enterprises have been accorded excessive immunity under the existing Constitution.[17] An effective arrangement for the future must include some satisfactory compromise between completely territorial jurisdiction and complete immunity of federal enterprises from provincial laws. We shall return to this problem later in the paper.[18]

The special position of national parks and federally supervised historic sites within the provinces should perhaps be commented on at this point. A purist might argue that there would be no justification for such properties in a federal system that assigned responsibilities for environmental protection and enhancement on a territorial basis. In the case of national historic sites, the argument clearly has little merit. Every Canadian, regardless of residence, can justifiably expect the national government to ensure the preservation of, and accessibility to, such unique and nationally significant places. The validity of federal government involvement with recreation areas and wilderness preserves is less obvious, but no less real or important. It is in the interest of all Canadians that representative samples of our natural heritage be preserved in all parts of the country as living museums accessible to both Canadians and foreign visitors: Quebecers have as legitimate an interest in the Rocky Mountains as Albertans have in the Plains of Abraham.

While it is true that the provinces could perform this function (and do so to a considerable degree), only the Government of Canada could guarantee its being carried out to uniformly high standards and to an extent that includes examples of all the country's major natural features. Moreover the present existence and successful administration of national parks over a long period of time, in itself argues for their continuance; constitutions cannot ignore history. Provincial laws, environmental and otherwise, should, however, be applicable within the parks, subject to the paramountcy provisions to be discussed later.[19]

Another difficulty inherent in the territorial principle is the identification of extraprovincial concerns. Where pollution actually crosses provincial borders, it is obvious that the situation has an extraprovincial dimension, but it is not nearly so clear which elements of the problem would therefore fall under federal jurisdiction. Would federal jurisdiction apply to every aspect of the polluting activity? Or to those aspects with respect to which the province would be powerless to act unilaterally because of the territorial limitations on its powers? Or only to those aspects with which the province is unable to deal unilaterally and has so far failed to deal with through co-operation with other affected jurisdictions?

It is submitted that the approach most closely consonant with the principles of federalism would be the last mentioned: that is, the restriction of federal involvement in trans-boundary situations to jurisdiction over those aspects of the problem with which the provinces cannot cope unilaterally and have not dealt co-operatively.[20] This involvement could be accomplished by employing the currently unfashionable notion of federal responsibility for problems having a 'national dimension'.[21] A matter would be considered to have a 'national dimension' only to the extent that it would be beyond the power of the provinces to deal with it. Suppose, for example, that smoke from a factory in British Columbia created air pollution in the State of Washington. The Parliament of Canada would have prima facie jurisdiction under its 'national dimension' power[22] to regulate that factory's activities to the extent necessary to reduce or prevent the trans-boundary contamination since the avoidance of breaches of international law and other international controversies is a matter of national interest. However, if the province reached accord with American authorities on appropriate control measures such as permissible pollution levels and so on, there would no longer be a problem with a national dimension that justified federal legislation. The matter might not end there, of course; if Parliament then decided that it would be in the national interest to 'trade off' a solution to the British Columbia–Washington situation for a reduction of American pollution of Lake Erie or of air pollution from Detroit and Chicago, another national dimension would appear, and federal legislation sufficient to implement such an international bargain would be in order.

If the territorial principle were applied in an entirely unqualified manner, yet another difficulty could arise. To give the provincial governments (or the Government of Canada, in the case of the Territories) complete autonomy with respect to the protection of their own internal environments might, in some circumstances, diminish the likelihood that the protection afforded would be adequate. The risk would be particularly acute in situations where the exploitation of a resource would benefit a large majority of the population living a long way from the area where the resulting environmental damage would occur. The Churchill River diversion project in northern Manitoba offers a good illustration. Manitoba Hydro, a provincial Crown corporation, decided that rather than develop hydro-electric generating facilities on the Churchill River, it would be much more economical to divert water from the Churchill to the Nelson River, where it could be run through existing and projected generators. The scheme involved widespread environmental damage both because the lower Churchill would be deprived of its natural flows, and because massive flooding of lakes, streams, and forests would take place along the diversion route. Since the area was remote, the individuals and communities adversely affected were relatively few, and the project would be economically advantageous for the majority of Manitobans in the south of the province, the provincial government raised no serious opposition. It was only after the federal government intervened, claiming jurisdiction by virtue of its powers over navigation, fisheries, and so on, that some ameliorative measures were taken, and even they are regarded as inadequate by many critics.

This is not to suggest that provincial governments are inherently less likely to be sensitive to environmental concerns than the Government of Canada. The point is that as a rule, any government having general responsibility for an area is influenced more by the wishes of the majority of its constituents than by those of minorities. Since the territorial principle would place primary environmental responsibility on provincial shoulders, this rule, as it relates to the environmental sphere, would apply chiefly to provincial governments. It would, however, be equally applicable — perhaps more so — to the Government of Canada's responsibility for the northern Territories.

To provide satisfactory protection against environmental degradation, this tendency should be counteracted. Two possible methods for achieving this suggest themselves: a counterpoise of related powers by the order of government that does not have territorial jurisdiction, as it partly has now, and an overriding constitutional guarantee of certain environmental rights. Both possibilities will be explored further in the next section.

General Constitutional Characteristics

Foremost among the factors that must be taken into account in deciding on suitable treatment of environmental matters in a new constitution are the general characteristics of that constitution itself. It has already been observed that since any new arrangement is likely to involve some form of federalism, the distribution of governmental powers should, to the extent permitted by other constitutional imperatives, be directed to achieve the federal ideal of having local matters dealt with locally and national matters centrally. In a later section of this paper, consideration will be given to alterations to this scheme that may be called for in the event that the future constitution permits special status for one or more provinces, or in the event that Quebec becomes independent or stands in a relationship of sovereignty-association with the rest of Canada. In this section, the discussion will concern several other important features of the general constitution that could influence the selection of appropriate provisions with respect to the environment.

Entrenchment of Environmental Rights

No constitution serves only a single purpose or seeks to uphold only a single value. While the British North America (BNA) Act recites a desire of Canadians to be "federally united,"[23] and generally achieves that goal, the federalist ideal has been deliberately compromised in certain respects in the interests of other goals regarded as more important than the attainment of perfect federalism. To cite only two examples that still command wide support, section 93 significantly qualifies provincial autonomy in the field of education in order to guarantee certain rights to denominational schools, and section 133 limits the ability of Quebec to determine the language to be used in its legislature and courts. The BNA Act, 1971 and the new Canadian Charter of Rights and Freedoms places like limits on the powers of the Manitoba and New Brunswick Legislatures. It is probable that any new Canadian constitution would similarly deviate from pristine federalism by placing certain highly cherished values beyond the reach of otherwise autonomous Legislatures. It would be possible to include within this group of constitutionally entrenched rights some that would protect against the type of environmental dangers illustrated by the Churchill River diversion.

What environmental rights would be appropriate for constitutional entrenchment? One writer, who called for an "Environmental Bill of Rights," proposed that it include the following guarantees:

1. Public hearings when maximum effluent levels are being set.
2. A requirement for environmental impact statements to be filed by any private person or government agency undertaking projects likely to affect significantly the environment, well in advance of start-up, outlining possible environmental changes and alternatives. These statements would be linked with public hearing procedures where there is opposition to the project.
3. Concrete guidelines from the Legislature against which environmental agency action (or lack thereof) can be reviewed by an environmental ombudsman and the courts, and drastic restriction on environmental agency discretion.
4. Guaranteed access by the public to governmental information and expertise, removal of the civil service secrecy oath, and the provision for financial support to assist those persons appearing in the public interest before environmental tribunals.
5. An environmental ombudsman, whether one person or an environmental council, to advise on policy, demand review of Environment Ministry decisions, report periodically on the state of the provincial environment, and act as a watchdog on environmental abuse.
6. Procedural Law Reforms would also be assured.

a) Any citizen would be allowed to sue
   i) in the civil courts in regard to a public nuisance; and
   ii) to obtain an injunction to stop any project or environ-
       mental proceeding not conducted according to law.
b) The threat of having to pay costs when a person is suing
   for public nuisance or law enforcement would be removed, except where the suit is completely frivolous.
c) The requirement that the plaintiff give an undertaking to
   pay damages to obtain a temporary injunction would be
   eliminated, or the amount limited to a sum which the
   ordinary citizen can afford, such as $500.
d) If a plaintiff or prosecutor shows, in a suit or private
   prosecution, that there are probable grounds to support
   his case, the burden of proof would shift to the defendant
   or accused. That is, it would be up to the defendant to
   show that the contaminant or other harmful activity was
   not the result of his actions.

                          . . .

e) All environmental laws would be amended so that once
   the plaintiff or prosecutor has demonstrated that environmental harm has occurred or is likely to occur, the
   defendant or accused should prevail only if he proves that
   there is "no feasible alternative to [his] conduct and that
   such conduct is consistent with the promotion of the
   public health, safety, and welfare . . ."[24]

Others have compiled roughly similar lists.[25] It should be
obvious that although these items may all be appropriate for
inclusion in the environmental protection legislation enacted by
particular jurisdictions, most of them would not be suitable for
constitutional entrenchment. At this level of administrative
detail, the legislators should be free to experiment with various
techniques. Some of the items would lend themselves to
constitutional guarantee, however. Access to public information
and standing to challenge unconstitutional, or otherwise illegal,
public actions in the courts are, for example, rights that many
believe should be guaranteed to every citizen. Of course the
importance of such rights is not restricted to the field of
environmental protection; if included in a future constitution,
they would merit general applicability. The most specific form
of entrenchment relating to the environment that might realistically be expected in a new constitution would be a vague and
sweeping statement akin to constitutional declarations of freedom of speech or rights of privacy: that every citizen has the

right to enjoy a reasonable standard of purity in the natural environment. The drafting of such a guarantee would be a difficult task, and its judicial interpretation would be even more challenging. Nevertheless, in view of the fact that American courts have relatively successfully translated highly generalized constitutional guarantees of civil liberties into precise judicial remedies, and that the Canadian Constitution now contains a wide range of entrenched rights and freedoms, neither task would appear to be beyond the capacities of Canadian lawyers and judges.

The probability that environmental rights would be entrenched in a new Canadian constitution is not very high, however. The proposal for an "Environmental Bill of Rights" and other suggestions for the guarantee of citizens' rights mentioned above were all advanced as models for ordinary legislation, not as constitutional imperatives binding on the Legislatures themselves. The writer favours the entrenchment approach, and it can be expected to appeal to other idealists and environmental enthusiasts, but it would be surprising if so novel a notion were to command majority support. Entrenchment of more general procedural rights, such as freedom of public information and standing to sue for unconstitutional conduct, would be a realistic expectation, however. The essential point to appreciate is that the fewer environmental guarantees, specific or general, substantive or procedural, that the constitution contains, the more important it will be to avoid unilateral governmental powers and to counterbalance the environmental responsibilities of the two orders of government. Some implications of such counterbalancing will be considered next.

Jurisdiction Overlap

A new constitution's tolerance for overlap between the two orders of government is an important component in the task of allocating environmental responsibility between them. Reference has already been made to its effect on the protection of rights. Another important implication is that if federal and provincial powers can be exercised concurrently, there is less need to be concerned about their precise definition than there would be if they involved exclusive jurisdiction.

The present Constitution permits a high degree of overlap, both generally and with respect to environmental matters. This concurrency takes two different forms, but it is submitted that for practical purposes they amount to the same thing. The only concurrency formally recognized by the BNA Act relates to immigration and agriculture[26] and to old age pensions.[27] However, many other fields of constitutional jurisdiction also involve considerable overlap of a type often referred to as 'functional concurrency'. Functional concurrency flows from a judicial recognition that a single subject matter of legislation can have both federal and provincial aspects. A law prohibiting the pollution of lakes and streams could be passed by a provincial Legislature on the basis of provincial responsibility for "the management . . . of public lands,"[28] while an identical law could be enacted by the Parliament of Canada pursuant to its jurisdiction over "fisheries"[29] or "criminal law."[30] With one exception,[31] any conflicts between the provisions of federal and provincial legislation in situations of either formal or functional concurrency are presently resolved by according paramountcy to the federal provision.

Concurrency is not complete, of course. Despite the extensive overlap between federal and provincial powers in the environmental area, some gaps exist. The decision of the Supreme Court of Canada in the *Interprovincial Cooperatives* case[32] is illustrative. That case concerned the power of the Manitoba Legislature to enact laws with respect to pollution of Manitoba waters by extraprovincial sources. A majority of the Court held that the enactment was invalid, despite the absence of contradictory federal legislation. The reasons were divided. Three of the majority judges held that legislation seeking to deal with interprovincial pollution could only be enacted by the Parliament of Canada.[33] The other majority judge and the three dissenters were of the view that such legislation could be passed provincially, but they differed on whether the transmitting or receiving province could do so.[34] All the judges ignored or rejected the solution that functional concurrency seemed to dictate: that although the federal Parliament might have pre-emptive jurisdiction, in the absence of contradictory federal legislation both provinces had the power to make laws effective within their own territories concerning aspects of the problem occurring within them. The failure of the Court to endorse functional concurrency in this instance left an unfortunate lacuna in Canada's environmental protection armour.

It was, apparently, to seal such gaps that the Joint Parliamentary Committee on the Constitution of Canada recommended in its 1972 *Report* that a new constitution acknowledge formal concurrency with respect to air and water pollution:

100. Control over the pollution of air and water should be a matter of concurrent jurisdiction between the Provincial Legislatures and the Federal Parliament, and, as in section 95 of the British North America Act, the powers of the Federal Parliament should be paramount.
101. The concurrency of jurisdiction over air and water pollution would necessitate both Federal-Provincial and Province-to-Province planning and coordination of programs.[35]

This suggestion has been opposed on the ground that the existing distribution of powers in the environmental field is satisfactory, and the introduction of formal concurrency would be undesirable: "Ce rapport sérieux et intéressant contient plusieurs recommandations qui emportent notre adhésion. Cependant au chapitre de la pollution nous écartons l'idée d'une compétence commune. Car il faudrait alors stipuler une prépondérance en cas de conflit; et, cette prépondérance dans une matière aussi diffuse et tentaculaire risque de détruire le jeu normal des articles 91 et 92 et de porter une atteinte très sérieuse à la dimension fédérale de la Constitution. Il vaut beaucoup mieux que les deux ordres de pouvoirs publics légifèrent en la matière en se repliant sur les compétences que la Constitution leur a reconnues."[36] The fear that the proposal would result in some aggrandizement of federal powers is well founded. Formal concurrency with respect to 'pollution' would permit federal authorities to move into some areas, such as purely local waste disposal, for which there is no existing excuse for federal involvement, and federal paramountcy would allow provincial and municipal legislation on the subject to be pushed aside. Two qualifying observations should be made, however. First, even in the absence of formal concurrency, there is, and will inevitably continue to be, a vast area of functional overlap. Under any conceivable future constitution, for example, federally owned and regulated operations will always affect provincial environments, and federal operational legislation will continue to cover common ground with provincial environmental protection legislation. Secondly the danger in the proposal of the Joint Parliamentary Committee lies not so much in the concept of concurrency as in the provision for total federal paramountcy. A constitution that sought to avoid jurisdictional gaps by a formal recognition of concurrency, but acknowledged provincial paramountcy on matters where local and provincial concerns should be predominant, would not unduly jeopardize provincial autonomy. The next section will deal with various methods of allocating paramountcy and otherwise dealing with jurisdictional conflicts.

Paramountcy and Conflict Resolution

The inevitability of jurisdictional conflicts over environmental issues has already been touched on. There will always be situations in which enterprises under federal control make an impact on the environment of the provinces in which they operate and activities carried on within one province affect the environment of another province or another country.

To assist in the discussion of the various ways in which these conflicts might be resolved, let us assume two hypothetical situations:

A. The provinces are given jurisdiction over air pollution within provincial boundaries, and the federal Parliament retains responsibility for extraprovincial trucking and rail operations. A province passes legislation requiring all internal combustion engines employed in the province to have certain pollution-control devices that unfortunately reduce the efficiency of the engines by five per cent. Parliament, concerned about energy shortages and the effect of increased fuel consumption on transportation costs, enacts a statute prohibiting the use of such devices on trucks and locomotives engaged in interprovincial traffic.

B. The provinces have jurisdiction over intraprovincial water quality, and Parliament has the power to make laws with respect to interprovincial pollution. A Quebec regulatory body, acting in accordance with provincial legislation, permits a factory to discharge a certain effluent into the headwaters of the St. John River. Considerable environmental damage results downstream in New Brunswick, and there is also a possibility of such damage in the State of Maine, although no complaint has yet been made by American authorities.

We shall return to these illustrations as different methods of dealing with jurisdictional conflicts are discussed.

Before proceeding to that discussion, however, it would be well to deal with a technique by which unnecessary conflicts would be avoided. Reference was made earlier to the problem of interjurisdictional immunity: the fact that certain enterprises operated or regulated by one order of government (usually federal) are sometimes held to be exempt from certain laws of the other order (usually provincial).[37] These situations often arise in the absence of any indication by Parliament that such immunity would be desirable. Such unnecessary immunity could be eliminated by a constitutional stipulation that all enterprises owned, operated, or regulated by one government in Canada, whether federal or provincial, are subject to the laws of every other jurisdiction within whose territory they operate unless and to the extent that the legislation regulating a particular enterprise expressly or by necessary implication provides to the contrary. In that way there would be no 'accidental' exercises of paramountcy. Where immunity was claimed, its validity would then be determined by the applicable paramountcy provisions, to which we now turn.

Federal paramountcy

The present Constitution handles conflicts between federal and provincial statutes by giving a power of pre-emption to the federal order of government in almost every situation. With the exception of old age-pension legislation under section 94A, the Parliament of Canada now has paramountcy whenever a federal law clashes with a provincial law in an area of formal or functional concurrency.[38] This means that in example A hypothesized above, the federal statute would override the provincial anti-pollution legislation, and that in example B, Parliament would have the authority to pass laws for the regulation of any aspect of the factory's operation whose regulation would be necessarily incidental to the control of interprovincial or international pollution.

The Joint Parliamentary Committee on the Constitution of Canada that called for concurrent federal and provincial powers with respect to air and water pollution, recommended what would, in effect, be an entrenchment of the *status quo* as far as paramountcy is concerned in those areas: an express stipulation that federal air- and water-quality legislation be paramount in the case of conflict. Although the Committee stressed the desirability of federal-provincial co-operation, their proposal would, in the final analysis, give Parliament even broader powers than it now has. Their reasons were as follows:

> Apart from the purely legal considerations which call for a paramount Federal power in the area of air and water pollution, there are compelling economic arguments. Because of the disparities in economic terms which exist between the Provinces in

Canada, to fail to have a paramount Federal power would be to invite Provinces to compete for industrial development on the basis of more relaxed pollution laws. It is only recognizing the obvious to suggest that some economically weaker Provinces would be unable to resist the temptation.

. . .

Although we have provided for Federal paramountcy, this does not mean that we contemplate a total and complete Federal occupation of the field of air and water pollution. Indeed we expect legislative coordination between the two levels. We support Federal paramountcy to ensure, however, that should the national interest require it, the Parliament of Canada can ensure that no Province could become a pollution haven. Of course, it would also ensure that pollution of the air and water of one Province by another, and pollution with international effects, could be governed by Federal legislation if deadlock arose or if there was irreconcilable legislation. [39]

While such an arrangement has the undeniable advantages of simplicity and certainty, it could produce regrettable results in some circumstances.

In type-A situations, the major fault of the *status quo* is that it accords automatic priority to Parliament without regard to functional considerations. It may be that energy conservation and transportation economics should take priority over environmental quality in some instances, but that surely depends on the particular circumstances, which vary from one occasion to another: What is the present condition of the environment in the territory affected? To what extent would exemption of federal transportation enterprises worsen the situation? How seriously would the Canadian economy be injured if those enterprises were forced to comply with the provincial law? To allocate legislative paramountcy without regard to such variables would result in the establishment of regulatory schemes that are out of touch with reality. While it may be contended that Parliament can be counted on to weigh all relevant factors when deciding whether or not to exercise its paramountcy, it is not likely to perform that task with impartiality. Because the basis of federal jurisdiction is usually entrepreneurial (interprovincial transportation, defence, atomic energy, and so on), Parliament can normally be expected, when conflicts arise, to display a bias in favour of entrepreneurial considerations over environmental ones. Even when the basis of federal jurisdiction is primarily environmental — as in the case of the present fisheries power — Parliament is unlikely to weigh the competing interests impartially; one bias merely replaces another.

In situations like example B, where the federal government has no direct interest in the matter, it may be slightly more plausible to regard Parliament as a neutral arbiter of interprovincial disputes. Even in those circumstances, however, absolute objectivity is illusory; such *sub rosa* factors as the relative numbers of Quebec and New Brunswick voters at the next federal election who are likely to be pleased or offended by the decision will seldom be ignored in any politically based technique of conflict resolution. Where there is an international component to the problem, the case for automatic federal paramountcy is strong, provided that the foreign connection is both genuine and significant; a merely formal international element should not be allowed to characterize matters that are substantially intranational in nature.

Provincial paramountcy
Priority could be given to provincial legislation. This is now the case with old age pensions,[40] and both the Joint Parliamentary Committee on the Constitution of Canada[41] and the Task Force on Canadian Unity[42] seem to have approved an expansion of provincial primacy beyond the *status quo*. Although no one ever seems to have proposed it seriously, it would be at least theoretically possible to give the provinces total paramountcy.

Automatic provincial paramountcy in environmental matters would, however, be subject to all the shortcomings of automatic federal paramountcy, with the exception that the bias would more frequently favour environmental protection than entrepreneurial advancement, where the threat to the environment came from enterprises under federal control. And there would be the added problem in interprovincial situations of selecting *which* province should be given priority.[43]

Entrepreneurial paramountcy
It would promote efficiency in resource exploitation and technological development to provide that legislative conflicts be resolved in favour of the jurisdiction having principal responsibility for the operational aspects of the activity involved. This would mean, for example, that in hypothesis A (above) the federal legislation would prevail, and that in hypothesis B, Quebec would have the final word. The economic advantages would be obvious: the easy avoidance of interjurisdictional conflicts would eliminate delays and facilitate long-range planning. It would probably also lead to more sophisticated, better

rounded, government regulation of the enterprises involved if one authority were ultimately responsible for all aspects of the operations, including their environmental impact. Greater regard for environmental factors by those in charge of operations would encourage the design of less destructive operating techniques, and greater awareness of operational needs by those responsible for the environment would discourage unrealistic restrictions.

The problem with entrepreneurial paramountcy, of course, is that even more than federal paramountcy (which, for practical purposes, it would closely resemble), it would seriously jeopardize environmental considerations by entrusting them to the care of authorities with a primarily operational orientation. Even the most enlightened hydro-electric engineer or designer of oil pipelines is likely to place a higher value on 'his' or 'her' project than on the surrounding wilderness.

Environmental paramountcy
The last word could be given to the environment by stipulating that, in the event of contradictory legislation, the laws of the jurisdiction whose environment was affected would prevail. If entrepreneurial paramountcy could be described as the 'co-ordination' model, in which ultimate responsibility for both operations and their environmental impact would be under integrated control, this could be called the 'competitive' model: operational and environmental aspects would be in competition whenever multiple jurisdictions were involved, with the former being subjugated to the latter in the event of irreconcilable conflicts.

This arrangement would clearly promote environmental protection, but probably to an unjustifiable extent. There are circumstances in which environmental considerations should properly yield to other, more pressing, needs. In hypothesis A, for example, the damage caused to the environment by exempting federal transportation enterprises from provincial vehicle-pollution laws might be insignificant compared to the resulting benefits to the national economy. Why, in that event, should an important national objective be frustrated by a relatively minor provincial environmental concern? By having to deal with environmental impact in isolation from entrepreneurial benefits, authorities might place a disproportionate emphasis on the former. Moreover the time and expense involved in having to satisfy two competing orders of government could be unduly wasteful for the enterprise concerned. Another problem would be the difficulty of selecting, in multiterritorial situations like hypothesis B, the *particular* affected jurisdiction that would exercise control, and of deciding the extent to which those controls should apply beyond that jurisdiction. Moreover, in international settings, it might involve the surrender of some degree of sovereignty to a foreign Legislature.

Paramountcy divided by subject

As mentioned previously, both the Joint Parliamentary Committee and the Task Force on Canadian Unity appear to have approved a division of paramountcy between the federal and provincial orders of government, presumably on the basis of subject matter. It is difficult, however, to visualize the application of such a provision in many circumstances.

Suppose that the Constitution provided, as the Joint Committee has recommended, that the power to make laws about "air and water pollution" should be concurrent, with federal paramountcy, and that it bestowed provincial paramountcy with respect to "the law of torts and delicts." If Parliament then passed a law permitting private citizens to sue by class action with respect to public nuisance caused by pollution of air or water, would that enactment take precedence over the present Manitoba statute that states that a nuisance action may not be brought with respect to most industrial odours?[44] On the one hand, the federal law should be paramount as 'pollution' legislation; on the other, the provincial law should be paramount as 'tort' legislation. Or suppose that the Constitution gave the provinces paramountcy with respect to "pollution in the province" and gave Parliament paramountcy concerning "interprovincial transportation." Which of the statutes described in hypothesis A would be given priority?

No doubt the courts would be able to decide in many situations that the subject matter of the conflicting legislation related predominantly, in "pith and substance," more to one jurisdiction than to the other; but there would be many instances in which it would be impossible to avoid the conclusion that the subject was as closely related to one field as to another. To deal with such situations of competing paramountcies, it would be necessary to allocate a last-resort 'superparamountcy' to one or other order of government, and all the problems associated with automatic paramountcy devices would resurface.

Paramountcy divided functionally by adjudication

It was suggested earlier that it is impossible to decide in the abstract whether federal or provincial paramountcy would be more satisfactory in situations like hypothesis A; it would depend on the circumstances prevailing at the time. To take another example, in time of war federal 'defence' legislation authorizing the military to devastate a provincial wilderness area for the purpose of tank training or gunnery exercises should have priority, in the writer's view; but this should not be so in peace time, when there is less urgency, and time can be taken to find less destructive training sites and techniques.

The only satisfactory way to distribute paramountcy in order to take account of such variables would be to entrust the task on a discretionary basis to some case-by-case adjudicator. A court or tribunal could be empowered to determine, in situations like examples A and B or the one just mentioned, whether federal or provincial priority would be more suitable, having regard to all relevant circumstances. It would also be able to decide which of competing provincial statutes should prevail in the case of interprovincial conflicts.

It does not require much prescience to foresee objections that would be raised to so radical a proposal. Some would object that it would introduce an intolerable degree of uncertainty into the Constitution. Flexibility unquestionably involves uncertainty. But uncertainty is endemic to constitutions. Certainty is often sacrificed to achieve a variety of other goals, not the least of which is the ability to continue providing good government in a wide variety of unforeseeable future circumstances. If a more flexible paramountcy principle would result in a more effective allocation of constitutional responsibilities than the present automatic rule, it may be worth the cost in added uncertainty.

Many can be expected to protest, as well, that this proposal would thrust on the courts an essentially legislative task for which they are ill suited. Little purpose would be served by rehearsing at length the hoary debate about whether courts can, should, or do legislate generally. In the present context the question is considerably narrower: Are adjudicative bodies well suited to determine which of two contradictory statutes applicable to a particular activity should be permitted to prevail?

It is submitted that the answer to this question is 'Yes'. Indeed a strong case can be made to the effect that courts are *better* suited to perform the task than are legislatures. Courts are sure to be provided by the competing interests with expert evidence on all aspects of the question — social, economic, and so on — thought by any interested party to be relevant. Their facilities for receiving such information are generally superior to those of legislatures. Moreover they are unencumbered by the considerations of politics and patronage that sometimes interfere with impartiality in the legislative arena. Administrative tribunals are often called upon to make similar policy-based decisions, and they generally carry out the function effectively and fairly.

Since a fairly high level of consistency would be required in these decisions, it might not be wise, however, to leave the task to low-level courts. Perhaps conflicts between competent federal and provincial statutes would be best handled by a special constitutional disputes tribunal, with appeal lying to the Supreme Court of Canada.

Delegation

Two factors will dictate a continuing need for large-scale federal-provincial co-operation under any new constitution: the fantastic complexity of many environmental problems, and the fact that any realistic scheme for allocating environmental responsibilities must entrust both orders of government with substantial powers. Careful co-ordination of all governmental control programs will be required. Moreover it will sometimes be convenient for certain functions normally within the ambit of one government to be exercised temporarily or permanently within a particular region by another government or by some intergovernmental body. The *Report* of the Joint Parliamentary Committee on the Constitution of Canada recognized this need, and called for both federal-provincial and interprovincial consultation and co-ordination.[45]

An important technique for achieving intergovernmental co-operation is delegation of legislative and administrative powers. While the existing Constitution permits satisfactory delegation of administrative functions, direct delegation of law-making powers is not possible.[46] This is a shortcoming that should be remedied in any new constitution. Although the Joint Parliamentary Committee did not approve of legislative delegation,[47] and proposed that environmental co-operation be accomplished by other means,[48] there seems to be wide support for the idea.[49] It will be assumed for the purpose of this essay that both administrative and legislative delegation would be possible under a new constitution.

Spending Power

In the past the wealth of the Government of Canada has enabled
it to enter fields of provincial responsibility, including some
local aspects of environmental management, by means of
financial grants or loans conditional on compliance with federal
regulations. The Joint Parliamentary Committee on the Constitution of Canada saw a continuation of this federal spending
power as a means of achieving federal-provincial co-operation in
environmental matters.[50]

   This would be a mistake. Any new constitution should attempt
to match the governmental responsibilities of each government
with adequate financial powers to carry out those responsibilities
independently and well. Economic imbalances between the
provinces should be rectified by satisfactory fiscal equalization
procedures rather than by federal handouts. This is, no doubt, a
counsel of perfection; money is never likely to lose its voice
altogether. Nevertheless, when Canadians are attempting to
design a constitutional instrument for the future, every effort
should be made to assign powers on a functionally efficient
basis, with equivalent assured financial resources. Although this
goal is never likely to be fully achieved, the end product is likely
to be considerably closer to perfection than the approach
proposed by the Joint Parliamentary Committee. To acknowledge in advance that the constitutional distribution of powers
may be frustrated whenever the federal government is willing to
pay a suitable price would be a counsel of defeat for those who
see value in federalism. It will be assumed for the purposes of
this paper that a new constitution would assure all governments
the financial resources necessary to carry out their responsibilities and would restrict the federal spending power to uses
within federal legislative competence, including, of course, any
powers it may receive by delegation.

Four Futures

An attempt will now be made to apply the foregoing thoughts in
the context of the four different constitutional options for the
future that were postulated at the outset.

Federalism

The most satisfactory allocation of responsibilities for environmental quality in a federal system of a type roughly similar to that which now prevails in Canada seems to be one based fundamentally on the territory affected, but with certain non-territorial features.

The provinces should have primary jurisdiction with respect to the protection of their own internal environments, and the federal Parliament should be responsible for extraprovincial aspects of environmental protection. By 'extraprovincial' is meant those aspects of interprovincial and international pollution that the provinces are incapable of dealing with unilaterally or co-operatively, or that they have not so dealt with, as well, of course, as conditions in the northern Territories. Provincial jurisdiction should extend to the intraprovincial aspects of situations with extraprovincial components so that in circumstances such as those that arose in the *Interprovincial Cooperatives* case,[51] provincial legislation would operate within the province, subject to being pre-empted by contradictory federal legislation aimed at the interprovincial aspects of the problem.

In addition to its responsibility for extraprovincial aspects of environmental protection, the Parliament of Canada would retain operational jurisdiction over various enterprises of national significance located within the provinces; some of these (such as interprovincial railways and pipelines) would endanger the environment, and others (such as national parks and wilderness preserves) would enhance it.

Formal concurrency of federal and provincial powers concerning the environment should be avoided for reasons already stated.[52] However, functional concurrency is unavoidable between provincial environmental powers and federal jurisdiction over both extraprovincial aspects of environmental control and the many federally regulated activities that affect environmental quality within the provinces. To reduce unnecessary conflicts between federal and provincial legislation, the Constitution should declare that all enterprises owned, operated, or regulated by one government in Canada, whether federal or provincial, are subject to all laws of every other Canadian jurisdiction within whose territory they operate, except to the extent that the legislation regulating a particular enterprise provides to the contrary, either expressly or by necessary implication.

Where federal and provincial statutes are incompatible with respect to a given situation or operation, the automatic federal paramountcy that presently applies should be replaced by a discretionary judicial determination stipulating which law should prevail in the circumstances. While many different procedures for making such a determination are conceivable, the task could probably be best performed by a special constitutional conflicts tribunal functioning one level below the Supreme Court of Canada. This tribunal would deal with disputes between provinces, as well as with those between the federal and provincial orders, and it would base its decisions on functional considerations relevant to the particular situation rather than on formal pre-ordained criteria.

Federal-provincial and interprovincial co-operation should be facilitated by making possible intergovernmental delegation of both administrative and legislative powers. The decision to delegate should not be influenced by financial considerations, however; fiscal resources should be adequate to fund any governmental responsibility found to be functionally justified.

To some extent the phenomenon of functional concurrency would operate as a safeguard against the risk that a government with primary environmental jurisdiction might sacrifice environmental quality for some more tempting, but less worthy, short-term benefit. If another government had authority to enact competing legislation that could be accorded paramountcy, the danger that environmental considerations might be abandoned would be somewhat reduced. The involvement of another government is no guarantee of purity, however; both governments may be equally unconcerned about environmental quality. Moreover functional overlap would never be complete; there would remain many areas in which one government had exclusive control. This would be especially true in the northern Territories, where federal authority would extend even to the matters normally within provincial jurisdiction, and where there would therefore be no significant provincial counterpoise to federal powers. To provide some protection against governmental shortsightedness in such one-sided situations, some constitutionally entrenched guarantees would be beneficial.

Three different constitutional safeguards were discussed earlier: liberal access to public information, standing to challenge unconstitutional laws, and a general guarantee of the right to a pure environment. The first two are not peculiar to environmental questions, and it is to be hoped that they would

be written into a new constitution in any event. The third, an
entrenched right to environmental purity, which would stand
beside such rights as freedom of speech, would be both more
specific and more radical. It is submitted (though not very
optimistically) that it should be no less acceptable on either
account. Without it the other two guarantees would not in
themselves constitute adequate environmental protection.
Another way to achieve such protection would, of course, be to
empower the Parliament of Canada to establish minimum
standards of environmental quality for the entire country, but
such paternalism would be alien to the principles of federalism.
If both paternalism and substantial risk to the environment are
to be avoided, I see no plausible alternative to a judicially
enforceable, general, constitutional guarantee of environmental
purity.

Special Status

It is difficult to imagine that a province with the right to special
constitutional status in certain respects would choose to alter the
basic pattern of jurisdictional allocation outlined above. Of
course, if the basic scheme adopted involved more extensive
federal powers than has been suggested (say, federal responsibility for air pollution or for the quality of major lakes and
streams), a desire on the part of some provinces for greater
environmental autonomy might lead to claims of special status.
It seems both unlikely and undesirable, however, that the
fundamental division of powers relating to the environment
would be significantly different from what has been indicated.

A province might be more likely to opt for special status with
respect to paramountcy provisions or constitutional guarantees.
If the constitution adopted the adjudicative paramountcy provision suggested, or one that would give automatic primacy to
federal legislation, it would not be surprising to find one or
more provinces seeking a special status whereby provincial
paramountcy would be substituted. Similarly some provinces
might not wish to go along with any entrenched rights respecting the environment that might be guaranteed to citizens by the
national constitution.

The wisdom of special status in general is beyond the scope of
this essay. As far as the limited forms of special status discussed
herein are concerned, they could probably be tolerated without
extreme detriment. A constitution that featured entrenched

environmental rights in some provinces, but not in others, and one kind of paramountcy provision for some provinces and another for others, could function reasonably satisfactorily, though the complexity would produce inevitable confusion. However, if the provisions out of which some provinces opted were significant environmental protections, as they would likely be, the cost of special status would include, in addition to the inevitable confusion, a regrettable risk of deterioration in environmental quality.

Separation of Quebec

If Quebec became a completely independent state, the appropriateness of the above remarks to the rest of Canada, assuming that it remained federally united, would not be greatly affected. Their applicability to Quebec would be radically altered, of course.

As far as purely intraterritorial situations were concerned, Quebec would be in an even more powerful position than the provinces of Canada, because her control over the environment would not be counterbalanced by functional concurrency with any federal responsibilities. The case for the entrenchment of environmental rights in the constitution would accordingly be even stronger in relation to Quebec than it would be in relation to Canada.

As far as extraterritorial situations are concerned, international law would replace constitutional law. Questions of interjurisdictional immunity would be replaced by those of sovereign immunity. The Government of Canada, instead of acting as legislator and adjudicator, would become adversary and negotiator on behalf of itself and the provinces bordering Quebec. In view of Quebec's geographic position — virtually surrounded by Canadian territory, its boundaries defined to a significant degree by waters shared with Canada, central Canada's chief route to the Atlantic flowing through its territory, its major air currents and weather systems shared with Canadian provinces and American states — the frequency of international environmental disputes would increase dramatically. Quebec's involvement with Canada and the United States in the International Joint Commission (IJC) or some similar body would be essential. (Conceivably, by the way, the addition of a third party to the IJC might strengthen that organization and make it easier to carry out impartial adjudication, at least in bilateral disputes.) The IJC has had considerable experience — and some success — in dealing with problems of trans-boundary pollution.[53] It suffers, however, from the major weakness of all voluntary international organizations: that on most matters its rulings are advisory only and are not binding on the parent governments. Unless the powers of the IJC were increased, the legal protections available against environmental hazards crossing Quebec's borders in either direction would accordingly be reduced by independence. Those for whom environmental quality is important would therefore have reason to be concerned, at least on that account, by the complete separation of Quebec.

Sovereignty-Association

Inasmuch as sovereignty-association would involve such sharing of powers as two sovereign nations might freely negotiate, it is impossible to say much that would be helpful at this stage about a suitable arrangement of environmental jurisdictions. The white paper issued by the Parti québécois Government of Quebec in 1979 to explain the implications of sovereignty-association dealt only with the economic aspects of environmental matters. The only clues that can be gleaned from the paper concerning its authors' approach to appropriate inter-governmental arrangements for the protection of environmental quality are the facts that:

- The paper places great emphasis on the importance of Quebec's exploiting its own resources independently.[54]
- It is stated that Quebec would "become a full partner in the International Joint Commission."[55]
- The European Economic Community (EEC) is frequently referred to as a suitable model for future Canada-Quebec relations.[56]

The reference to the International Joint Commission would indicate no significant difference, as far as protection of environmental quality is concerned, between sovereignty-association and complete separation. The EEC references may, however, hold out hope that a sovereign Quebec would be willing to enter into arrangements in the environmental field that would involve the surrender of some autonomy to common legislative and judicial bodies with powers greater than those of the chiefly voluntary IJC. It would be a mistake to be overly sanguine on this score; even if Canada and Quebec agreed to emulate the EEC, that organization's environmental protection activities have been relatively recent and, so far, rather limited.[57] Nevertheless, the EEC paradigm would offer two important improvements over the IJC model: its edicts would be binding, and they could embrace intraterritorial, as well as trans-boundary, environmental problems.

Should Environmental Jurisdiction Be Treated Separately?

We are now in a position to reconsider the question that was deferred at the beginning of this essay: Is it necessary or desirable to deal with environmental protection and enhancement as a discrete item in a new constitution?

The answer seems to be that although discrete treatment cannot hurt and might even be beneficial in avoiding confusion, it is necessary only to the extent that it is desirable to entrench a constitutional right to environmental purity. Any federal constitution is likely to distribute legislative responsibilities on a roughly territorial basis, and all the other provisions suggested above — that is, elimination of unnecessary interjurisdictional immunity, a new paramountcy provision, guaranteed freedom of public information, and standing to litigate public wrongs — would be general stipulations not limited in their scope to environmental matters.

Nevertheless, since I have advocated the creation of a constitutional guarantee of environmental quality, and since it would be beneficial, in any event, to clarify environmental responsibilities in the new constitution, it is submitted that separate treatment should be accorded to environmental matters.

Appendix

Selected Proposals Concerning the Future Constitutional Position of Environmental Management

1. *Quebec's Traditional Stands on the Division of Powers (1900–1976)*, Province of Quebec, 1976:

   > *Environment*
   > 1970 — Mr. Bertrand states that Quebec cannot allow the federal government to act unilaterally to settle the watercourses question. (Federal-Provincial Conference)
   >
   > 1971 — Quebec calls for a constitutional provision granting the provinces jurisdiction over environmental protection policies. (Constitutional Conference)

2. *Environmental Management — A Constitutional Study Prepared for the Government of Canada*, J.W. MacNeill, 1971:

   [This lengthy study, the most thorough yet prepared on the subject, does not make specific proposals for constitutional reform, and therefore does not lend itself to extraction and quotation. It must not be overlooked, however. It tends to support a much wider federal role than has been proposed in this paper.]

3. *Final Report of Special Joint Committee of the Senate and the House of Commons on the Constitution of Canada*, 1972:

Chapter 36 — Air and Water Pollution
Recommendations

100. Control over the pollution of air and water should be a matter of concurrent jurisdiction between the Provincial Legislatures and the Federal Parliament, and, as in section 95 of the British North America Act, the powers of the Federal Parliament should be paramount.
101. The concurrency of jurisdiction over air and water pollution would necessitate both Federal-Provincial and Province-to-Province planning and coordination of programs.
102. We endorse the work of the Resources Ministers Council as a means of continuing consultation on matters of renewable resources.

In recent years a totally new challenge has developed from the growing global crisis of the environment. Not only is man learning that the world's resources are finite, but also that their ever increasing consumption, particularly by the economically-developed nations, may even threaten our long-run physical and psychological survival. The dimensions of our ecological crisis are both potentially awesome and immediately urgent.

The rapid growth of population, the immense expansion of industry, and the urbanization of life have been intensified by an exploding and seemingly ungovernable technology. It is not surprising, therefore, that this subject matter, unknown and unthought of in 1867, has emerged in the current review of the Constitution.

In the evidence we heard, several themes dominated: first of all, there was a sense of urgency; also, there was a growing, militant and popularly based anti-pollution movement. The overriding feeling was that positive and extensive governmental action is needed.

Because pollution control is so urgently needed, we feel that any confusion which exists in constitutional powers should be ended as quickly as possible.

Canada is seriously affected, although there is clearly a global scope to the phenomenon of environmental pollution. Lake Erie, we are told, is in danger of dying and her sister lakes may gradually succumb. Wildlife is being poisoned by pesticides. Cities are enveloped in smog affecting health. Rising crescendos of noise threaten tranquillity everywhere. Clean air, clear water and the purity of our soil and our sea products can no longer be assumed in Canada.

Our evidence revealed a deep concern to protect that peace and beauty essential to sustain the human spirit. Our witnesses also recognized that, increasingly, havens of peace and beauty are being surrounded and eliminated by air and water pollution.

It was conceded by virtually all witnesses that concerted action on the international, national, provincial and urban levels of government will be required. Any constitutional approach must, therefore, be flexible.

There seems to be widespread agreement that jurisdiction over pollution is at present complicated at best and confusing at worst. Federal and Provincial sources in the B.N.A. Act for pollution control are many. For example, Provincial jurisdiction may stem from "Property and Civil Rights in the Province", "Municipal Institutions in the Province", "Local Works and Undertakings", "Generally all Matters of a merely local or private Nature in the Province". Federal jurisdiction, on the other hand, depending on the class of subject dealt with in the legislation, might arise from "The Criminal Law", "Navigation and Shipping", "Sea Coast and Inland Fisheries", and "The Regulation of Trade and Commerce".

The possibilities for jurisdictional overlapping here revealed show the difficulties of determining constitutional and political accountability. Although the respective powers are legally and narrowly "exclusive" in the strict sense, pollution problems do not always fit into such neat, compartmental packages. Consequently, the lines of political accountability are not clear. The voter is left with his annoyance; the politician with his constitutional enigmas. What is clear is that the witnesses who appeared before us recognized that pollution has local, provincial, national and international aspects. Rather than getting bogged down as to whether the pollution to be cured was a "Fisheries" or a "Navigation" or a "Management of Public Lands" or a "Local Works and Undertaking" problem, they felt that pollution itself should be the subject matter of concern to Parliament and the Legislatures. They felt that pollution of air and water, because of their many facets, should be a concurrent power shared by both Parliament and the Legislatures.

The object in making air and water pollution a specific head of power is to avoid, as completely as possible, jurisdictional conflicts based on existing powers: for example, whether the legislation is, in pith and substance, in relation to "Public Lands" (Provincial) or "Inland Fisheries" (Federal). The same reasoning compels us to acknowledge that, in the event of conflict between the new concurrent Federal and Provincial powers in the area of air and water pollution, Federal legislation should be paramount. Consequently, we recommend a similar concurrent formulation for jurisdiction over pollution of air and water as already exists in section 95 of the British North America Act, with respect to Immigration and Agriculture. A similar power in this area might read this way:

> In each Province the Legislature may make Laws in
> relation to the control of air and water pollution in the
> Province, and it is hereby declared that the Parliament of
> Canada may, from Time to Time, make Laws in relation to
> the control of air and water pollution among the Provinces;
> and any Law of the Legislature of a Province relative to the
> control of air and water pollution shall have effect in and
> for the Province as long and as far only as it is not re-
> pugnant to any Act of the Parliament of Canada.

Apart from the purely legal considerations which call for a
paramount Federal power in the area of air and water pollution,
there are compelling economic arguments. Because of the
disparities in economic terms which exist between the Provinces
in Canada, to fail to have a paramount Federal power would be
to invite Provinces to compete for industrial development on
the basis of more relaxed pollution laws. It is only recognizing
the obvious to suggest that some economically weaker Provinces
would be unable to resist the temptation.

We would envisage, because the new pollution power would
be concurrent, that necessarily greater Federal-Provincial and
Province-to-Province planning and coordination would result.
The superior financial and research capabilities of the Federal
Government, especially in relation to the smaller Provinces, can
be brought into play through the concurrent power itself and
through the Federal spending power, if necessary.

Although we have provided for Federal paramountcy, this
does not mean that we contemplate a total and complete Federal
occupation of the field of air and water pollution. Indeed we
expect legislative coordination between the two levels. We
support Federal paramountcy to ensure, however, that should
the national interest require it, the Parliament of Canada can
ensure that no Province could become a pollution haven. Of
course, it would also ensure that pollution of the air and water
of one Province by another, and pollution with international
effects, could be governed by Federal legislation if deadlock
arose or if there was irreconcilable legislation.

The whole question of environmental management is a very
broad one. It covers not only pollution control but many other
subjects such as land use control, control over mining, lumber,
wildlife and fish, agriculture, land reclamation and abandon-
ment, weather forecasting and weather modification, recreation
and leisure activities, transportation, electric power, multiple-
use water management, housing and urban planning and noise
abatement.

It is not possible, at the moment, to see how far this concept
goes. Consequently, we have rejected the idea of describing the

specific pollution power in the Constitution as a power over "environmental management". That is why we have limited our recommendations to a constitutional formulation to cover jurisdiction over air and water pollution.

4. *Communiqué, Regina Premiers' Conference*, 1978:

. . . the Premiers, in the course of their discussion in Regina, have reached agreement upon a number of additional substantive matters, on which federal views are invited:

- the establishment of an appropriate provincial jurisdiction with respect to fisheries.
- confirmation and strengthening of provincial powers with respect to natural resources . . .

5. *Harmony in Diversity — A New Federalism for Canada*, Province of Alberta, 1978, p. 24:

6. That the existing sections in the British North America Act protecting provincial ownership and control of natural resources be strengthened.

. . .

12. That sea coast and inland fisheries be a concurrent power in the Constitution, with provincial paramountcy.

6. *Towards a New Canada*, Canadian Bar Association, Committee on the Constitution, 1978, Chapter 19, p. 107:

Recommendations

1. The Constitution should expressly provide that the provinces have exclusive legislative power respecting the exploration, exploitation, conservation and management of all natural resources in the province.

2. The natural resources of the public domain in the provinces should continue to belong to the provinces.

3. The federal Parliament should have exclusive legislative power respecting seacoast fisheries; the provinces should have exclusive legislative power respecting inland fisheries in the province.

4. The provinces should have exclusive legislative power respecting water resources in the provinces, subject to the concurrent and paramount power of the federal Parliament to legislate respecting situations having extraprovincial effects.

. . .

7. The federal Parliament and the provincial legislatures should have concurrent legislative power respecting atomic energy, with federal paramountcy.

7. *A Future Together — Observations and Recommendations*, Task Force on Canadian Unity, 1979, pp. 125–26 (emphasis added):

    32. The principal roles and responsibilities of the provincial governments should be:
       i — the social and cultural well-being and development of their communities;
       ii — provincial economic development, including *the exploitation of their natural resources*;
       iii — property and civil rights; and
       iv — *the management of their territory.*

          . . .

    40. In devising a new distribution of powers, the following steps should be taken:
       i — broad areas of governmental activities should first be identified. Such broad areas might include external affairs, defence, economic policy, transportation, communications, natural resources, administration of justice and law enforcement, the status and rights of citizens, culture, health and welfare, *habitat and the environment*.

8. *A New Canadian Federation*, Quebec Liberal Party Constitutional Committee, 1980, pp. 98 and 118:

   Recommendations 21

    1. The constitution should affirm the priority rights of all Canadians to the natural resources of their country.
    2. The constitution should affirm the provinces' right of property over natural resources found on their territories and should maintain their exclusive jurisdiction in the management and regulation of natural resources including, among other things, mining resources, oil, gas, hydro-electric resources, lands and forests, save for the exception stated in the following paragraph.
    3. The constitution should entrust to the provinces the right to manage and regulate nuclear energy, limited by the legislative paramountcy of the central government in those matters pertaining to defence, national security, pollution and international responsibility which are implied in the use of fissionable matter.

          . . .

    7. The constitution should entrust to the provinces the right to manage and regulate the underwater resources situated in territorial waters as well as the right to manage and regulate the underwater resources located on the continental shelf.

8. The constitutional reform process should provide for a mechanism to define borders in order to precisely define the territorial waters of each province as well as the continental shelf areas which fall under their respective jurisdictions.

9. The constitutional [reform process] should allocate to the provinces the right to manage and regulate interior and coastal fisheries provided that the provinces' coastal fisheries be subject to the federal government's jurisdiction over navigation, protection of the species and the environment.

Recommendations 25

. . .

3. The constitution should make the provinces responsible for the protection of the environment, especially for plant and animal life and water, and for the management of these resources, as well as for the regulation of hunting, subject to those restrictions flowing from international treaties.

4. There are four exceptions to the general principle stated in the preceding recommendation and the federal government should have jurisdiction over these matters:

   a) the right to impose penalties on the more serious pollution offences which threaten personal safety and property, by virtue of its power to enact a Criminal Code;

   b) the protection of coastal, interprovincial and international waters;

   c) nuclear pollution; and

   d) the prevention and punishment of pollution offences arising from maritime or aerial navigation.

9. *Québec-Canada: A New Deal*, Gouvernement du Québec, 1979, p. 56:

   . . . Québec will respect the agreement on the St. Lawrence Seaway and will become a full partner in the International Joint Commission.

Notes

1. British North America Act, 1867, 30 and 31 Vict., c. 3, s. 91(12); "sea coast and inland fisheries."

2. *Ibid.*, s. 92(5): "The management and sale of the public lands belonging to the Province and of the timber and wood thereon."

3. *Ibid.*, s. 109: "All lands, mines, minerals, and royalties belonging to the several Provinces . . . at the union . . . shall belong to the several Provinces . . . in which the same are situate or arise . . . "

4. See Dale Gibson, "Constitutional Jurisdiction Over Environmental Management in Canada," *University of Toronto Law Journal* 23 (1973): 54–73.

5. For example, Gibson, "Constitutional Jurisdiction . . .," and Gerald A. Beaudouin, "La protection de l'environnement et ses implications en droit constitutionnel," *McGill Law Journal* 23 (1977): 207–24. Not everyone is satisfied with the present balance, however; see, for example, Paul Emond, "The Case for a Greater Federal Role in the Environmental Protection Field: An Example of the Pollution Problem and the Constitution," *Osgoode Hall Law Journal* 10 (1972): 647–80. See generally J.W. MacNeill, *Environmental Management: A Constitutional Study Prepared for the Government of Canada* (Ottawa: Information Canada, 1971).

6. See, in addition to the works quoted in the Appendix and the articles cited in note 5, Stanley B. Stein, "Environmental Control and Different Levels of Government," *Canadian Public Administration* 14 (1971): 129–44; Henry Landis, "Legal Controls of Pollution in the Great Lakes Basin," *Canadian Bar Review* 48 (1970): 66–157; R.T. Franson and P.T. Burns, "Environmental Rights for the Canadian Citizen: A Prescription for Reform," *Alberta Law Review* 12 (1974): 153–71; Paul Emond, "Participation and the Environment: A Strategy for Democratizing Canada's Environmental Laws," *Osgoode Hall Law Journal* 13 (1975): 783–837; David Trezide, "Alternative Approaches to Legal Control of Environmental Quality in Canada," *McGill Law Journal* 21 (1975): 404–27.

7. Criminal Code, R.S.C. 1970, c. C–34, s. 176.

8. For example, Fisheries Act, R.S.C. 1970, c. F–14. The constitutional limits of this power were examined by the Supreme Court of Canada in two recent decisions: *Northwest Falling Contractors Ltd.* v. *The Queen*, (1981) 113 D.L.R. (3d) 1 (S.C.C.) and *Fowler* v. *The Queen*, (1981) 113 D.L.R. (3d) 513 (S.C.C.)

9. S.C., 1970–71–72, c. 47.

10. R.S.C. 1970 (1st Supp.), c. 5.

11. British North America Act, s. 91(27).

12. *Ibid.*, s. 92(13): "property and civil rights in the Province"; s. 92(16): "generally all matters of a merely local or private nature in the Province."

13. *Ibid.*, s. 92(14): "the imposition of punishment by fine, penalty, or imprisonment for enforcing any law of the Province made in relation to any matter coming within any of the classes of subjects enumerated in this section." See, for example, *Re Nakashima and the Queen*, (1975) 51 D.L.R. (3d) 578 (B.C.S.C.)

14. Direct authority in support of this proposition is surprisingly difficult to find, especially in the environmental field. The power of Parliament to tamper with civil real property rights as a necessary incident of railway legislation was, however, upheld in *Attorney-General of Canada* v. *C.P.R. and C.N.R.*, [1958] S.C.R. 285. That Parliament may legislate respecting civil remedies for interprovincial water pollution seems implied in the reasons for judgment of at least Pigeon, Martland, and Beetz, JJ., in *Interprovincial Cooperatives Ltd.* v. *The Queen*, (1975) D.L.R. (3d) 321 (S.C.C.) Even in *MacDonald* v. *Vapour Canada Ltd.*, (1976) 66 D.L.R. (3d) p. 1 at p. 25 (S.C.C.), where a federal provision resulting in a civil remedy was struck down, and there are dicta (for example, at p. 25) attacking the civil nature of the provision, the *ratio decidendi* was the absence of any basis for federal legislation on the subject, and other civil remedies included in the statute were left intact.

15. The airspace was held not to be within the province by the Manitoba Court of Appeal: *Re The Queen and Air Canada*, (1978) 86 D.L.R. (3d) 631. On appeal the Supreme Court of Canada found it unnecessary to deal with the question: (1980) 111 D.L.R. (3d) p. 513 at p. 521.

16. *Cardinal* v. *Attorney-General of Canada*, (1974) 40 D.L.R. (3d) 553 (S.C.C.)

17. Dale Gibson, "Interjurisdictional Immunity in Canadian Federalism," *Canadian Bar Review* 47 (1969): 40–61.

18.   See text p. 130.

19.   See text pp. 130–31.

20.   See Dale Gibson, "Measuring 'National Dimensions'," *Manitoba Law Journal* 7 (1976): 15–27, where it was argued that such is the test under the present Constitution. Although the reasoning of Pigeon, Martland, and Beetz, JJ., in *Interprovincial Cooperatives Ltd.* v. *The Queen*, (1975) 53 D.L.R. (3d) 321 (S.C.C.) and perhaps also the majority reasons in *Reference Re Anti-Inflation Act*, (1976) 68 D.L.R. (3d) 452 (S.C.C.) seem to refute this view, it is submitted that it is, in any event, a principle that should be embodied in a new constitution.

21.   British North America Act, s. 91 (preamble).

22.   Assuming, of course, that the constitution contained no more specific power relating to international relations.

23.   British North America Act, preamble.

24.   David Estrin and John Swaigen, eds., *Environment on Trial: A Citizen's Guide to Ontario Environmental Law* (Toronto: Canadian Environmental Law Research Foundation, 1974), pp. 311–13.

25.   See, for example, Franson and Burns, "Environmental Rights for the Canadian Citizen."

26.   British North America Act, s. 95.

27.   *Ibid.*, s. 94A.

28.   *Ibid.*, s. 92(5).

29.   *Ibid.*, s. 91(12).

30.   *Ibid.* s. 91(27).

31.   *Ibid.*, s. 94A, old age pensions. In this case provincial legislation has priority.

32.   *Interprovincial Cooperatives Ltd.* v. *The Queen*, (1975) D.L.R. (3d) 321 (S.C.C.)

33.   *Ibid.*, per Pigeon, Martland, and Beetz, JJ. at p. 351 ff.

34.   *Ibid.*, per Ritchie, J., p. 343 ff.

35.   Canada, Parliament, Special Joint Committee of the Senate and the House of Commons on the Constitution of Canada, *Final Report* (Ottawa, Queen's Printer, 1972), p. 91. (Hereinafter cited as Special Joint Committee, *Report*.) The report was careful to restrict its recommendations to air and water pollution, noting at p. 92 that the more general question of "environmental management" is as yet too broad and uncertain to be dealt with as a whole.

36.   Beaudouin, "La protection de l'environnement . . . ," p. 224. The Task Force on Canadian Unity, on which Dean Beaudoin served, was generally sceptical of formal concurrency: "Concurrent jurisdiction should be avoided whenever possible through a more precise definition of exclusive powers." Task Force on Canadian Unity, *A Future Together* (Ottawa: Minister of Supply and Services Canada, 1979), p. 126, recommendation 38(i).

37.   See text p. 130.

38.   See Bora Laskin, "Occupying the Field: Paramountcy in Penal Legislation," *Canadian Bar Review* 41 (1963): 234–63 and W.R. Lederman, "The Concurrent Operation of Federal and Provincial Laws in Canada," *McGill Law Journal* 9 (1963): 185–99.

39.   Special Joint Committee, *Report*, p. 92.

40.   British North America Act, s. 94A.

41.   Special Joint Committee, *Report*, recommendation 50. For air and water pollution they called for federal paramountcy, however: see p. 92.

42.   Task Force on Canadian Unity, recommendation 38(ii).

43.   The *Interprovincial Cooperatives* case, note 20, shows that the Supreme Court of Canada has not yet settled on a basis of selection in such situations.

44.   The Nuisance Act, C.C.S.M. 1976, c. N 120, s. 2.

45.   Special Joint Committee, *Report*, recommendations 101 and 102.

46.   *Attorney-General of Nova Scotia* v. *Attorney-General of Canada and Lord Nelson Hotel*, [1951] S.C.R. 31 (S.C.C.)

47.   Special Joint Committee, *Report*, recommendation 51. The Canadian Bar Association's Committee on the Constitution agreed: *Towards a New Canada* (Toronto, 1978), Chapter 11, recommendation 5.

48.   Special Joint Committee, *Report*, p. 92. The methods suggested were the federal spending power and continued use of the Canadian Council of Resources Ministers.

49.   See, for example, Task Force on Canadian Unity, recommendation 5; Constitutional Committee of the Quebec Liberal Party, *A New Canadian Federation* (Montreal, 1980), recommendation 13.

50.   Special Joint Committee, *Report*, p. 92. It should be noted, however, that the same report called for certain general restrictions on the manner in which the spending power would be utilized (recommendations 56, 57, and 58), as well as for access of both orders of government to all fields of taxation (recommendations 54 and 55).

51.   *Interprovincial Cooperatives Ltd.* v. *The Queen*, (1975) D.L.R. (3d) 321 (S.C.C.)

52.   Task Force on Canadian Unity, recommendation 38(i).

53.   See L.M. Bloomfield and Gerald F. Fitzgerald, *Boundary Waters Problems of Canada and the United States (The International Joint Commission 1912–1958)* (Toronto: Carswell, 1958).

54.   Québec, Conseil exécutif, *Quebec-Canada: A New Deal* (Quebec: Éditeur officiel, 1979), p. 87 ff.

55.   *Ibid.*, p. 56.

56.   *Ibid.*, p. 48, for example.

57.   See, for example, P.S.R.F. Mathijsen, *A Guide to European Community Law*, 2d ed. (London: Sweet & Maxwell, 1975), p. 161; and Eric Stein *et al.*, *European Community Law and Institutions in Perspective: Text, Cases and Readings* (Indianapolis: Bobbs-Merrill, 1976).

The Author

DALE GIBSON is a Professor of Law, specializing in Constitutional Law and Torts, at the University of Manitoba. He has served as Constitutional Adviser to the Governments of Canada and of Manitoba and has been a member of the Law Reform Commission of Manitoba for seven years; he is currently Chairperson of the Manitoba Human Rights Commission. Professor Gibson has published numerous articles on a wide variety of legal subjects. He is the author, with Lee Gibson, of *Substantial Justice: Law and Lawyers in Manitoba 1670–1970*, and has edited a recent collection of essays entitled *Aspects of Privacy Law*. A forthcoming book, *The Man Who Tried To Steal Manitoba*, describes the life of a very influential, but little known, lawyer of Canada's Western frontier.

Foreign Policy

DENIS STAIRS
Centre for Foreign Policy Studies
Dalhousie University

Contents

Foreign Policy

Introduction

The purpose of this paper is to consider the four projected options for a new Canadian constitution in terms of their implications for foreign policy. By agreement with other contributors, however, the analysis will exclude questions of economics and international law, which are considered elsewhere in the work, and will give only cursory attention to national defence.

It might reasonably be argued that this restriction precludes effective treatment of the subject that I have been assigned, for there is a sense in which little remains of 'foreign policy' after its legal, economic, and security ingredients have been removed. Moreover it is hard to make predictions pertaining to what does remain, subject as that is to the influence of a host of causal forces that are themselves constantly changing. In these circumstances even the most daring of forecasters is wise to begin with provisos. They protect his flank. They also remind his readers that the study of politics is an untidy discipline and one not very forgiving of those who use it to reconnoitre the future. A statement of hesitations — and of working assumptions — therefore follows. It is, necessarily, incomplete.

Assumptions and Cautions

It is difficult, first of all, to decide what to include under the heading of 'foreign policy'. The problem stems partly from the complexity of the modern international agenda. Scholars and foreign service officers alike once thought it reasonable to consider foreign affairs primarily in politico-security terms. In appropriate instances, they might recognize the international distribution of economic interests and capabilities as an important causal or motivating force, but the focus of their analytical

157

attention was on the political and military behaviour to which that force gave rise. Such a perspective made possible, not only an intellectual division of labour among academics, but also a functional division of labour among departments of government. Foreign offices were regarded by their domestic equivalents as entities apart.

In recent decades, however, there have been dramatic increases in both the range and intensity of the relationships between different national communities. Few enterprises of government are now immune to influences from abroad. Almost every ministry of government, therefore, has developed an interest in external affairs. Far from being entities apart, foreign offices have come to be viewed more often as obstacles in the way. A list of subjects considered by intergovernmental conferences in the past few years would include the control of crime, the sharing of satellites, the construction of habitats, the distribution of food, the constraint of terrorism, the management of populations, the pricing of petroleum, the regulation of multinational firms, the conservation of wildlife, and the cleansing of the environment. Such a list would show at once how fuzzy the edges of 'foreign policy' have become. To distinguish foreign policy from the conduct of public policy at large thus requires, more than ever, arbitrary decisions.

Defining 'foreign policy' involves conceptual difficulties, too. Should foreign policy be considered in relation to specific problems or *in toto* as an 'across-the-board' abstraction? Should it be identified by its objectives, direct or indirect, short-term or long-term? Or by its strategies of alignment? Or by its diplomatic tactics and methods? Or by some patterned combination of these, as implied, for example, in the notion of an international 'role' or 'orientation'?[1] In practice all these criteria and doubtless more are very common, and sometimes they appear together in the same exposition, depending on the evolving purposes of a particular analysis. Even if all of them were employed, however, they would not fully solve the present analytical problem since to inquire into the foreign policy implications of optional constitutional arrangements is to ask, first, what pertinent changes each option would bring about in the international (and domestic) environment, and secondly how these changes would affect, not merely the agenda of the decision makers, but also their capabilities. The ensuing foreign policy behaviour, however its tenor is determined, thus becomes a secondary, rather than a primary, effect, a 'dependent variable' that is one step removed from its primary cause.

It is obviously impossible to deal here with the international aspects of all the many fields of public policy that would be affected by each of the constitutional options considered in this work. The treatment, therefore, will be very general, and it will focus largely on the impact that these various options might have on diplomatic capabilities and effectiveness. It should be understood that to approach the problem from this perspective may prejudice the issue to some extent since, from the standpoint of diplomatic efficacy, 'big and centralized' may be better than 'small and devolved'. In any event the reader should certainly be aware that an enterprise of this sort puts many balls in the air, and not all jugglers would seek to keep the same selection aloft.

There is another obvious difficulty best identified by the question, "Foreign policy implications *for whom*?" For Canada inclusive of Quebec? For Canada without Quebec? Or for Quebec alone? Objectivity and detachment, as well as the structure of the project's research design, together suggest the answer, "For all three." It should be understood, however, that the composition of the 'states' or 'régimes' whose 'foreign policies' are being examined is itself undergoing constant change, and this circumstance not only complicates the exposition, but leads to confusing shifts of focus. The problem is aggravated slightly by the asymmetry of the options list. While this list identifies four broad types of potential constitutional development within Canada, from the international point of view it really serves to distinguish only two: that is, the situation in which Quebec would act as a sovereign power in international affairs (Options C and D) and the situation in which it would not (Options A and B). The 'independent variable' is thus being manipulated, at least in the area of external affairs, in asymmetrical degrees.

Still another difficulty common to most hypothetical constructions in the social sciences arises from the presence of hidden assumptions. The survey of constitutional options calls, in effect, for the fourfold manipulation of one complex independent variable: the constitutional arrangements governing Canada and Quebec. It is clear, however, that the implications for foreign policy of constitutional change depend heavily on many other factors both at home and abroad. Imagine, for example, a constitutional change that happened to coincide with an abrupt termination of foreign shipments of oil to North America. The results in that circumstance might be very

different from those that would follow if the change occurred at
a time when external oil supplies were secure. It is impossible in
an analysis of this kind to take into account the potential impact
of all such hypothetical developments. To resolve the problem,
therefore, the analyst must put most of the forces of history 'on
hold' and assume that other environmental conditions will
remain more or less constant while he manipulates in his
imagination the variable in which he is particularly interested, in
this case, the Constitution. I shall try from time to time to call
explicit attention to some of the more significant assumptions,
but it will be obvious that numerous others, many of them
hidden, are implicit in the discussion. Except when I indicate
otherwise, it will be assumed that no fundamental changes have
occurred within the international environment and that the
current general patterns of international politics are still in
place.

It may be useful to notice, incidentally, that the problem of
implicit assumptions goes beyond the impact of completely
extraneous factors, for in the real world of politics, the way in
which a given constitutional change comes about might very well
be as significant, at least in the short and medium terms, as the
change itself. A transition to Option C (sovereignty for Quebec),
for example, might yield very different results if it developed
through processes of amicable negotiation from those that it
would yield if it developed in circumstances of deepening
political enmity or, even worse, of military or para-military
conflict. For the most part the present analysis assumes that the
transition to a new constitutional arrangement has been peaceful and that the political conflicts involved have been prosecuted
by normal constitutional processes rather than by military,
para-military, or other extra-constitutional means. It is possible
to argue that without this assumption, the option of
sovereignty-association would not be feasible at all. Nonetheless,
the premise is fundamentally significant to the analysis as a
whole, and it might well prove to be highly unrealistic if a serious
drive for independence were to develop again in Quebec.

Option A: Reformed Federalism

Option A contemplates a re-arrangement of the division of
governmental powers under a federal structure. It amounts to a
continuation of the present system, albeit with adjustments and

reforms designed to accommodate the ever more conflicting interests of the two principal levels of government. The option assumes that the diversities within Canada are not great enough to prevent their reconciliation by means that are consistent with the principles and practices of constitutional democracy as interpreted in Western liberal societies, and in a way that supports a sufficient measure of national unity to sustain a single state. It makes the further assumption that national unity can be achieved most effectively through a system in which all of the second-level units of government (in this case, the provinces) are formally invested with the same constitutional powers and responsibilities, despite their different political and economic resources, and ethnic, social, and cultural characteristics.

Since peaceful internal adjustments of this kind do not alter the number or the weight of the international 'personalities' involved, they offer no particular difficulty from the perspective of the international community. Foreign governments and international organizations could be expected to regard such changes as essentially domestic matters. Some of the relevant authorities in foreign countries would be interested in the implications of the modified system for Canadian *policies* in various fields, and in a few capitals, at least, there might be moderate concern about their eventual impact on Canadian diplomatic practice and on the flexibility of Canadian negotiators. But, in the final analysis, constitutional amendments of the sort projected under Option A would have, at most, a negligible effect on the international environment within which Canadian foreign policy is conducted and to which it must respond.

The significance of Option A for foreign policy, therefore, would be expressed primarily in its impact on the processes whereby Canadian decisions about external affairs are made and implemented. These processes might undergo quite significant changes in detail, and this development could have substantive policy implications in particular fields: that of energy, for example. But it seems improbable that in broad outline decision-making practices would differ substantially from the present ones. The likelihood that innovations in this area would be minimal stems from the fact that, no matter how the division of powers and responsibilities is arranged internally, as long as only one federal government is recognized internationally as the legal 'spokesman' for Canada, mechanisms broadly similar to those already in place will *have* to be maintained in order to permit the provinces to be actively involved in the making and conduct of 'foreign policies' that impinge on provincial areas of jurisdiction. Such mechanisms are also necessary to ensure that Canada's negotiating positions abroad are as consistent and coherent as possible.

Most of the ingredients of the current system were developed in the late 1960s. Initially they were the result of the conflict between Ottawa and Quebec over the latter's claim to the right to conduct its own relations directly with foreign powers in areas of provincial jurisdiction. The federal government considered the issue particularly important because the governments of France and of a number of francophone states in Africa were apparently willing to give *de facto* support to Quebec's diplomatic aspirations. If this support went unchallenged, it might eventually lead to recognition of Quebec as an independent state capable of acting unilaterally under international law. The problem was not confined entirely to Quebec, however, since other provinces, too, had begun to discover that matters falling within their spheres of constitutional responsibility were increasingly subject to international influences and hence to the outcomes of international diplomacy. The control of pollution, the conservation of energy and of other resources, the management of communications, the exploitation of the sea and seabed, the production and distribution of food: all these issues and many others like them had been catapulted into the international arena as a result of a host of technological, economic, demographic, and other developments, but they were all of direct and constitutionally legitimate interest to provincial authorities. In short, while Quebec's demands might pose the most dramatic of the provincial challenges to the ultimate survival of the Canadian state, they have had their counterparts in other provinces as well.

The mechanisms that evolved as part of the federal response to this challenge fell into two main categories.[2] The first category included legalistic mechanisms developed primarily to protect the federal government's position in the international community. More specifically these mechanisms were designed, on the one hand, to safeguard Ottawa's international status as the recognizably 'sovereign' Canadian authority abroad and, on the other, to protect federal agencies from being held responsible for the implementation of international agreements that had been reached entirely through provincial action. They included, for example, exchanges of notes between the federal government and the interested foreign power; these notes (the so-called '*Ad Hoc* Covering Agreements') give explicit federal assent to arrangements concluded between the latter and a provincial régime. Notes of this kind could also be drafted less restrictively in order to provide an umbrella authorization for the conclusion in the future of broadly similar arrangements (General Framework Agreements or *Accords Cadres*) within specific fields. Mechanisms in this category also included a system by which the federal government could act on behalf of a given province as the signing agent *vis-à-vis* a foreign power while at the same time concluding explicit 'indemnity' agreements with the provincial authorities. The latter thereby effectively guaranteed to implement the terms of the treaty and to accept liability for any default.

Devices within the second category were more procedural than legalistic. They were designed to accommodate provincial governments by directly involving them, as constitutionally appropriate, in the processes by which foreign policy decisions were made. One of the devices, for example, consisted of a general federal commitment to consult with provincial authorities before acceding to international conventions affecting provincial interests, and to circulate for information purposes the documentation of international agencies concerned with matters under provincial jurisdiction. Ottawa also promised to include in Canadian delegations to international conferences with provincial relevance representatives of the provinces, sometimes as chairmen or in other positions of leadership, and to consult generally with the provinces in the development of federal programs abroad that had an impact on provincial responsibilities. These arrangements would apply, for instance, to the design of external assistance programs involving the recruitment and assignment overseas of large numbers of teachers from provincial school systems.

Again, the purpose of these various procedures was to protect Ottawa's position as the authoritative and ultimate representative of Canada in intergovernmental dealings abroad, while making it possible for provincial authorities to play active roles in initiating, developing, and even negotiating policies that had international dimensions bearing on provincial responsibilities. The entire system, however, was and still is heavily dependent on the presence of a substantial measure of goodwill and commonality of over-all purpose among the federal and provincial authorities, as well as on the willingness of federal politicians and officials to give genuine meaning to their promises of consultation. It requires that foreign policy conflicts between the two levels of government be resolved either by processes of mutual give-and-take or by the full retreat of one of the parties. The alternative is a sectoral breakdown in the foreign policy process with the result that the question at issue is either lost abroad by default or is left indefinitely on the shelf. Since most issues that are important enough to generate significant domestic intergovernmental conflict also hazard substantial political, diplomatic, or other penalties if they are left in a policy vacuum, such breakdowns are relatively rare, although they do sometimes occur.[3] But the possibilities for an escalation of federal-provincial tensions, short of a total breakdown, are obviously very great, and the willingness of the parties involved to accept the politics of give-and-take therefore remains essential to the effective operation of the system.

The point of this discussion is not to argue past history or current affairs, but to stress that the same general arrangements that now exist would still be necessary in the wake of the kinds of constitutional amendments envisaged under Option A. These arrangements might differ in detail and in degree, but not in kind. International affairs have come to impinge directly or indirectly on almost every activity of government. In these circumstances no practicable internal division of powers is available that would resolve the problem of jurisdictional overlap in dealings abroad. If the basic structure of a single state is to be maintained, therefore, mechanisms will still be required that are designed to accommodate the two principal levels of government in the policy-making process and to provide legal cover for provinces wishing to conclude their own agreements with foreign powers. Moreover it is reasonable to argue that the importance of these devices would be significantly increased to the extent that constitutional amendments produce an even greater decentralization of powers and responsibilities than we have now. It is also possible that these devices would function less easily since the opportunities for policy disagreement would be enlarged, and the areas of federally controlled consensus reduced.

When the various legal and procedural arrangements described above are working effectively, they do, in some sense, 'solve' the problem. But they also have costs. For example they can introduce significant delays into the policy-making process, particularly when more than one province is involved, and when provincial views are diverse. They may also reduce both the flexibility and the credibility of Canadian negotiators abroad. The first reduction may come about because the difficulty of securing an agreed position at home may make adjustments in response to the bargaining initiatives of foreign governments more difficult; the second reduction may occur because it may become known internationally that Canadian diplomats cannot always guarantee the acceptance at home of the foreign commitments they undertake.[4] The procedures can lead, in short, to a condition of 'co-ordination overload' that can seriously damage the capacity of the foreign service to respond with maximum tactical effectiveness to external needs and opportunities. This incapacity intensifies a problem already made serious enough by the accelerating involvement in activities abroad of nominally 'domestic' departments of government and by the consequently weakened capacity of the Department of External Affairs to maintain effective surveillance, much less control, of the full range of Canada's international relations.

In addition the process of reaching concerted policy positions through mechanisms of federal-provincial negotiation can help to erode the foundation of public accountability on which the parliamentary system is based. This is partly because the negotiations themselves must often be conducted behind closed doors. Otherwise the give-and-take required for the resolution of disagreements may become politically difficult for the participants, and there may be an inconvenient loss of bargaining advantage to interested foreign powers. The result, however, is that legislative institutions at both the federal and provincial levels are presented with a *fait accompli*. Ministers, moreover, who in other circumstances might be held unequivocally responsible for their 'decisions', are now in the position of being able to 'pass the buck', asserting, in effect, that they have done their best, given the intransigent attitudes of their provincial adversaries. In this they may be right if, indeed, 'power' has passed, not from Ministers to mandarins (although that is a factor, too), but from persons to processes.

Ultimately, of course, a system that lays such emphasis on establishing a consensus among so many powerful governments, each with its own peculiar mix of political constituencies, is bound to have an impact on the substance of policy itself. In some contexts there may be no disagreement at all. In others only one or two provinces may be interested. But in many agreement will be possible only at the level of the lowest common denominator, and this may inhibit, where it does not actually prevent, the development of an effective national policy.[5]

The significance of these various liabilities is difficult to measure with precision in terms of substantive 'national interest', although indicators are easily obtained in the form of lamentations by officials in the foreign service and by their negotiating counterparts abroad.[6] The problems, in any event, have to be weighed against the benefits that have ensued for the maintenance of federal-provincial amity and the preservation of the present division of powers. The ultimate defence of any decentralized system of government rests, after all, on the assumption that in certain fields 'the people' are better served by policies obtained from regional, rather than from national, rulers. It should be understood, however, that if the current arrangements were applied in the context of an even greater measure of decentralization, their 'foreign policy' costs, as defined by the general criteria of diplomatic efficacy discussed above, would be correspondingly increased. Whether these increases would matter very much would depend on the nature of the decentralization. Even if they did not, the evaluation could be expected to vary with the political preferences of the assessor, as well as with his empirical judgement. To the extent, for example, that the changes led to a significant improvement in the psychic or other satisfactions of Québécois, among others, it could be held that they were worth the diplomatic price.

In the absence of a clear indication of the areas in which the decentralization would occur, it is difficult to be more specific about its implications. It seems obvious, however, that decentralization would be most noticeable, not in the politico-security field, but in the 'functional' areas of trade in raw materials and finished goods and services, capital movements, tourism, cultural activities, environmental interdependencies, and the like. Politico-security matters could be expected to remain in federal hands under *any* constitutional framework premised on the continuation of Canada as a single state. It seems highly improbable, for example, that defence policy would be directly influenced, although there might be an indirect impact if the new arrangements produced major changes in federal tax revenues or otherwise altered Ottawa's capacity for defence spending. Setting aside the pertinent 'functional' international organizations such as, for example, the specialized agencies of

the United Nations, this means that the principal impact of
decentralization would be experienced in relation to the countries with which Canada has the greatest number of 'functional'
interactions. The principal impact, then, would be perceived
most immediately and most pervasively in Canada's relations
with the United States, followed, at some considerable distance,
by those with the countries of Western Europe, including the
United Kingdom, and Japan. Relations with the Third-World
members of *la francophonie* already constitute a special case and
probably would not be much affected. In most other contexts
the impact of decentralization on Canadian foreign relations
would be marginal.

The special case of the United States, however, might well
have very great significance, particularly from the viewpoint of
Canadians who are anxious about the pervasive American
impact on Canadian life. Even now the development of a clearly
defined strategy for dealing with this problem seems as daunting an administrative challenge as it is a political one,[7] and there
is little doubt that the problem would be exacerbated by almost
any additional decentralization of powers within Canada. The
recent and continuing quarrel between Ottawa and Alberta over
the volume and pricing of sales of Canadian energy resources to
the American market provides an obvious and startling indi-
cator of the potential difficulties. There can be no doubt, either,
that the Americans would obtain substantial bargaining advantages, even within the confines of specific issues, from the
increased opportunity to 'divide and conquer' that a still greater
measure of Canadian devolution would give them.[8] The same
phenomenon could be expected to arise in lesser degree in
relation to the European Economic Community and in other
contexts in which hard-bargaining ('Yankee trading') over
substantive functional issues is common. The cumulative effect
of such developments over the long term is hard to predict, but
there is certainly a very great risk that they would ultimately
strengthen, rather than weaken, the centrifugal economic and
psychological forces of Canadian politics and hence encourage
the process of national disintegration. From the 'federalist'
point of view, the danger would presumably be greatest if the
decentralization were to include a complete federal abandon-
ment to the provinces of the regulation of foreign direct
investment, as well as control over the export of energy and
other natural resources including those in the coastal economic
zone.[9] But the danger would also be present in cultural fields

and in areas of indirect economic significance: for example the control of electronic media and communications, and the regulation of industrial pollution.

To repeat, however, these complications of Option A arise largely in the domestic Canadian environment. Although further measures of decentralization might create exploitive opportunities for foreign powers (and for certain non-governmental agencies such as multinational corporations), from the point of view of international politics they would be essentially non-controversial. At particular international conferences, the composition of Canadian delegations and the status of provincial representatives assigned to them might sometimes cause confusion, and occasionally even irritation.[10] But assuming the visible preservation of the legal primacy of the federal government through protective mechanisms similar to those already in place, this would not be an insurmountable problem.

Option B: Special Provincial Status

Option B is concerned with the possibility of assigning special status to one or more provinces or regions; it implies a devolution of powers and responsibilities to the provincial or regional level in one or a few instances, but not in the same degree to all. While at first glance Option B seems to define a situation in which at least one of the provincial or regional authorities would obtain powers greater than those it holds under present constitutional arrangements, theoretically it does not preclude a system much more centralized than the existing one. The only formal requirement is that at least one provincial or regional authority have more jurisdiction than the others. In theory, too, the special status need not be confined to Quebec. It could apply, for example, to both Quebec and Ontario because they are the largest provinces, or to Ontario, Alberta, and British Columbia because they are the richest provinces, or to the Atlantic provinces because they are the poorest, or to Newfoundland because it is geographically isolated and has a claim to certain special historic rights.[11] In practice, however, the argument in support of special status has been legitimized on grounds of linguistic and cultural differences, and these distinctions have been considered to apply in sufficient degree only to Quebec. In what follows, therefore, Option B has been taken to mean special status for Quebec alone and to imply for that province a significantly greater measure of decentralization than currently exists.

In purely domestic terms Option B appears to raise three basic questions:

- *Would special status be unjust?* That is, would it lead to constitutionally induced, but nonetheless morally unacceptable, inequities in the treatment of citizens from different parts of the country by their respective provincial or regional governments?
- *Would it sell?* That is, would the conferring of special powers on the Government of Quebec, whether or not it actually produced just results, be acceptable politically to the rest of Canada?
- *Would it intoxicate the beneficiaries?* That is, by conceding the legitimacy of the cultural-linguistic argument and by whetting the appetites of Québécois, would it set in motion an irreversible train of thought and a matching array of political forces that would ultimately lead to the separation of Quebec from Canada?

Answers to these fundamental problems may become more evident from the studies of domestic policy issues appearing elsewhere in this collection.

If one takes the point of view of foreign policy, however, and assumes a benignly disinterested international community, the basic issues posed by Option B appear similar in principle to those raised by Option A. Because a smaller portion of the total store of national resources would be affected, and because consultation and co-ordination might be more easily arranged with one provincial government than with ten, the difficulties of the system could even be substantively less significant and procedurally more manageable than those associated with Option A. Depending on the nature of the issues subject to the special status arrangements, Option B might also seem less confusing to the representatives of foreign governments. In time these representatives might be more easily educated to comprehend and accept the idea of Quebec as a special political entity than they could the far more daunting notion that in foreign affairs Canada speaks, not with one voice, but eleven.

Because Option B assumes Canada's survival as an integrated and sovereign power, the same sorts of legal and procedural mechanisms between the two levels of government for co-ordinating foreign policy would still be required. If, however, greater policy latitude were given to Quebec as a special status province, it seems probable that the legal devices would be emphasized at the expense of the procedural ones, at least with respect to the policy fields affected. In other words, the devolution of policy-making authority in particular foreign policy fields might somewhat reduce the requirement for day-to-day consultation in the policy process. (In substantive terms, fewer of the decisions would be Ottawa's business.) At the same time there might be an increased need for umbrella agreements to give Quebec the necessary legal cover abroad. Assuming amity, trust, and integrity of purpose on the part of both the federal and provincial authorities, and assuming also that the government in Quebec did not attempt to expand its turf by 'stretching' the agreed interpretation of the new jurisdictional rules, it is conceivable that the arrangement under Option B would work more smoothly than either the present system or a variant under Option A. In theory, certainly, Option B would diminish the number of potential friction points in specified policy areas since Ottawa would simply have abandoned the field.

Many of the disadvantages of Option A also apply to Option B, although in the second instance their distribution would probably be more uneven. In the case, for example, of negotiations that fell under the special status arrangements and that were of interest only to Quebec,[12] the policy process would not be delayed by the need for federal-provincial consultation, and the flexibility and credibility of 'Canadian' negotiators (suitably covered by legal instruments) would presumably not be affected.[13] In special status areas in which other parts of Canada also had an interest, however, the potential disadvantages would be greatly compounded since the international community might find itself confronting a potentially quarrelsome 'Canadian' delegation that included a federal authority, a clearly defined Québécois subdivision with substantial powers, and perhaps a collection of other provincial government representatives as well. The havoc created by this sort of situation could lead to despair and protest abroad; it could also work to the disadvantage of *all* the 'Canadian' bargainers. Experience might quickly instruct the various Canadian governments of the wisdom of working out their internal disagreements well in advance of their appearance in diplomatic public. But it seems clear that in fields of interest not entirely confined to Quebec, special status arrangements could have seriously disruptive results for the effective pursuit of Canadian interests abroad.

Similarly the problem of maintaining effective processes of public accountability would remain and might be intensified in those areas that were not visibly of interest to Quebec alone; so, also, would the complications arising generally for the conduct of 'national' policy in the affected fields.

These considerations suggest that from the foreign policy point of view, the special status option offers the greatest promise in fields that can be identified with interests peculiar to the Province of Quebec. In other areas it could hamstring the policy community at home, debilitate its negotiators abroad, and both at home and abroad substantially increase, rather than diminish, the intensity and frequency of federal-provincial conflict.

This prospect, in turn, raises the question of whether it is possible to identify specific fields of 'foreign policy' that are exclusively or primarily of interest to Quebec. Politico-security problems, for example, would seem not to meet the test. Certainly defence policy does not. The most obvious possibilities are those arising in fields that bear on social and cultural affairs: fields, that is, that provide Quebec with the distinctive characteristics on which the rationale for special status is ultimately founded.[14] These are precisely the fields in which the Quebec government has been particularly active since the early 1960s, and the existing umbrella agreements are, for that reason, concerned primarily with educational, cultural, technical, and scientific affairs in the context of *la francophonie*. The apparent success of these arrangements[15] may suggest, however, that the effective defence of the Quebec interests involved can be satisfactorily accomplished under existing arrangements or arrangements modified under Option A, and that special status is not really required. Even Quebec's interest in the encouragement and processing of francophone immigration is being smoothly accommodated under the present system.[16]

The 'foreign policy' argument for special status might be strengthened, however, if Quebec's claim to a unique socio-cultural interest were buttressed by arguments from economics. It could be held, for example, that culture is a camp-follower of commerce, and that if Quebec is to enrich its heritage and make its own mark on the francophone world, it must be free to influence the movement of goods and services and the flow of investment. But even here the authorities in Quebec City are at liberty now to engage in any promotional activities for their province that they think appropriate,[17] and it is difficult to see

how they could be given the power to do more without depriving
the federal government of the basic instruments of macro-
economic policy.

It can be argued that there is, perhaps, one area of foreign
policy in which the socio-cultural and economic aspects of
statecraft come together, and in which Quebec could be given
special powers without causing these other difficulties. This area
consists of the administration of international development
assistance to francophone countries. Again, this is not really so
much a matter of the Constitution as of public policy. The
Quebec government is already involved in modest development-assistance programs of its own,[18] and even within the
present framework, it is open to the federal authorities to
delegate administrative powers in the foreign aid field to
provincial governments as they already do to certain non-
governmental organizations. In principle, however, there is
nothing to prevent the assignment of such powers to Quebec
from becoming a matter of constitutional right. To the extent
that this change removed the policy from the field of federal
discretion, it would give the arrangement a comforting measure
of security from Quebec's point of view. It would also provide a
guaranteed flow of federal funds into the provincial 'foreign
aid' budget, which suffers at present from being inadequately
financed. The Quebec authorities could then design and
administer the program in a manner consistent with their own
priorities and resources, and in a way that would promote their
cultural, educational, economic, and other interests. In short the
arrangement would give them an opportunity to maintain a
significant presence abroad in precisely the areas where they
have the most distinctive interests. This presence, in turn, would
presumably help to expand the international horizons of
Québécois.

It is probable, of course, that the federal government would
resist this sort of proposal quite vigorously. Foreign aid depends
in part on humanitarian considerations, but it is also an
instrument of foreign policy, and the federal authorities are
unlikely to welcome a further weakening of their already limited
diplomatic arsenal. An examination of the history of Canada's
development-assistance effort would show that the francophone
portion of the program has been that most directly linked to
immediately visible political objectives. Its purpose has been
partly to provide francophone Canadians with a sense of
involvement in the projection of Canada abroad, and this

objective would still be served — perhaps better served — under a decentralized system. But the program has also been aimed at cross-pressuring any other francophone powers that might be tempted from time to time to give a measure of *de facto* diplomatic recognition to Quebec as an independent power in world affairs. In effect Ottawa, with its substantially greater resources, has been trying to create in such countries a significant 'stake' in the survival of Canada's constitutional unity while seeking to dilute the influence of France, which would otherwise enjoy the enviable position of a near-monopoly donor. Quite apart, therefore, from the threat that an expansion of Quebec's role in foreign aid programs would pose to the domains of federal bureaucratic fiefdoms, officials in Ottawa could be expected to fear the loss of the bargaining leverage it would bring about in the event of future contests with foreign powers sympathetic to the aspirations of the more radically nationalist element in Quebec. For federal officials, in short, to give Quebec this kind of expanded power would seem at best a calculated risk.

This particular federal anxiety draws attention to the underlying assumption of both Options A and B that the objectives of a reasonably stable majority of Québécois are ultimately limited and therefore satiable. If this assumption is removed, and if it is further postulated that at least some members of the international community might be willing to give active diplomatic or other forms of support to an independence drive within Quebec,[19] it can then be argued that a greater measure of decentralization would serve to increase Quebec's opportunities for taking independent 'foreign policy' initiatives and for creating protocol incidents that could be interpreted as precedents in a gradual progress towards its achievement of international sovereign status.[20] As the disputes of the late 1960s clearly suggest, this possibility is a danger from the federal point of view even under the present system. The risk might well be aggravated by a special status constitution that would not only widen the area of potential jurisdictional 'aggression', but also concede the validity of the fundamentally significant premise that ethnic, linguistic, and cultural differences legitimize a special allocation of sovereign power. Once this concession is made, it can lead by logical extension to the notion that only a full measure of sovereignty will suffice, and that all arrangements short of complete constitutional independence inevitably threaten or compromise the ethno-cultural interest. The concession may thus seriously weaken the 'functional' argument in defence of the federal system. Whether this should be regarded in practice as a decisive consideration is a matter for long-term political judgement.

The reaction abroad to a movement in favour of Option B would probably be much the same as that to a movement in favour of Option A since either movement would be viewed as an essentially domestic constitutional adjustment. Some countries — for example, Belgium — would doubtless be curious about the details of the system and its practical implications. There might also be a degree of alarm in Africa and elsewhere at the prospect of ambitious minorities closer to home using the Canadian experiment as a precedent. There might, too, be some confusion in a variety of international contexts over the *locus* of final authority within Canadian delegations to conferences. For the reasons discussed earlier, however, this difficulty might be more readily overcome in the circumstance of special status for Quebec than in that of a further decentralization of foreign policy powers among all the provinces. In general, therefore, the international reaction could be expected to range from the faintly curious to the benignly indifferent.

At the same time it also seems probable that the substance of Canada's relations with at least a few members of the international community would be moderately affected. The Americans, for example, might find their bargaining position in some areas marginally improved along the lines discussed under Option A. More noticeably, perhaps, the countries of *la francophonie* would find themselves dealing more exclusively than they do now with Quebec's government, a circumstance they would presumably regard as more or less attractive depending on the impact of the arrangement on the flow of development assistance. Ottawa, in turn, could once again be expected to concentrate its own bilateral foreign aid initiatives in the traditional Commonwealth areas. It might also shift its own cultural, scientific, and educational exchange programs in the direction of non-francophone countries on the understanding that the francophone field would be taken over by Quebec. Depending on the exact terms of the devolution, 'Canadian' policies in particular fields — for example, the exploitation of international satellite-communications systems or even such controversial questions as the sale of uranium — might also be affected, and this could be of particular interest to Western Europe. Assuming, however, that the federal government retained control of the basic instruments of macro-economic policy, as well as responsibility for the politico-security aspects of Canada's external affairs, a special status arrangement could be expected to have a relatively limited impact on the international community at large. Like Option A, Option B is thus more interesting for its domestic than for its international implications.

Option C: Sovereignty for Quebec

From the international point of view, Option C (sovereignty for Quebec) and Option D (sovereignty for Quebec and formal association with Canada) differ very substantially from Options A and B in that the former pair would lead to the creation of two new international 'personalities' where previously there had been only one.[21] The focus of analysis must therefore shift from the question of how foreign policy decisions would be made and implemented in the context of variations on Canada's existing constitutional framework to the questions of how the international positions of Quebec and Canada-without-Quebec would be affected, and what direction their *policies* would take following Quebec's acquisition of fully sovereign status. Economic issues aside, it is not clear that the conclusion of an agreement of sovereignty-association would have a very significant impact on foreign policy. On the other hand, the general political atmosphere within which Quebec's constitutional independence was actually achieved and the degree to which its claims were subsequently contested by Ottawa could very well be centrally important factors. It will be assumed here that the transition, while painful, has been conducted in a manner recognized by both parties as constitutionally legitimate, and that it has not been accompanied by military or para-military violence. In these circumstances much of what is said about Option C would apply as well to Option D.

Turning first to Quebec, it seems obvious that the decision makers for the new state's foreign policy would quickly encounter some very clearly defined constraints on its freedom of action in world affairs. These would include, in particular, Quebec's geo-political location in North America and its consequent dependence on the continuation after partition of healthy patterns of economic and financial exchange with the United States, as well as with what would remain of 'Canada'.

There is little doubt that the relatively limited dimensions of Quebec's own internal sources of national power abroad,[22] and the existing way of life and expectations of its domestic constituency would be basic determinants of its foreign policies. It would be essential for Quebec to avoid any initiative that would risk causing hostility or alarm in governmental, industrial, or financial circles in the United States. It would also be important for Quebec to maintain as conciliatory a relationship with 'Canada' as possible, if only to minimize the very serious possibility of vengeful Canadian reactions to the original separation decision.[23]

The outcome of these considerations would be most readily evident in the fields of defence and security and in economic affairs, none of which are examined in detail in this paper.[24] In broad outline, it is apparent that the need to maintain friendly relations with the Americans would preclude alignment with members of the Soviet or Chinese worlds, even in the unlikely event that such a stance seemed an attractive option within Quebec itself; the same need would also rule out any policy of neutralism that would involve denial of Quebec airspace to North American defence forces. An independent Quebec would be far more likely to adopt a strategy of maintaining co-operative defence arrangements with both Canada and the United States; these arrangements could be expressed, among other means, by formal membership in NORAD and perhaps also in NATO.[25] It is probable, on the other hand, that the new state would keep its military contribution at a relatively low level, for it is obvious to everyone concerned that Quebec's forces could have, at most, a symbolic significance in East-West military affairs, and that Quebec's territory, like all of Canada, will be protected by the United States whether Quebecers or Canadians like it or not. When soldiers are used to buy diplomatic credit rather than to meet real security needs, the temptation is to provide them in minimal numbers and to rejoice in the luxury of the 'free ride'. The result of such a tactic would be a military establishment designed essentially to maintain territorial sovereignty and provide aid-to-the-civil-power. The Americans, provided that their own continental defence were not obstructed, could be expected to respond with no more than token expressions of disappointment.

In economic matters, too, the new Quebec régime would have to take into account its need to maintain confidence abroad, particularly in the United States. Ultimately, this requirement could be expected to have a conservative impact on its social and fiscal policies, as well as on official attitudes towards foreign capital and the general regulation of private enterprise.

Aside from these basic areas of public policy, a newly independent Quebec could be expected to exercise a particularly distinctive role in its relationships with other francophone countries since this is where the cultural and linguistic foundations of the independence movement would find their most obvious external expression. Such a development would be especially noticeable in relation to educational, cultural, scientific, and technological issues, where Quebec's involvement even now is very substantial. While the arrival of the new state would doubtless be welcomed by the Government of France, it is not inconceivable that over time rivalry would develop between the two powers in their Third-World relationships. Such difficulties might easily arise, for example, if the somewhat romantic view of Quebec that has been evident in France in recent years, but that now seems to be subsiding, were replaced in the post-separation period by France's more traditional posture of cultural arrogance and condescension. This development might be encouraged by the fact that, once Quebec's independence had been fully achieved, its usefulness as an instrument for causing discomfort among the 'Anglo-Saxons', already devalued by the death of de Gaulle, would be finally destroyed, and its heart-warming status as a hapless victim of anglophone oppression dissipated. It is possible, too, that developing countries in *la francophonie* would be tempted to possess themselves of diplomatic leverage by playing the two governments off, each against the other. On balance, however, the impact of this sort of development would almost certainly be marginal and, in any event, it would not be of significant interest to countries outside the francophone world.

A more serious consequence from the point of view of *la francophonie* might be the effect of the partition on the total flow of Canada-Quebec development assistance. Under present circumstances the federal government has a significant incentive for assigning considerable portions of Canadian foreign aid to the francophone sector of the Third and Fourth Worlds. Even with the special arrangement envisaged as a possibility under Option B, Ottawa would be required to supply Quebec with substantial resources allocated to precisely this purpose. In the post-separation period, however, it is almost certain that the francophone portion of the Canadian aid program would be brought to an end if only because its continuation would be politically unacceptable at home.[26] Quebec would therefore have to assume full financial responsibility for bilateral disbursements in the francophone world. It seems improbable, however, that it would be able to allocate for this purpose resources comparable to those previously available from Ottawa. This could be a particularly serious problem in the early years of the new régime when the economy might be suffering from severe transitional dislocations, and when domestic expectations for expensive public policy initiatives at home might well be euphorically high. The potential recipients of Quebec's assistance would doubtless accept for a time the argument that delays were unavoidable during so dramatic a period of adjustment, but eventually the pressures on the new régime to offer substantial amounts of development aid would almost certainly intensify. To the extent that Quebec failed to respond, its popularity would fade.

Difficulties with *la francophonie* could also arise in the field of immigration, although this development is not as easy to predict.[27] It is probable that the new government would take a special interest in immigration from French-speaking communities. Certainly such action would be consistent with that government's cultural objectives, however worrisome it might be to the English-speaking minority within its own constituency. It is not inconceivable, however, that a policy of this sort would produce a particularly large number of applications from the poorer countries of the francophone world, leading in turn to the adoption of a relatively restrictive policy on admissions. Resentments might very well result, especially if the restrictions were administered in a way that aggravated the 'brain-drain' from the Third World, or produced the practical effect of discrimination among applicants along racial lines. This problem would by no means be peculiar to Quebec, but if it gave rise to charges of implicit racism, the fact that the new state had been legitimized primarily on linguistic and cultural grounds might make the charges even more difficult to evade or refute. It could not, in short, be assumed that Quebec's relationships with the rest of the French-speaking world would be entirely free of tension.

The new state's relations with other members of the international community could be expected to be essentially uncontroversial. They would reflect Quebec's basic politico-security alignment with the West, its geographical location under the continental defence umbrella of the United States, and its general characteristics as a *status quo* power with modest ambitions, limited resources, and an unblemished historical past. The régime would certainly seek full membership in the United Nations and any other international bodies that it considered useful and appropriate.[28] If its sovereign status were not being contested in principle by Ottawa, its admission to each international organization would probably be secured without the inconvenience of serious opposition. In sum an independent Quebec would be received by the world at large as an inoffensive and, in global terms, not very substantial, offspring of the Western bloc.

This over-all characterization calls attention again to the fact that in many areas, including most of the 'functional' ones, the ultimate bargaining power of the new régime would be relatively limited. Quebec would no longer suffer at home from the disadvantage of having to filter through the federal policy-making process the pursuit of its interests abroad. On the other hand, the practical weight of its international interventions would not be amplified, as before, through their espousal by an experienced middle power. This might lead Quebec's government to be particularly distrustful of bilateral mechanisms for dealing with foreign countries and encourage it to follow Canada's own post-war strategy of supporting the resort to multilateral forums for international problem solving. With the exception of the principal Western security organizations, however, these multilateral forums tend to be dominated by coalitions of Third- and Fourth-World powers with which the new régime would have relatively little in common. In many important fields — for example, the pursuit of secure supplies of petroleum resources or the conduct of international trade negotiations — this situation might lead Quebec's government to attempt to increase its influence by acting politically and diplomatically in concert with Canada and the United States. It is not inconceivable that the advantages of having Canadian and American support in such dealings overseas would to some extent inhibit Quebec's bargaining with its neighbours at home.[29] Taken together with the compromises in domestic policy that would arise from the need to accommodate American capital and security interests, the situation might also create a measure of dissatisfaction among nationalist Québécois in the domestic constituency. The balancing of such internal and external pressures might be one of the more difficult of the political challenges that would confront the new régime.

For the development of all these international relationships, of course, it would be necessary for Quebec's government to create its own professional foreign service, but this does not appear to be a particularly intimidating prospect. The basic machinery is to some extent already in place in the form of the Department of Intergovernmental Affairs and the various Quebec Delegations-General abroad.[30] It is also possible that francophone diplomats could be attracted from the present Department of External Affairs.[31] In any case the demand would be relatively limited in the sense that the régime would require independent missions in only a handful of capitals and could administer its other relationships through multiple accreditations, special arrangements with the diplomatic services of other foreign powers, personnel assigned to multilateral organizations, and other such devices. The reciprocal representation of foreign powers in Quebec City would lead to the development there of a small diplomatic corps, although it seems probable that most countries would seek double-duty arrangements through their existing missions in Ottawa,[32] Washington, or New York.

For 'Canada' the loss of Quebec to independent sovereign status would probably not have fundamental significance for the general direction of foreign policy decisions, particularly if the transition to the new arrangement were negotiated by processes acceptable to both sides and, therefore, to the international community at large. The country's fundamental strategic interests and, in most respects, its economic interests would remain the same as before, and to that extent basic shifts in policy would be unlikely. On the other hand, Canadian diplomats would probably experience a perceptible decline in their influence in certain areas, including those concerned with the politics of security. This decline would result partly from the fact that Quebec's departure would represent a reduction in the store of real national assets, including military forces, under ultimate federal control and partly from the spectacle of the partition process itself. This spectacle would provide foreign governments with a highly visible bench-mark on which to base Canada's demotion in the international hierarchy. To some degree this is an intangible matter of socio-psychological perception, and it is difficult to estimate its effects in concrete terms. Nonetheless, it seems highly probable that Quebec's separation would be taken abroad as a signal of Canadian weakness or failure even if the comparative civility of the atmosphere within which it was accomplished were admired overseas. The problem would not be evident in every field — the country's position as a grain producer, for example, would be unaffected — and in a few cases there might be gains in bargaining leverage. Unless, for example, 'Canada' undertook an obligation to continue the arrangements currently in place or projected for supplying Quebec with Albertan oil, Ottawa might discover that it had, at least for a time, a greater measure of 'export room' in the petroleum area. To some extent, too, the damage might be limited by arrangements for acting in concert with Quebec in international negotiations. Over all, however, there seems to be little doubt that Canada would lose status abroad as a protagonist in world affairs, and that this would diminish its credibility in such multilateral contexts as the United Nations and the North Atlantic alliance.

Ottawa might also lose some bargaining power with the United States, particularly in areas in which the Americans were able to exploit competing interests of Canadians and Québécois, or where they were in a position to take tactical advantage of the desire of both powers to develop and maintain independent diplomatic and political credibility in Washington. On the other hand, awareness of this very danger might give both Ottawa and Quebec City an overriding incentive to form diplomatic alliances in dealing with their much more powerful neighbour.[33] Perhaps the safest conclusion is that *all* of these patterns would be evident, both simultaneously and consecutively, depending on issue and context.

Economic adjustments aside, the one area in which significant changes would probably occur would be in relation to *la francophonie*. In spite of the substantial francophone communities in New Brunswick, Ontario, and some other provinces, the departure of Quebec would effectively remove the principal reason for Canada's presence in francophone Africa as a source of development assistance, and it is conceivable that the continuation of such programs would arouse the active hostility of the anglophone Canadian population. It is possible that this reaction would be accompanied by a renewed emphasis on the Commonwealth connection, although this is more difficult to determine. It is also conceivable, but by no means certain, that there would be a resurgence in Canada of English-Canadian nationalism; this could affect cultural policy abroad, particularly in relation to the United States. The Quebec nationalist argument that Quebec's separation would be liberating for

English Canada as well as for Québécois is based on the notion that Canadian cultural policy would no longer have to suffer from the diluting inhibitions hitherto forced on it by the need to accommodate two nationalities. On the other hand, it also seems possible that the existing network of functional north-south linkages would be greatly strengthened by the division of the country if only because of the damage it would do to the political psychology that results from the maintenance of a single polity "from sea to sea." It can be argued, as well, that the cultural differences that now exist between Canada and the United States are precisely the result of the duality to which nationalists in Quebec are so strongly opposed. How these conflicting forces would affect the eventual status of Canada and Quebec, and to what extent they would be influenced by the more general geo-political considerations of statecraft, it is impossible to predict.

Option D: Sovereignty-Association for Quebec

Economic issues aside, it is not clear that Option D, that is, sovereignty-association, would have international or foreign policy implications significantly different from those entailed by Option C. Option D can therefore be considered quite briefly. Since sovereignty-association would make the break with Canada appear less 'clean' and open it up to greater ambiguities of interpretation, it might pose a slightly more puzzling problem for foreign powers during the transitional phase when international recognition of Quebec's new status was being pursued. This would be a temporary difficulty at most, however, and it is even possible that the situation would work the other way: that is, to the extent that formal association with Canada would demonstrate Ottawa's acceptance of Quebec's decision for independence, it could help to lessen the delicacy of the situation from the viewpoint of foreign powers by making it easier for them to recognize Quebec

From the tactical point of view, on the other hand, an association agreement might have considerable significance for foreign policy if only because it would indicate that Canada and Quebec intended to concert their positions on many foreign policy issues and perhaps maintain an integrated defence establishment. Both countries might thereby rescue some of the bargaining power that each of them would otherwise have lost as a result of their separation. They would be in a better position, in particular, to deal with the 'divide-and-rule' tactics that might become tempting to Washington. They might also be able to economize on representational facilities and personnel.[34] To the extent that they were able to hold substantive policy positions in common, there might be circumstances in which the separation actually served in a marginal way to increase their combined power; for example they would now exercise two votes instead of one in multilateral international organizations. Since this sort of co-operation might disappoint the more ardent of Quebec's nationalists, as well as the more resentful of the divorced Canadians, both governments might find it difficult for domestic political reasons to carry the policy very far, particularly in highly visible situations and especially at the beginning. In time, however, the pattern of co-operation, once successfully initiated, would probably grow.

All this assumes, of course, that Quebec's acquisition of sovereignty has been achieved by more or less amicable means, and that no deep-seated residue of bitterness and hostility remains in anglophone Canada. From the point of view of practical self-interest, there may be little doubt that in the foreign policy field, as in others, the most sensible arrangement after separation would be the maintenance of closely co-operative working relationships. From the political point of view, however, the assumption that the 'Canadians' would be so moderately disposed in the wake of a separation agreement that they would accept such a relationship appears to be highly unrealistic, especially since many of the basic societal determinants of the 'brokerage style' in Canadian politics would have been undermined by the separation itself. A spirit of vengeful hostility might well follow the partition, and if it led to policies that had the effect of creating a reciprocal measure of ill will on Quebec's side, there would be a genuine possibility of these attitudes becoming permanently ingrained. The difficulties, moreover, could arise as much from policies *within* the two countries as from relations between them: for example, in reference to their respective treatments of English- and French-speaking minorities in the post-separation period. A foreign policy corresponding to sovereignty-association might, therefore, be easily executed; it would not be easily instituted.

Conclusions

It should be clear from the foregoing that in terms of foreign policy, each of the four options considered is viable, assuming appropriate circumstances of domestic politics. In other words, none of the constitutional possibilities envisaged in the project appears to pose a *conclusive* disadvantage in terms of foreign policy for either 'Canada' or Quebec, although the precise distribution of probable costs and benefits obviously varies marginally from one arrangement to the next, particularly if one moves from Option A or B to Option C or D. That the options are internationally workable is a reflection ultimately of Canada's relatively modest size and unusually secure geopolitical position. The international community must be regarded as benignly indifferent to the constitutional relationships between Canada and Quebec. Some of the members of that community — for example, the United States — may have preferences, but given the existing political and economic realities, which would act as constraints on Canada-Quebec policies abroad under *any* constitutional circumstance, other nations are unlikely to regard their own preferences as vital to their national interests. From the purely international point of view, therefore, Canadians — and Quebecers — are free to devise whatever constitutional arrangements they like. They should not assume, however, that devising the constitution they like will automatically allow them to choose the foreign policies they wish.

Notes

1. For a discussion of these and related concepts, see K.J. Holsti, *International Politics: A Framework for Analysis*, 2d ed. (Englewood Cliffs, N.J.: Prentice-Hall, 1972), especially Chapters 4, 5, and 6.

2. The following paragraphs are adapted from Denis Stairs, "Devolution and Foreign Policy: Prospects and Possibilities," in *Options: Proceedings of the Conference on the Future of the Canadian Federation* (Toronto: University of Toronto Press, 1977), especially pp. 143–45. For the official Ottawa view, see the Honourable Paul Martin, *Federalism and International Relations* (Ottawa: Queen's Printer, 1968) and the Honourable Mitchell Sharp, *Federalism and International Conferences on Education: A Supplement to Federalism and International Relations* (Ottawa: Queen's Printer, 1968).

3. The 'textbook' example is provided by Canada's inability to ratify a number of internationally negotiated labour conventions. The country has avoided international censure partly because the record of other powers is also mixed, but more because provincial labour codes already meet or exceed international standards.

4.   The Americans have a similar difficulty arising, not from the power of state governments, but from Congress's independence of the executive. There are occasions, of course, when inability to make firm commitments is tactically helpful for hard-pressed negotiators.

5.   The weakness of the Foreign Investment Review Agency seems to be due in part to this factor.

6.   Officials of the Commission of the European Community, for example, sometimes complain that negotiations with Canada over such matters as fisheries are inconveniently prolonged by Ottawa's need to consult with Newfoundland and other Atlantic provinces. (Brussels, confidential interviews, Autumn 1979.)

7.   This results from the number and range of intergovernmental dealings with American authorities. Melancholy officials in the Department of External Affairs have been known to comment that on matters of Canadian-American relations, "The Ambassador in Washington is often the last to know."

8.   It has been argued that one of Canada's bargaining advantages under current circumstances is that Ottawa is able to arrange its positions much more easily than Washington. See Gilbert R. Winham, "Choice and Strategy in Continental Relations," in W. Andrew Axline *et al.*, *Continental Community? Independence and Integration in North America* (Toronto: McClelland and Stewart, 1974).

9.   This possibility is exemplified by the Clark government's commitment to give Newfoundland full ownership and control of the resources under its coastal waters.

10.   This would not be entirely new. Such difficulties arose, for example, in some of the francophone conferences in Africa in the late 1960s when a number of African governments complained about the procedural harangues over the status of the Quebec delegation. (Ottawa, confidential interviews, 1972–1973.)

11.   In relation, for example, to resources of the sea and the seabed.

12.   As in the context of francophone cultural issues. Even here, however, it could be argued that New Brunswick and Ontario also have a substantial stake in the outcomes of pertinent negotiations.

13.   There might, however, be spill-over effects in other policy areas as a result of the confused perceptions of other powers.

14.   Acadians in New Brunswick might wish, of course, to challenge the exclusivity of this claim.

15.   It should be understood, however, that at least some officials in Ottawa are convinced that even the existing umbrella agreements have given the Quebec authorities too much latitude. They would like to see these agreements more restrictively defined. (Confidential interviews.)

16.   Paris, confidential interviews, November 1979. There is a problem, of course, in that once immigrants are admitted to Quebec, there is nothing to prevent them from moving to other parts of Canada.

17.   For a brief account, see Louis Sabourin, "Quebec's International Activity Rests on Idea of Competence," *International Perspectives* (March/April 1977), pp. 3–7.

18.   These are primarily in educational and related fields. Details can be obtained from the annual reports of the Ministry of Intergovernmental Affairs. The activities involved are not usually identified as 'development assistance'. (Variations on the term 'co-operation' seem to be preferred.) But the flavour is made very explicit in the Quebec government's white paper on sovereignty-association. See Québec, Conseil exécutif, *Québec-Canada: A New Deal* (Quebec: Éditeur Officiel, 1979), p. 96.

19. France is the obvious possibility, although its present official posture is to treat the matter as a domestic issue.

20. Thereby following a pattern earlier established by Canada itself. See R. MacGregor Dawson, *The Development of Dominion Status, 1900–1936* (London: Oxford University Press, 1937).

21. This assumes, of course, that the balance of 'Canada' has remained united. It is conceivable that the country would balkanize.

22. As measured by population, gross national product, standing armed forces, and the like.

23. The Parti québécois has always assumed that such reactions could be contained. This could well be a fundamental miscalculation.

24. For my own views, such as they are, see Stairs, "Devolution and Foreign Policy," pp. 123–34.

25. This is made explicit in Québec, Conseil exécutif, pp. 56–57, 95–96. The references to NATO, however, are slightly ambiguous, and there is some indication that the régime might regard its involvement in NORAD as sufficient practical fulfilment of its NATO commitments. The association of NORAD with NATO is an old Canadian custom usually overlooked by other NATO allies.

26. Ottawa might in any case encounter a practical difficulty in that it would have lost its principal source of francophone technical assistance personnel.

27. The white paper on sovereignty-association deals with such questions as citizenship and arrangements for the movement of labour, but makes no mention of immigration policy.

28. See Québec, Conseil exécutif, pp. 56–57.

29. This would depend to some extent on the degree to which issues were 'linked' during the course of negotiation, but, even without explicit linkages, the Quebec government would presumably be interested in maintaining a warm climate of diplomatic credit in Washington.

30. See Sabourin, "Quebec's International Activity . . ."

31. These diplomats might be encouraged to make the move in part by changes in 'Canadian' attitudes towards francophone public servants in general. Talent might also be available from other foreign service departments, for example, Industry, Trade and Commerce.

32. That is, assuming that this arrangement would not be diplomatically awkward.

33. The possible effects of changes in the structure of the North American state system are considered briefly in Daniel LaTouche, "Quebec and the North American Subsystem: One Possible Scenario," *International Organization* 28 (Autumn 1974): 955–59.

34. The white paper on sovereignty-association notes that it "does not exclude the possibility that ... Québec ... may share with Canada some of its responsibilities toward foreign countries." Québec, Conseil exécutif, p. 95.

The Author

DENIS STAIRS is Professor and Chairman of Political Science at Dalhousie University. He was Director of Dalhousie's Centre for Foreign Policy Studies from 1970 to 1975. His research interests are in the field of Canadian defence and foreign policy. Professor Stairs is past-President of the Canadian Political Science Association.

Les affaires extérieures :
la perspective juridique

IVAN BERNIER
Université Laval

Table des matières

Les affaires extérieures :
la perspective juridique

Introduction

Avant de chercher à dégager, dans le domaine des affaires extérieures, les implications juridiques des quatre options constitutionnelles que nous connaissons, il importe d'abord de bien se situer par rapport au droit existant, tant au plan constitutionnel qu'international. Les éléments essentiels à envisager, de ce point de vue, sont le statut international du Canada, la répartition des pouvoirs extérieurs en droit interne canadien ainsi que le statut international des provinces.

Au regard du droit international, le Canada, depuis l'adoption du Statut de Westminster en 1931, constitue un État souverain doté de la pleine personnalité internationale, juridiquement égal aux autres États souverains et responsable, vis-à-vis la communauté internationale, pour tous les actes contraires au droit international commis sur son territoire[1]. De ce point de vue, il ne peut en aucune façon se réfugier derrière sa constitution fédérale pour échapper aux obligations qui lui incombent en vertu du droit coutumier international ou de traités en vigueur[2]. S'il est incapable, pour des motifs de compétence interne, de s'engager dans un domaine donné, il doit ou bien s'abstenir ou bien négocier un traitement particulier dont le contenu sera explicité dans une clause typique dite *clause fédérale*. De fait, le Canada, à plusieurs reprises dans le passé, a dû avoir recours à de tels expédients. Encore tout récemment, dans les derniers accords rattachés à l'Accord général sur les tarifs douaniers et le commerce (GATT), il préférait s'abstenir de tout engagement en ce qui concerne les politiques d'achat des provinces et obtenait, pour ce qui est du Code sur les obstacles techniques au commerce, que son engagement se limite à prendre toutes les mesures raisonnables en son pouvoir pour assurer le respect de celui-ci par les provinces. Ainsi donc, nonobstant son statut d'État souverain en droit international, le Canada apparaît à certains égards handicapé dans la conduite de ses relations extérieures, et les États étrangers se voient contraints d'une certaine façon d'en tenir compte.

Dans de telles conditions, il est presque inévitable que la reconnaissance d'une personnalité internationale restreinte au profit des provinces soit perçue comme une solution possible à des problèmes précis. Le droit international, nonobstant ce que certains constitutionnalistes canadiens ont pu affirmer[3], n'a pas d'objection fondamentale à ce type de solution. Mais ainsi qu'il est apparu lors des discussions qui ont entouré la rédaction de l'article 6 de la *Convention de Vienne sur le droit des traités*, le fondement premier de cette personnalité internationale restreinte ne peut résider ailleurs que dans la constitution interne de l'État concerné. Au point de départ, donc, seul l'État souverain qu'est le Canada peut être considéré comme sujet de droit international; les provinces, pour leur part, peuvent être acceptées comme des sujets dérivés de droit international dans la mesure où la constitution du Canada le permet, et où les autres États souverains consentent à traiter avec ces dernières[4].

Mais que dit la constitution du Canada sur le partage des compétences dans le domaine des affaires extérieures[5]? La seule disposition de l'Acte de l'Amérique du Nord britannique 1867 qui porte explicitement sur le sujet est devenue caduque en 1931 : elle octroyait tout simplement au Parlement fédéral le pouvoir de mettre en œuvre au Canada les traités de l'Empire. Depuis, la théorie, la jurisprudence et la pratique constitutionnelles sont venues préciser les données fondamentales du partage des compétences dans ce domaine. S'agissant d'abord du *treaty-making power*, l'opinion la plus répandue veut que l'exécutif fédéral, à titre d'héritier de la prérogative royale en matière de relations extérieures, soit le détenteur unique du pouvoir de conclure des traités avec l'étranger. Bien que ce point de vue ait parfois été contesté, particulièrement chez les auteurs québécois, et bien que la question n'ait jamais été résolue judiciairement, la prépondérance quasi absolue du pouvoir central, à l'heure actuelle, apparaît en pratique difficilement contestable, au moins au niveau des contacts officiels entre les États. Au niveau des échanges informels ou des relations transnationales, si l'on préfère, les provinces, en revanche, ont eu tendance à multiplier les contacts avec diverses institutions dans plusieurs pays de telle sorte qu'à l'heure actuelle, un vaste réseau de relations s'est tissé entre celles-ci et l'étranger[6]. S'agissant d'autre part de la mise en œuvre des traités du Canada au plan interne, la jurisprudence a clairement établi que celle-ci relevait du point de vue législatif de l'autorité compétente suivant l'objet du traité. Dès que le gouvernement canadien s'engage vis-à-vis un autre État dans un domaine qui ne relève pas de la compétence législative du Parlement fédéral, il s'expose à de sérieux problèmes, à moins évidemment qu'une clause fédérale n'ait été insérée dans l'accord en question ou qu'il ne se soit assuré à l'avance la collaboration des provinces. Nonobstant les nombreuses critiques formulées à l'endroit d'un tel partage des compétences en matière d'affaires extérieures et certaines allusions de la part du juge en chef Laskin à l'effet qu'un nouvel examen de la position de principe de la jurisprudence dans ce domaine pourrait être justifié, cette dichotomie fondamentale décrit parfaitement l'état actuel du droit au Canada.

Compte tenu de l'attitude du droit international vis-à-vis les États fédéraux en général et compte tenu des règles de droit constitutionnel décrites précédemment, les provinces canadiennes peuvent-elles prétendre à un quelconque statut international à l'heure actuelle? La réponse à cette question, en principe, relève de la pratique internationale. Or, cette pratique n'est pas très claire dans la mesure où elle est interprétée différemment par le gouvernement fédéral et par les provinces, particulièrement le Québec. En effet, s'il est vrai que cette dernière province a effectivement conclu des « ententes » culturelles avec la France en 1964 et 1965, sous le parapluie d'un accord France-Canada, et a été admise, à titre de « gouvernement participant », à l'Agence de coopération culturelle et technique, qui regroupe la plupart des États francophones, il faut ajouter qu'une interprétation diamétralement opposée de la signification de ces faits a été proposée dans deux livres blancs, l'un fédéral, l'autre québécois. À part la France, cette controverse paraît surtout avoir agacé les pays étrangers impliqués qui, bien que réceptifs à une solution de droit international, ne veulent en aucune façon intervenir dans les affaires canadiennes. Finalement, avec l'élection du parti québécois à la tête du gouvernement du Québec en 1976, le débat a été largement relégué à l'arrière-plan, compte tenu du désir de ce parti de réaliser l'indépendance de la province[7].

Telles sont donc, dans les grandes lignes, les données essentielles qui décrivent le cadre juridique actuel dans lequel s'insère l'action internationale du Canada. Face aux quatre grandes options constitutionnelles que l'on connaît, soit le fédéralisme renouvelé, le statut particulier, la souveraineté-association et l'indépendance, il va de soi que ce cadre est appelé à être modifié. Mais le droit lui-même a certaines exigences qui font que les possibilités de modification ne sont pas infinies : au-delà de certaines limites, la règle de droit n'a tout simplement plus d'utilité. Il faut préciser, cependant, que le rôle du droit, de même que ses exigences, varie suivant le degré d'intégration politique de la société dans laquelle il s'insère. Au niveau de la société internationale, qui est encore relativement peu intégrée, la sécurité demeure la préoccupation première. Aussi est-ce surtout par rapport à des concepts fondamentaux comme ceux de souveraineté, de responsabilité et de consentement que seront appréciés, à ce niveau, les changements envisagés au Canada. À l'intérieur même des sociétés étatiques, en revanche, le droit vise d'abord et avant tout à l'efficacité. Les principales qualités de la règle de droit seront alors la précision, la cohérence et le réalisme, et c'est en fonction de ces qualités que seront jugées, au plan interne, les diverses solutions proposées.

Dans les pages qui suivent, nous allons envisager tour à tour chacune de ces options à la lumière de ces critères généraux de sécurité et d'efficacité, en suivant dans chaque cas un cheminement identique : la dimension interne des changements proposés sera d'abord envisagée; viendra ensuite l'examen de leur dimension externe. Dans le cas du fédéralisme renouvelé et du statut particulier, l'analyse portera essentiellement sur les conséquences d'une centralisation ou d'une décentralisation accrue des pouvoirs dans le domaine des affaires extérieures. Dans le cas de la souveraineté-association et de l'indépendance, c'est le processus même de désintégration qui retiendra davantage notre attention.

Le fédéralisme renouvelé

Dans l'optique d'un fédéralisme renouvelé, l'objectif primordial qui est poursuivi, de façon générale, est la révision de la constitution, non pas dans ses données essentielles, mais plutôt sur des points précis où des changements paraissent s'imposer à la lumière de l'expérience acquise. Or, le domaine des affaires extérieures est précisément un de ces secteurs d'activité qui semblent, de l'avis général, exiger certains changements. À la source de cette insatisfaction, on peut relever en particulier deux problèmes.

Le plus fréquemment mentionné, surtout chez les juristes et les politicologues anglophones[8], a trait à la distinction traditionnelle entre le pouvoir de conclure et le pouvoir de mettre en œuvre un traité : on considère que cette distinction n'a plus sa place de nos jours et contribue à affaiblir le Canada au plan international. On fait valoir également, toujours dans le même sens, que le Canada, seul responsable au plan international, doit être en mesure de respecter tous ses engagements s'il veut conserver la confiance de ses partenaires. L'idée que les provinces puissent agir au plan international est totalement rejeté, car le Canada ne doit s'exprimer qu'avec une seule voix à l'extérieur. Déjà, à cet égard, la multiplication des contacts informels entre les provinces et l'étranger, y compris dans certains cas la mise en place de véritables réseaux de délégations, est perçue comme un danger.

Pour certains[9], cependant, particulièrement chez les juristes et les politicologues québécois, mais aussi, à l'occasion, parmi leurs confrères des provinces de l'Ouest, le véritable problème réside davantage dans l'absence d'une compréhension réelle des données provinciales et régionales de la part des autorités centrales. Cette incompréhension, souligne-t-on, a contribué à fournir une image déformée du Canada à l'étranger, surtout en matière culturelle, et a parfois même desservi carrément les intérêts des provinces.

Entre ces deux positions opposées, certains,[10] persuadés de la nécessité d'une plus grande cohésion dans la formulation de la politique extérieure canadienne, reconnaissent que l'octroi au Parlement fédéral d'un pouvoir législatif absolu en matière de mise en vigueur des traités constituerait une menace très grave à l'autonomie des provinces. Pour eux, la seule solution possible est la mise en place de mécanismes efficaces de coordination, tout en conservant le *statu quo* en ce qui concerne le partage des compétences.

Pour l'essentiel, les changements envisagés dans le cadre d'un fédéralisme renouvelé tournent autour de trois hypothèses : un pouvoir fédéral complet en matière de conclusion et de mise en vigueur des traités; un pouvoir provincial partiel en matière de conclusion des traités, correspondant au champ de compétence des provinces; le *statu quo* en ce qui regarde le partage des compétences, mais avec des mécanismes plus élaborés en ce qui regarde la coordination. Il reste maintenant à envisager l'impact de ces changements au plan interne et au plan externe.

La perspective interne

L'hypothèse d'un pouvoir fédéral complet en matière de conclusion et de mise en vigueur des traités apparaît à première vue comme une solution simple et radicale au problème de la relative incapacité du Canada au plan international. Libéré de la crainte de s'engager dans un domaine hors de sa compétence, en effet, le gouvernement canadien serait nul doute plus en mesure d'élaborer des politiques qui répondent de façon globale aux préoccupations du Canada au plan international. Sa liberté de manœuvre dans des négociations complexes comme la Ronde Tokyo s'en trouverait élargie, tout comme serait accrue de façon positive sa capacité d'agir au sein d'organismes internationaux comme l'Organisation internationale du travail ou encore sa capacité de prendre des initiatives dans des domaines comme celui des relations culturelles. En ce qui regarde, par ailleurs, l'exécution de ses engagements internationaux, la situation juridique serait claire, et une véritable cohérence enfin serait réalisée.

Mais cette solution, théoriquement très efficace, est-elle réaliste? Dans une étude récente, Donald C. Story, tout en se prononçant en faveur de celle-ci, se voit contraint d'admettre qu'elle risque pour le moment d'être assez mal reçue. « *It is indeed the third possibility, total federal authority — interestingly the least politically palatable option to many Canadians at this time in our history — which presents the fewest complications and, most important, seems to hold the greatest promise for unity in the long run* »[11].

Il est difficile de voir comment le Québec, pour ne prendre que cette province, accepterait un changement qui irait à l'encontre de toutes ses prises de positions antérieures. Même pour les autres provinces et même à long terme, cette solution paraît douteuse. Il se peut, effectivement, qu'elle soit la plus favorable à une certaine conception de l'unité canadienne, mais elle peut aussi être considérée, dans une autre perspective, comme une menace à cette même unité. Ici comme dans bien d'autres domaines, le jugement de valeur varie en dernier ressort suivant le point de vue que l'on adopte et l'objectif ultime que l'on poursuit. Le mieux que l'on puisse dire, dans les circonstances, c'est que la solution envisagée, théoriquement efficace par rapport à un problème donné, soit celui de l'unité canadienne, ne l'est pas en pratique parce qu'elle ignore que cette même unité repose sur la diversité.

Aux yeux du Québec, du moins tel qu'il s'est exprimé de 1965 à 1975, la solution la plus réaliste, dans le contexte politique canadien, consisterait à reconnaître aux provinces le droit de conclure des accords internationaux dans leurs domaines de compétence propre[12]. Cette solution, tout comme la précédente, présente l'avantage de mettre en relation le pouvoir de conclure un traité et le pouvoir de l'exécuter : à cet égard, elle peut facilement être qualifiée de cohérente. Malheureusement, toujours au strict plan interne, elle souffre d'un double défaut. D'abord, elle est moins claire qu'il ne peut paraître à première vue. Fréquemment, en effet, il arrivera qu'une question abordée au plan international implique à la fois des aspects de compétence provinciale et des aspects de compétence fédérale. Qui alors, du fédéral ou des provinces, sera constitutionnellement responsable des négociations? La réponse à cette question n'est pas simple et, quelle que soit sa nature, risque de soulever des désaccords. Et, il n'est pas sûr qu'elle intéresse vraiment d'autres provinces que le Québec. Seul l'Ontario, jusqu'à date, a exprimé un souhait semblable, et, même là, l'exercice de cette compétence nouvelle dans le domaine des affaires extérieures est rendu sujet à l'approbation préalable des autorités centrales[13]. Au surplus, comme il est prévisible que certaines provinces seraient difficilement en mesure d'assumer adéquatement une telle responsabilité, il faudrait prévoir un mécanisme quelconque de délégation.

Dans ces conditions, il n'est pas surprenant de constater que la position commune de la plupart des projets de révision constitutionnelle est à l'effet qu'un *treaty-making power* provincial n'est pas nécessaire, une collaboration plus étroite entre les autorités fédérale et provinciales devant suffire à assurer une représentation plus réelle des particularismes provinciaux[14]. De façon générale, donc, ces projets suggèrent le *statu quo* en ce qui concerne la dichotomie entre le pouvoir de conclure et le pouvoir de mettre en œuvre un traité, mais créent à la charge du gouvernement fédéral une obligation de consultation préalable dans les domaines de compétence qui intéressent les provinces, et prévoient dans certains cas une ratification par une deuxième chambre de type fédéral. Dans cette même perspective, les accords informels à caractère administratif de la part des provinces, tels qu'ils se pratiquent actuellement, seraient officiellement reconnus de même que le droit des provinces à une représentation à l'extérieur, mais à condition que ces dernières agissent à l'intérieur des grandes lignes de la politique canadienne.

Toutefois, entre cette position et celle d'un Québec préoccupé par sa survie et désireux de faire connaître au reste du monde, mais particulièrement aux pays francophones, qu'il existe, la distance est manifestement assez grande. Dans ces circonstances, on en arrive à se demander si la recherche d'une solution uniforme, valable pour l'ensemble du Canada, qui soit en même temps claire, cohérente et réaliste, n'est pas une illusion. À cet égard, on serait tenté de conclure que le fédéralisme renouvelé n'offre, en ce qui concerne les relations extérieures, que des solutions de type *second best*. Mais peut-être ce genre de solutions, dans un contexte fédéral, est-il le seul possible au regard du droit international?

La perspective externe

Il va de soi que, si le Canada devait modifier sa constitution dans le sens d'une intégration plus complète des pouvoirs dans le domaine des affaires extérieures, les autres pays n'y verraient pas d'inconvénients. Au contraire, dans la mesure où ils n'auraient plus à envisager des arrangements spéciaux pour faciliter la participation du Canada à telle ou telle convention internationale, dans la mesure où ils n'auraient plus à redouter que le Canada n'utilise le prétexte de son partage des compétences au plan interne pour esquiver ses responsabilités au plan international, dans la mesure enfin où ils n'auraient plus à faire face à des « querelles de drapeaux » au sein d'organismes internationaux comme l'Agence de coopération culturelle et technique, les pays étrangers ne pourraient que s'en réjouir[15]. Pour ces derniers, en effet, toute solution simple qui élimine les incertitudes et les conflits inutiles est *a priori* souhaitable. Mais depuis longtemps déjà, ces pays savent également qu'au-delà des arrangements internes dans le domaine des affaires extérieures, c'est d'abord et avant tout le caractère fédéral d'un pays qui soulève, au plan international, des difficultés.

Par « caractère fédéral », il faut entendre cette réalité politique qui fait que, même si tous les pouvoirs dans le domaine des affaires extérieures sont dévolus, au sein d'un État fédératif, aux autorités centrales, dans certains cas, il demeure pratiquement impossible à celles-ci de s'impliquer dans un domaine ou un autre sans l'assentiment des gouvernements décentralisés, ou à tout le moins de représentants désignés des régions. L'expérience des États-Unis et de l'Australie, deux États fédéraux où les autorités centrales sont dotées de pouvoirs absolues en

matière d'affaires extérieures, paraît très significative à cet
égard. À plusieurs reprises, en effet, les gouvernements américains et australiens ont dû reconnaître que leur contexte
politique fédéral limitait leur marge de manœuvre au plan
international; tout comme le Canada, et pratiquement dans les
mêmes situations, ils ont été contraints de rechercher un
traitement particulier et parfois même de s'abstenir[16]. Parmi les
domaines où des difficultés communes se sont manifestées de
façon plus évidente, malgré les contextes juridiques distincts, on
peut mentionner ceux du travail et des droits de l'homme. À la
lumière de ces expériences, les États étrangers ont acquis une
certaine dose de réalisme qui fait que, même s'ils peuvent
préférer une solution simple et radicale au problème des États
fédéraux, ils demeurent néanmoins ouverts à toute hypothèse
de solution compatible avec le maintien d'un minimum de
sécurité juridique.

À cet égard, il faut reconnaître que l'hypothèse d'une
décentralisation du *treaty-making power* correspondant globale-
ment au partage des compétences législatives, accompagnée
d'un droit de légation des provinces, risque de recevoir un
accueil plutôt froid à l'extérieur. Au mieux, les États étrangers
accepteraient de conclure des accords bilatéraux avec les
provinces canadiennes dans des domaines relevant clairement
de leur compétence exclusive, ainsi qu'en témoignent les accords
informels assez nombreux conclus avec certaines d'entre elles.
Même là, la perspective d'avoir à négocier avec dix entités plutôt
qu'une pourrait suffire, dans certains cas, à décourager les
contacts, ou encore à les limiter aux provinces les plus importantes, avec le résultat que les autres, faute d'interlocuteurs, se
verraient coupées du monde extérieur. La possibilité d'une
délégation de compétence aux autorités centrales pourrait
toujours être envisagée dans ce dernier cas, mais elle ne ferait
que souligner l'existence d'un autre problème important, celui
de la responsabilité internationale.

Même si les pays étrangers acceptent de traiter directement
avec les provinces, il n'est pas dit qu'ils renoncent par le fait
même à tenir le gouvernement fédéral responsable pour les
engagements de ces dernières. Diverses hypothèses ont déjà été
envisagées à cet égard, allant d'une responsabilité exclusive de
l'État fédéral à une responsabilité exclusive des États membres,
en passant par une responsabilité primaire des autorités centrales et une responsabilité secondaire des gouvernements
régionaux ou *vice versa*[17]. Mais au regard du droit international,

compte tenu des principes fondamentaux de souveraineté et de responsabilité qui expriment cette préoccupation de sécurité dont nous avons déjà parlé, la solution qui s'impose *a priori* est celle de la responsabilité de principe de l'État fédéral, sauf renonciation des États étrangers qui acceptent, lorsqu'ils traitent avec les provinces, de tenir ces dernières seules responsables. Vu l'existence de dix provinces, et vu la variété de comportements que peuvent adopter les États étrangers, on perçoit facilement le danger de confusion qui pourrait en résulter. Évidemment, si une seule province était impliquée, ce danger ne serait plus le même.

En ce qui concerne le droit de légation des provinces, sa concrétisation dépendra ultimement de la volonté des États étrangers d'établir des relations de droit international avec ces dernières. Plusieurs provinces, ainsi qu'on l'a déjà mentionné, ont des délégations à l'extérieur. En général, ces délégations ne bénéficient d'aucun traitement diplomatique ou consulaire; en pratique, toutefois, il serait probablement assez facile de les faire accéder au statut de consulat. La situation se complique lorsqu'on envisage une participation directe des provinces à des organisations internationales. Dans la vaste majorité des cas, en effet, la charte constitutive de ces organisations ne prévoit pas la participation d'entités autres que des États souverains. Or, il est pratiquement impensable que ces chartes soient modifiées pour faire place aux dix provinces canadiennes, d'autant plus qu'un tel procédé accorderait au Canada une place hors de proportion avec son importance réelle dans le fonctionnement de ces organisations[18]. La seule hypothèse réaliste que l'on puisse envisager à cet égard est qu'une province comme le Québec agisse, dans certains cas, comme représentant du Canada au sein d'organismes culturels francophones.

De façon générale, donc, une décentralisation accrue des pouvoirs dans le domaine des affaires extérieures qui s'alignerait sur le partage des compétences législatives paraît pour le moins problématique au plan externe. La solution idéale, aux yeux des États étrangers, serait que le Canada invente des mécanismes de collaboration interne qui soient de nature à faciliter son action au plan international et à assurer l'exécution de ses engagements dans quelque domaine que ce soit. Comme cette solution, pour être vraiment efficace, implique un minimum de contrôle politique des provinces sur les décisions des autorités centrales en matière de politique extérieure, il n'est pas certain que les États étrangers puissent s'en tirer sans quelques inconvénients. Dans la mesure où ce contrôle politique des provinces s'exercerait vraisemblablement par l'intermédiaire d'une deuxième chambre, l'expérience du Sénat américain ne peut qu'inciter à une certaine prudence.

Le statut particulier

La notion de statut particulier, entendue dans un contexte fédéral, signifie juridiquement qu'un ou plusieurs des gouvernements locaux bénéficient d'un statut distinct au regard même de la constitution. Au Canada, c'est d'abord et avant tout en rapport avec le Québec qu'un tel concept a été mis de l'avant. Dans le domaine des affaires extérieures plus particulièrement, cette notion de statut particulier implique presque nécessairement la reconnaissance d'un *treaty-making power* restreint en fonction de certaines matières précises. À titre d'exemple, on peut facilement imaginer une situation où le Québec assumerait la responsabilité première de ses relations culturelles avec les pays francophones; à la limite, il est même permis d'envisager une situation où le Québec agirait au nom du Canada tout entier. Dans un cas comme dans l'autre, cependant, on considère qu'une reconnaissance constitutionnelle de ce statut particulier serait requise, surtout vis-à-vis l'extérieur.

Pour certains, l'octroi d'un statut particulier ne nécessite pas obligatoirement une atteinte, dans la constitution, à l'égalité de principe de toutes les provinces. Ainsi, pour la Commission de l'unité canadienne, il suffirait, pour arriver au même résultat, que l'on donne

> (...) à toutes les provinces accès aux compétences dont le Québec a besoin pour préserver sa culture et son héritage particuliers, mais d'une manière qui leur permette, si c'est leur volonté, de ne pas exercer ces compétences et d'en confier l'exercice à Ottawa. Deux méthodes permettent d'emprunter cette voie. L'une grouperait ces matières sous le manteau de la compétence concurrente, assortie de la prépondérance provinciale, ce qui aurait pour effet de laisser aux provinces le choix d'exercer ou non leur pouvoir prépondérant en ces domaines. L'autre méthode consisterait à inscrire dans la constitution un mécanisme de délégation législative ou interparlementaire[19].

Assez curieusement, un des seuls exemples d'une telle façon de procéder a trait au domaine des affaires extérieures, plus particulièrement à celui de l'immigration. Ce dernier domaine en est un de compétence concurrente — le Parlement fédéral aussi bien que les assemblées législatives provinciales peuvent légiférer en matière d'immigration — mais avec prépondérance fédérale. Jusqu'à tout récemment, les autorités fédérales occupaient pratiquement l'ensemble du champ, ne laissant aux provinces que de maigres pouvoirs en matière d'accueil des immigrants. Toutefois, à la suite de demandes réitérées de la part du Québec, le gouvernement fédéral, en 1978, acceptait de conclure avec cette province une entente aux termes de laquelle la sélection des ressortissants étrangers désireux de s'établir en permanence au Québec s'effectuerait sur une base conjointe et paritaire, selon des critères québécois et canadiens[20].

Une telle entente, autorisée par l'article 109(2) de la *Loi sur l'immigration*, vient donc préciser la portée de la Loi en définissant la marge de pouvoir normatif et décisionnel laissée au Québec. Dans la mesure où aucune autre province n'a manifesté d'intérêt pour un arrangement semblable, on peut donc voir là une forme atténuée de statut particulier.

Quelle que soit la méthode utilisée pour réaliser le statut particulier, il est clair que celui-ci soulève des problèmes assez délicats, tant en ce qui concerne l'élaboration interne de la politique étrangère canadienne qu'en ce qui concerne la réalisation externe de cette politique.

La perspective interne

L'hypothèse d'un statut particulier dans le domaine des affaires extérieures fait appel, en droit, à des critères de démarcation suffisamment précis pour permettre de distinguer une province des autres. Dès l'abord, on peut sérieusement se demander si, mis à part le Québec, il existe d'autres provinces au Canada qui peuvent prétendre à un tel statut. En effet, il est difficile de voir ce qu'une quelconque province anglophone pourrait réclamer dans le domaine des affaires extérieures qui ne pourrait pas également être réclamé par toutes les autres. Ainsi, s'il est vrai que la plupart des provinces ont des intérêts économiques relativement distincts qu'elles ont cherché à faire valoir de plus en plus énergiquement à l'extérieur ces dernières années, il demeure que toute solution formelle à ce problème vaudrait vraisemblablement pour chaque province, quelle que soit la nature exacte de l'intérêt économique en cause. Dans le cas du Québec, en revanche, sa spécificité culturelle paraît offrir à première vue un critère susceptible de justifier l'octroi d'un statut particulier à cette province dans le domaine des affaires extérieures. Mais en est-il vraiment ainsi, et comment arriver à délimiter de façon précise le domaine de compétence du Québec, à supposer qu'il en soit ainsi?

Il ne suffit certes pas, dans un tel contexte, d'en référer à la compétence générale du Québec dans le domaine des affaires culturelles : toutes les provinces à cet égard sont sur un pied d'égalité. La notion de francophonie, si elle permet de mieux cerner le champ d'intérêt particulier du Québec, ne nous éclaire pas davantage sur la spécificité des besoins du Québec en matière de relations extérieures. En réalité, le seul besoin qui puisse justifier pour la province un statut particulier est de nature d'abord et avant tout psychologique : pour sa survie et son développement en tant que minorité culturelle, le Québec a besoin d'un reflet de lui-même à l'extérieur. À l'encontre des minorités francophones de Suisse et de Belgique, le Québec, en tant que principal représentant de la minorité francophone canadienne, se trouve enclavé dans un milieu culturel qui lui est étranger. À l'encontre des autres provinces du Canada, il ne se voit qu'imparfaitement dans l'image que projette le Canada à l'extérieur. C'est pourquoi le Québec a tant insisté depuis une vingtaine d'années pour avoir des rapports directs avec l'étranger, surtout en ce qui concerne les relations avec les pays francophones[21]. À la suite des disputes occasionnées par les ententes culturelles France-Québec, le Canada a voulu ignorer cette réalité essentielle en signant une entente culturelle avec la Belgique sans le concours du Québec. Or, l'entente est restée lettre morte jusqu'à ce qu'un nouvel arrangement avec la Belgique autorise la création d'une sous-commission culturelle Québec-Belgique directement responsable des relations entre les deux gouvernements[22]. De là à admettre un statut particulier au Québec en matière de relations culturelles avec les pays francophones en général, il n'y a qu'un pas. Mais pour franchir ce dernier, encore faut-il circonscrire en termes juridiques ce besoin essentiel de la province de communiquer directement avec le courant francophone international.

La tâche n'est pas facile. Dans la mesure où les relations culturelles ne sont qu'un aspect de la politique extérieure d'un pays, il est manifeste que le Québec pourrait difficilement agir en toute liberté dans ses relations avec les pays francophones sans que ne surgisse le risque de conflit avec la politique extérieure du Canada. Néanmoins, il y a des solutions à ce problème. On peut chercher à délimiter avec précision le type d'actes qui pourraient être posés dans le domaine des affaires extérieures de manière à minimiser les possibilités de conflits : on pourrait autoriser de façon générale les accords essentiellement administratifs, comme c'est déjà le cas en Suisse, par exemple, de même que tous les autres actes plus formels couverts par un accord-cadre entre le Canada et le pays étranger concerné. Il est douteux, cependant, qu'une telle solution soit perçue par le Québec comme la reconnaissance d'un statut particulier, car il s'agirait là essentiellement de la reconnaissance formelle de pratiques déjà existantes. Une autre solution serait de prévoir une compétence concurrente des gouvernements canadiens et québécois en ce qui concerne les relations culturelles avec les pays francophones, avec prépondérance au gouvernement fédéral. Une telle hypothèse aurait l'avantage de permettre au gouvernement central d'agir au nom des provinces autres que le Québec sans engager foncièrement le Québec. Mais le Québec se retrouverait dans une situation d'infériorité qui pourrait très bien s'avérer inacceptable au niveau des principes. Resterait alors une troisième possibilité qui est celle qui a été exploitée dans l'entente Québec-Canada sur l'immigration : une compétence concurrente aux gouvernements d'Ottawa et de Québec, avec droit de véto pour chacun d'eux. Cette solution aurait l'avantage de sauvegarder à la fois les intérêts du Québec et du Canada tout en les contraignant à un minimum de collaboration.

Quoi qu'il en soit, au-delà de ces diverses hypothèses axées sur l'octroi d'un statut particulier au Québec dans le domaine des relations culturelles, on comprendra que les deux principaux problèmes juridiques à résoudre au plan interne ont trait, d'une part, à la relation à établir entre le bénéficiaire de ce statut et les autres provinces (problème du critère de distinction) et, d'autre part, à la relation à établir entre ce même bénéficiaire et le pouvoir central (problème de la coordination des politiques). Or, ces deux problèmes ne sont pas du même ordre. Le premier, pour être résolu de façon efficace, exige que le langage utilisé pour désigner le bénéficiaire ne laisse aucune place à des demandes identiques de la part d'autres provinces : autrement, le statut particulier, plutôt que de répondre à un problème particulier, sera davantage source de nouvelles difficultés. À cet égard, il n'est pas nécessaire de rappeler jusqu'à quel point la notion de statut particulier semble soulever à prime abord un sentiment de méfiance, particulièrement chez les provinces anglophones. Un des documents mis de l'avant par la

Colombie-Britannique est fort éloquent : « *Flexibility should not be achieved by granting some subject matters to some provinces and denying those matters to other provinces* [23]. »

Le second problème, qui a trait aux relations entre la province bénéficiaire du statut particulier et le pouvoir central, exige la mise en place d'un mécanisme juridique qui garantisse à la fois l'autonomie décisionnelle de la province en cause et la prise en considération des grandes orientations de la politique étrangère du Canada. À défaut d'un tel mécanisme, le statut particulier sera considéré ou bien comme une structure dépourvue de toute signification ou bien comme une épine dans le flanc de la politique étrangère canadienne. Un équilibre délicat devra donc être réalisé pour que le statut particulier soit perçu en pratique comme une solution efficace.

Un tel statut, par ailleurs, vise à répondre à un problème précis qui n'est pas celui de la majorité des provinces. Dans la mesure où l'on considère la division traditionnelle entre le pouvoir de conclure un traité et le pouvoir de légiférer pour mettre en vigueur un traité comme un problème important, on devrait trouver une solution adéquate à celui-ci parallèlement à une solution au statut particulier. Cette dernière serait sans doute axée sur la mise en place de nouveaux mécanismes de consultation, car, si elle rejoint pour l'essentiel le contenu du statut particulier, celui-ci perd concrètement sa signification; on retombe alors purement et simplement dans la problématique du fédéralisme renouvelé.

La perspective externe

Au regard du droit international, le concept de statut particulier soulève sensiblement le même type de problèmes que le fédéralisme renouvelé. La différence essentielle est que l'incertitude et l'incohérence susceptible de résulter de la multiplicité de représentation internationale se trouve ramenée à un niveau beaucoup plus acceptable, dans le cas du statut particulier, qui n'implique en principe qu'une seule province. De fait, l'expérience passée démontre que le droit international n'est pas réticent à reconnaître divers types de statut particulier. Qu'il s'agisse simplement de la reconnaissance du fait que la signature d'un État n'engage pas automatiquement certaines parties de son territoire, qui bénéficient d'un statut d'autonomie, comme, par exemple, le Danemark et les Îles Féroé [24], ou qu'il s'agisse de l'admission officielle d'États membres de fédérations au sein d'organismes internationaux, comme ce fut le cas, pour des raisons pratiques, jusqu'en 1934 pour le Wurtemberg et la Bavière au sein de la Commission européenne[25], ou comme c'est le cas, pour des raisons essentiellement politiques, de l'Ukraine et de la Byolorussie au sein de l'ONU[26], il appert que la capacité d'adaptation du droit international est pratiquement sans limite, pourvu que les données juridiques essentielles soient claires.

Aussi peut-on considérer qu'un statut particulier pour le Québec, à condition qu'il soit délimité clairement au plan constitutionnel, aurait de bonnes chances d'être accepté et reconnu au plan international. En revanche, si ce statut devait découler essentiellement d'arrangements administratifs, il est plausible que la communauté internationale des États serait davantage réticente à en prendre acte. De ce point de vue, on peut considérer que la sécurité juridique essentielle au droit international impose des limites certaines à la façon de réaliser un statut particulier dans le domaine des affaires extérieures.

La souveraineté-association

L'hypothèse de la souveraineté-association implique d'abord, en droit interne, un processus de désintégration dont l'aboutissement ultime est l'apparition d'un nouvel ordre juridique parallèle et égal à l'ancien. Ce nouvel ordre peut se réaliser dans la continuité juridique, comme ce fut le cas pour le Canada vis-à-vis la Grande-Bretagne, ou il peut résulter d'une rupture complète avec l'ancien, comme ce fut le cas pour les États-Unis. Simultanément, la souveraineté-association implique aussi la mise en place de mécanismes de collaboration suffisamment développés pour permettre la réalisation d'une union économique ou à tout le moins d'un marché commun. Évidemment, ce double processus a un impact considérable à l'extérieur. Durant la période de négociations, d'abord, les États étrangers auront l'obligation de respecter la souveraineté du Canada en n'intervenant pas dans ses affaires internes. Par la suite, lorsque le démembrement du Canada sera un fait accompli, ils auront à se prononcer sur l'existence d'un nouvel État. Et comme ce nouvel État sera issu du démembrement d'un autre État, ils auront encore à s'interroger sur ce qu'il advient des engagements pris antérieurement par le Canada. Finalement, du fait que le Canada demeurera un territoire économique unique, ils auront à traiter avec certaines institutions dont les pouvoirs et les responsabilités demeurent encore à définir. En somme, parce qu'il implique essentiellement un passage du droit constitutionnel au droit international, c'est le processus même de réalisation de la souveraineté-association qui intéresse le domaine des affaires extérieures.

La perspective interne

Le premier problème que soulève l'hypothèse de la souveraineté-association concerne le droit de sécession des provinces. Lorsqu'il est envisagé plus particulièrement avec le Québec, référence est souvent faite au droit à l'autodétermination des Québécois; les deux concepts doivent cependant être distingués[27]. En premier lieu, le droit de sécession se présente essentiellement comme un concept de droit constitutionnel, alors que le droit à l'autodétermination est d'abord et avant tout un concept de droit international. En deuxième lieu, le droit de sécession est généralement identifié à un territoire donné, alors que le droit à l'autodétermination se rattache davantage à un peuple. Enfin, la sécession, si elle est l'expression ultime du droit à l'autodétermination, ne constitue pas la seule façon d'exercer ce droit[28]. D'un point de vue interne, et en rapport avec la souveraineté-association, le droit à l'autodétermination n'a de sens, en fait, que dans la mesure où il paraît appuyer une demande qui ne trouve point d'appui dans notre droit constitutionnel.

En effet, bien que l'A.A.N.B. 1867 ainsi que les textes constitutionnels subséquents n'interdisent pas précisément le droit de sécession, l'absence de toute mention à cet égard est généralement interprétée comme signifiant qu'un tel droit n'existe tout simplement pas[29]. Néanmoins, les auteurs sont aussi d'accord pour reconnaître que la sécession, en tant que résultat, pourrait être obtenue soit à la suite d'un amendement constitutionnel, soit à la suite d'une déclaration unilatérale d'indépendance dont l'efficacité serait internationalement reconnue. La première méthode, plus positive, implique d'une certaine façon un acquiescement, un arrangement à l'amiable avec le reste du Canada. Parce que la majorité des Canadiens, sans admettre nécessairement que le Québec bénéficie d'un quelconque droit à l'autodétermination, semblent prêts à admettre qu'une volonté clairement exprimée du Québec de se séparer devrait donner lieu à un arrangement en ce sens, cette première méthode est généralement favorisée. Quant à la seconde méthode, elle est davantage perçue comme une solution ultime dans l'hypothèse d'un désaccord complet entre le Québec et le Canada. Dans la mesure où la souveraineté-association implique, au-delà de l'indépendance du Québec, un traité d'association économique avec le reste du Canada, il paraît raisonnable d'affirmer que la déclaration unilatérale d'indépendance n'est pas compatible avec la réalisation de cette souveraineté-association. Reste donc, pour y arriver, la technique de l'amendement constitutionnel.

Un amendement d'une telle importance, cependant, ne manquerait pas de soulever de nombreux problèmes. Manifestement, le Québec ne pourrait y arriver seul en agissant en vertu de l'article 92(1) de l'A.A.N.B. 1867 : modifier la constitution du Canada pour permettre au Québec de se séparer dépasse de beaucoup la compétence accordée à la province de modifier sa propre constitution. Le Parlement fédéral ne pourrait guère plus y arriver en agissant en vertu du pouvoir d'amendement que lui reconnaît l'article 91(1). Ce pouvoir, en effet, se trouve sévèrement limité par l'interdiction qu'il comporte d'affecter de quelque façon que ce soit le partage des compétences ou encore les droits ou privilèges reconnus aux provinces ou à certaines catégories de personnes; il a été interprété de façon restrictive d'ailleurs par la Cour suprême dans son opinion dans l'*Affaire des questions soumises par le gouverneur en conseil sur la compétence législative du Parlement du Canada relativement à la Chambre haute*[30]. Dans la mesure où la sécession du Québec implique la remise à cette province de pouvoirs législatifs antérieurement détenus par le Parlement fédéral, il faudrait nécessairement avoir recours à la nouvelle procédure d'amendement que prévoit la Loi constitutionnelle de 1982[31]. Cette procédure veut qu'un amendement à la constitution ne soit adopté que sur proclamation du gouverneur général autorisé à la fois par des résolutions du Sénat et de la Chambre des communes ainsi que par les assemblées législatives d'au moins deux tiers des provinces dont la population confondue représente au moins cinquante pour cent de la population entière. Dans les cas particuliers prévus à l'article 41 de la même Loi, toutefois, il est stipulé qu'un amendement touchant à la reine, au gouverneur général ou au lieutenant-gouverneur, à l'usage du français ou de l'anglais, ou encore à la composition de la Cour suprême devra être approuvé par l'assemblée législative de chaque province. Comme la sécession pourrait théoriquement toucher à certains de ces sujets, il n'est pas interdit de penser que le consentement unanime des provinces pourrait être requis pour légaliser un tel changement.

Au-delà de cet aspect foncièrement de procédure, la sécession soulève également, au plan interne, le problème difficile du partage de l'actif et du passif de la Couronne aux droits du Canada. Diverses théories ont été élaborées en droit international pour répondre à ce problème, mais aucune n'a vraiment acquis une acceptation totale. Néanmoins, certaines conclusions très générales peuvent être dégagées. Ainsi, dans un article daté de 1978, Jean-Maurice Arbour, après avoir analysé le problème de la sécession du Québec à la lumière des données pertinentes du droit international, en arrive à formuler les quelques propositions suivantes[32]. S'agissant d'abord de la propriété publique fédérale sise dans les limites géographiques du Québec, l'actif passerait automatiquement au Québec, et ce sans compensation aucune, sauf accord spécial. En ce qui concerne la dette publique canadienne, le Québec, en se fondant sur la pratique internationale, ne serait pas obligé d'en assumer une part quelconque, bien qu'une répartition de dette ait effectivement été réalisée dans certains cas. Toutefois, l'auteur, de concert avec la plupart des publicistes, reconnaît l'existence d'une obligation morale à la charge de l'État nouveau. Dans le contexte de la souveraineté-association, il y a lieu de présumer, vue la dimension positive d'un tel arrangement, que le problème du partage de l'actif et du passif se réglerait à l'amiable.

Une fois le problème de la sécession réglé, il reste encore à envisager celui de l'association. Au plan de la procédure, le problème n'est pas exactement le même. La négociation de l'accord d'association, même si elle précède la sécession proprement dite, se situe au niveau du droit international et implique un statut d'égalité juridique entre les deux parties en cause. La conclusion d'un tel accord n'exigerait donc pas, en tant que telle, que l'on ait recours à la procédure d'amendement prévue dans la Loi constitutionnelle de 1982. Tout au plus peut-on envisager qu'un tel accord, vu son importance, serait soumis pour approbation à la Chambre des communes et au Sénat. En dehors de cette différence essentielle, cependant, il est permis de croire que la négociation de l'accord d'association procéderait plus ou moins de la même façon que les discussions sur la sécession, vu l'intime relation entre les deux au niveau du résultat recherché. Le gouvernement fédéral agirait-il en son nom et au nom des provinces, après consultations avec celles-ci? Une équipe spéciale de négociateurs serait-elle constituée, composée de représentants de chacun des gouvernements impliqués? La population canadienne serait-elle consultée, par référendum ou autrement? Le gouvernement fédéral, compte tenu de sa compétence exclusive dans le domaine du commerce international, pourrait-il engager les provinces contre leur volonté? Toutes ces questions demeurent évidemment sans réponse pour le moment.

Une fois la souveraineté-association réalisée, le Québec et le Canada, au plan interne, seraient libres de conduire leurs relations extérieures comme ils l'entendent, sujet, cependant, aux limites découlant de l'accord d'association. Dans la mesure où l'union économique entre le Québec et le Canada serait maintenue, il va de soi que la politique commerciale extérieure des deux États devrait être élaborée en commun, comme c'est le cas à l'heure actuelle au sein des communautés économiques européennes[33]. Les accords commerciaux engageant l'union économique seraient conclus au nom de celle-ci ou des deux États conjointement. Dans la mesure enfin où une monnaie commune serait maintenue, des conclusions similaires vaudraient pour la politique monétaire.

Au simple plan de l'efficacité, cependant, on peut sérieusement s'interroger sur le réalisme d'une structure décisionnelle essentiellement paritaire dans un domaine aussi lourd de conséquence que le domaine économique. L'exemple du marché commun ici n'est pas particulièrement utile; l'arbitrage susceptible de résulter des opinions diverses exprimées au sein d'un groupe de six ou neuf États ne peut tout simplement pas se réaliser dans une confrontation d'un à un. L'un ou l'autre doit éventuellement céder. À court terme, une volonté réelle de conciliation peut permettre de résoudre de nombreux problèmes; à long terme, cependant, les chances de rupture paraissent beaucoup plus grandes. Une façon possible de réaliser l'arbitrage entre les deux États serait de confier à des institutions communautaires indépendantes un rôle analogue à celui de la Commission au sein de la Communauté économique européenne : celle-ci, comme on le sait, a un droit d'initiative en matière de formulation de politiques, et un refus du Conseil des ministres, représentatif des États, renvoie tout simplement un projet devant la Commission[34]. Mais dans le contexte d'un passage du fédéralisme à la souveraineté-association, est-il encore possible de songer à des institutions communautaires indépendantes? Le livre blanc du gouvernement québécois sur la souveraineté-association fait très bien ressortir cette ambiguïté d'un système qui se veut d'abord et avant tout de droit international, mais qui au fond ne peut survivre que s'il repose sur une solide base de droit communautaire dont la parenté avec l'idée fédéraliste a toujours été évidente.

La perspective externe

D'un point de vue externe, la mise en branle des négociations devant conduire à la souveraineté-association ne manquera probablement pas d'attirer l'attention de plusieurs pays qui peuvent être tentés d'intervenir avant le fait de manière à influencer le cours des événements dans un sens favorable à leurs intérêts. Certains pourront voir d'un mauvais œil le démantèlement de l'État canadien; d'autres seront davantage préoccupés par la portée exacte de l'association économique à venir. Quoi qu'il en soit, ils se devront en principe de manifester une certaine retenue à cet égard, vu la règle de droit international qui veut qu'un État souverain ne s'immisce pas dans les affaires internes d'un autre État souverain. En pratique, il est permis de croire qu'en fait la vaste majorité des États respecteront cette règle. Toutefois, rien n'interdit aux parties canadiennes en cause d'établir de contacts discrets avec l'étranger dans le but de préparer un éventuel appui extérieur au cas où les négociations viendraient à échouer. Une telle hypothèse, cependant, si elle devait se concrétiser, augurerait très mal de l'avenir des négociations et ouvrirait toute grande la porte à une intervention étrangère.

Une fois les négociations sur la souveraineté-association complétées, le nouvel arrangement devrait pouvoir entrer en vigueur au plan interne sans trop de difficultés. Au plan international, toutefois, l'apparition d'un nouvel État, déjà économiquement intégré à un autre au moment de sa naissance, ne manquera pas de soulever certaines interrogations chez les États étrangers. Ceux-ci feront connaître leur réaction en reconnaissant ou ne reconnaissant pas le nouvel arrangement. Vu le caractère consensuel de l'arrangement en question, cette reconnaissance en pratique devrait suivre facilement. Néanmoins, il est à prévoir que la nouvelle association économique, surtout si elle implique une monnaie commune, posera certains problèmes en ce qui concerne la participation conjointe du Québec et du Canada à des organismes économiques tel le Fonds monétaire international. Il est difficile de voir, en effet, comment le Québec et le Canada pourraient prétendre représenter des intérêts distincts, avoir des comptes de tirages séparés et, de façon générale, bénéficier d'une double représentation au sein de ce dernier organisme, s'ils maintiennent une monnaie commune[35]. Pour les autres organismes internationaux à vocation économique, la portée exacte de l'union réalisée entre le Québec et le Canada déterminera le type de solution à adopter entre la représentation distincte et la représentation conjointe, compte tenu évidemment des statuts de chaque organisme. Dans le cas du GATT, il est à prévoir que la solution retenue serait de type communautaire, comme dans le cas de la Communauté économique européenne. Dans le cas de l'Organisation de coopération et de développement économique, par ailleurs, une représentation distincte paraîtrait beaucoup plus vraisemblable. Quoi qu'il en soit, la règle fondamentale qui guidera les décisions à cet égard est assez claire : la représentation sera conjointe ou séparée selon que la responsabilité au plan international sera assumée conjointement ou séparément.

Au-delà de ce problème de reconnaissance mais en relation étroite avec celui-ci, les États étrangers ne manqueront pas de s'interroger sur ce qu'il advient des engagements internationaux antérieurement assumés par le Canada. La réponse de principe du droit international à ce problème est assez simple : le nouvel État est entièrement libre d'accepter ou de refuser les engagements internationaux de l'État dont il est issu[36]. Quant à ce dernier, il demeurera lié par ses engagements, sauf dans la mesure où ces derniers sont affectés par la perte de territoire conséquente. L'acceptation de l'État sécessionniste, ou son refus, suivant les engagements, pourra prendre la forme d'une déclaration expresse ou résulter tout simplement de la conduite de l'État. Certains auteurs établissent une distinction entre la sécession radicale et violente, qui donnerait généralement lieu à un rejet global des accords antérieurs, et la sécession par négociation, où la continuité des engagements serait davantage la règle[37]. Il s'agit là essentiellement d'une constatation *a posteriori* et non d'une norme juridique; dans le cas de la souveraineté-association, néanmoins, il est plausible qu'elle se vérifierait à nouveau, particulièrement dans le domaine économique. Ainsi, peut-on facilement imaginer que le Québec maintiendrait l'accord entre le Canada et les États-Unis relatif à la voie maritime du Saint-Laurent. On peut présumer aussi que les accords de double fiscalité entre le Canada et nombre de pays étrangers seraient maintenus, car déjà le Québec les étend, sur une base purement volontaire, à ses propres taxes[38]. Enfin, toujours dans le cadre de la souveraineté-association, il faut prendre pour acquis que les accords de commerce avec les États étrangers ne seraient modifiés que d'un commun accord. Dans le domaine politique, et plus particulièrement dans le domaine culturel, par ailleurs, il est à présumer qu'un examen en profondeur de tous les traités conclus par le Canada serait effectué.

L'indépendance

D'un point de vue strictement juridique, l'indépendance pure et simple du Québec soulève fondamentalement le même type de problèmes que la souveraineté-association, à cette différence près que l'indépendance, contrairement à la souveraineté-association, peut résulter d'une rupture violente des relations entre le Québec et le reste du Canada. Dans cette perspective, les éléments essentiels ont trait, au plan interne, à la signification d'une déclaration unilatérale d'indépendance, et, au plan externe, au rôle de la reconnaissance internationale dans l'hypothèse d'un refus du Canada d'admettre la sécession du Québec.

La perspective interne

Si l'on prend pour acquis, en se fiant au livre blanc du gouvernement québécois sur la souveraineté-association, que l'indépendance pure et simple du Québec viendrait à la suite d'un échec des négociations avec le reste du Canada, on peut présumer que la procédure choisie pour y arriver serait celle de la déclaration unilatérale d'indépendance. Or, une telle déclaration, dans la mesure où elle remet en cause la souveraineté du Canada sur une partie de son territoire, appelle immédiatement une prise de position de la part du gouvernement canadien. Deux options s'ouvrent alors. Celui-ci pourrait d'abord donner un accord de principe à la déclaration du Québec, sous la forme d'une entente entre représentants des deux gouvernements. Cette entente pourrait subséquemment être transposée au plan interne par des lois du Parlement canadien d'une part, et du Parlement québécois d'autre part, un peu comme en 1922 un accord fut conclu entre l'Angleterre et l'Irlande qui conduisit à l'adoption, par le Parlement britannique, du *Irish Free State (Agreement) Act* quelques mois plus tard[39].

L'autre possibilité, qui pourrait se concrétiser particulièrement si le référendum sur l'indépendance ne paraissait pas
convainquant, serait que le gouvernement canadien rejette la
déclaration unilatérale d'indépendance du Québec et cherche à
faire invalider judiciairement et administrativement toute incursion de la province dans les domaines de compétence
proprement fédéraux. En d'autres termes, le gouvernement
canadien adopterait purement et simplement le raisonnement
formulé en 1968 par le Comité judiciaire du Conseil privé
relativement à la déclaration unilatérale d'indépendance de la
Rhodésie, dans l'affaire *Madzimbamuto* c. *Lardner-Burke*[40]. Il fut
jugé alors que les lois adoptées par le régime sécessionniste de
Rhodésie étaient illégales, compte tenu du fait que le gouvernement de Westminster, loin d'avoir renoncer à exercer sa
souveraineté sur la Rhodésie, avait pris des mesures concrètes
pour faire valoir cette souveraineté. Contrairement à
l'Angleterre, dont les moyens d'intervention en Rhodésie de-
meuraient limités compte tenu de l'éloignement, le Canada
serait certainement en bonne position pour réaffirmer sa
compétence sur le territoire québécois. À l'inverse, cependant,
cette réaffirmation de compétence ne pourrait demeurer aussi
longtemps inefficace : autrement, compte tenu encore une fois
des circonstances, il faudrait conclure à une renonciation
implicite du Canada. Les tribunaux québécois ne pourraient
certes suspendre leurs décisions au-delà d'une certaine limite de
temps, et, à défaut d'autres indications, il est à prévoir qu'ils se
fonderaient sur l'exercice réel du pouvoir politique pour
décider de la légalité ou de l'illégalité des gestes posés par le
régime sécessionniste québécois.

La perspective externe

Tout comme la déclaration unilatérale d'indépendance appelle
une réaction de l'État souverain en droit interne, l'apparition
d'un nouvel État, en droit international, appelle une réaction de
la part des gouvernements étrangers. Lorsque ce nouvel État
résulte d'un arrangement à l'amiable, son acceptation par les
États étrangers suit presque automatiquement, et le rôle exact
de la reconnaissance, en rapport avec l'apparition de ce nouveau
sujet de droit international, demeure alors une question
théorique. La situation est toute différente lorsque le nouvel
État en puissance voit son existence niée dès le départ par l'État
dont il prétend se séparer. Dans un tel cas, la controverse

classique entre la théorie de la reconnaissance « constitutive » et la théorie de la reconnaissance « déclaratoire » redevient actuelle[41]. Derrière cette controverse, qui tourne autour de la question de savoir si la reconnaissance conditionne la naissance d'un nouvel État ou si elle ne fait que la constater, le véritable problème qui se dessine est celui de l'efficacité, en droit international, d'une déclaration unilatérale d'indépendance. Force est bien de constater que, plus un État aspirant exerce un contrôle efficace sur son territoire, moins il a besoin d'une reconnaissance internationale pour assurer son existence, auquel cas la reconnaissance a surtout un effet déclaratoire; et, à l'inverse, moins un État paraît exercer un contrôle efficace sur son territoire, plus la reconnaissance semble essentielle à sa survie, auquel cas elle sera considérée comme ayant un effet constitutif. Le Bangla Desh et le Biafra sont deux précédents qui illustrent très bien l'une et l'autre hypothèse.

Dans le cas du Québec, le rôle de la reconnaissance sera donc conditionné dans une large mesure par l'attitude du gouvernement du Canada. Si celui-ci devait rejeter sans appel la déclaration unilatérale d'indépendance du Québec et utiliser tous les moyens à sa disposition pour maintenir son autorité sur le territoire québécois, la situation difficile dans laquelle se retrouverait le Québec rendrait d'autant plus essentielles les manifestations d'appui extérieures. Aussi longtemps que la situation ne sera pas clarifiée dans les faits, il est à prévoir que la vaste majorité des États étrangers s'abstiendront de toute reconnaissance hâtive susceptible d'être considérée, en droit, comme une intervention indue dans les affaires d'un État souverain. Pour le Québec, le risque serait donc grand de se retrouver alors isolé et sans appui. Si le Canada devait continuer à exercer ses compétences au Québec de façon ininterrompue, il faudrait très vite, comme dans le cas du Biafra, parler d'un échec de la tentative sécessionniste du Québec. À l'inverse, si le Québec devait s'assurer, pendant cette période transitoire, l'exclusivité de l'exercice de la compétence législative sur son territoire, un nombre croissant d'États reconnaîtraient probablement, avec le temps, le nouveau sujet de droit international.

Une fois le Québec séparé du Canada et admis en tant que nouvel État indépendant au sein de la communauté internationale, la conduite de ses relations extérieures, cela va de soi, ne serait plus sujette à des restrictions de nature juridique, du moins en dehors des exigences du droit international. Certains problèmes, tels que, par exemple, ceux découlant de la succession d'État ou encore celui du transit entre les parties est et ouest du Canada, exigeraient certes des solutions rapides dans l'immédiat. Mais il s'agirait là de questions à régler entre États indépendants et non plus de questions internes.

Conclusion

Au terme de cette étude, la conclusion fondamentale qui s'impose, en ce qui concerne les problèmes juridiques susceptibles d'être soulevés dans le domaine des affaires extérieures, a trait à la passivité relative de l'ordre juridique international face aux divers types de solutions envisagés. S'agissant d'abord de la souveraineté-association et de l'indépendance, la préoccupation essentielle du droit international concerne l'efficacité des changements opérés. Dans cette perspective, c'est avant tout le caractère consensuel ou conflictuel des changements qui déterminera le rôle exact du droit international en tant que contrainte extérieure. Une fois le problème de la reconnaissance réglé, la personnalité internationale des parties en cause sera pleine et entière, et donnera ouverture à une participation distincte aux organismes internationaux, à cette exception près que, dans le cas de la souveraineté-association, une participation conjointe à certains organismes à vocation économique s'imposera dans les faits.

Paradoxalement, ce sont les hypothèses du fédéralisme renouvelé et du statut particulier qui soulèvent, au regard du droit international, le plus de problèmes[42]. La préoccupation essentielle ici concerne la responsabilité de l'État canadien en tant que sujet de droit international. En effet, les contraintes inhérentes à la structure fédérale du Canada limitent la capacité du gouvernement canadien de s'engager de façon responsable au plan international, ce qui ne manque pas d'inquiéter les pays étrangers. Mais, par ailleurs, l'hypothèse d'une représentation multiple des intérêts canadiens au plan international entraîne le risque d'une dilution de l'obligation de responsabilité qui incombe au Canada comme à tous les autres États, ce qui semble tout aussi dangereux. Entre ces deux maux, le droit international souhaite seulement ne pas avoir à choisir. L'idéal serait donc d'en arriver à une solution qui soit efficace au plan interne et qui ne mette pas en cause le principe fondamental de la responsabilité internationale. À cet égard, la solution la plus logique, pour autant, évidemment, qu'on demeure dans un contexte fédéral, paraît aller dans le sens d'une amélioration des mécanismes de collaboration intergouvernementale dans le domaine général des affaires extérieures, d'une part, et d'une représentation distincte des intérêts culturels du Québec, d'autre part. Au-delà des prises de positions de principe, qui souvent n'offrent qu'un semblant de solutions valables, il y a là, croyons-nous, une possibilité de règlement efficace. À moins, bien sûr, qu'il ne soit trop tard et que le temps des décisions radicales ne soit venu.

Notes

1. Sur l'accession du Canada à l'indépendance, voir, de façon générale, George F.G. Stanley, *A Short History of the Canadian Constitution*, Toronto, Ryerson Press, 1969. Voir également Brian M. Mazer, « Sovereignty and Canada: An Examination of Canadian Sovereignty From a Legal Perspective », *Saskatchewan Law Review*, 42 (1977−78), pp. 1−15. Sur les implications du statut d'État indépendant en droit international, voir, de façon générale, Georg Schwarzenberger, *International Law*, 3ᵉ éd., Londres, Stevens and Sons, 1977, vol. 1, chap. 6.

2. La question de la responsabilité de l'État fédéral sur ses États membres au regard du droit international est étudié dans Ivan Bernier, *International Legal Aspects of Federalism*, Londres, Longman Group, 1973, chap. 2.

3. En 1965, le professeur Bora Laskin, avant qu'il ne devienne plus tard juge en chef de la Cour suprême du Canada, écrivait qu'en vertu du droit international général, « *only one juridical personality can be recognized in a federal state* » (« The Provinces and International Agreements », dans *Background Papers and Reports*, Ontario Advisory Committee on Confederation, Toronto, The Queen's Printer of Ontario, 1967, vol. 1, pp. 101−113).

4. Voir Bernier, *International Legal Aspects . . .* , chap. 1.

5. Voir, de façon générale, Anne-Marie Jacomy-Millette, *L'introduction et l'application des traités internationaux au Canada*, Paris, Librairie générale de droit et de jurisprudence, 1971.

6. Voir, par exemple, Ronald G. Atkey, « Provincial Transnational Activity: An Approach to a Current Issue in Canadian Federalism », dans *Background Papers and Reports*, Ontario Advisory Committee on Confederation, vol. 2, p. 161. On trouve une bibliographie assez complète dans Donald C. Story, « Government — A 'Practical Thing': Towards a Consensus on Foreign Policy Jurisdiction », dans *Canada Challenged: The Viability of Confederation*, R.B. Byers et Robert W. Reford, éd., Toronto, Canadian Institute of International Affairs, 1979, p. 119, n. 35.

7. Pour les plus récents développements, voir Anne-Marie Jacomy-Millette, « Le rôle des provinces dans les relations internationales », *Études internationales*, 10 (1979), pp. 285−320.

8. Voir, par exemple, N.A.M. MacKenzie, « Canada and the Treaty-Making Power », *La revue du Barreau canadien*, 15 (1937), pp. 401−454. Pour les écrits plus récents, voir Gerald L. Morris, « The Treaty-Making Power: A Canadian Dilemma », *La revue du Barreau canadien*, 45 (1967), pp. 478−512; et Story, « Government — A 'Practical Thing' . . . », p. 133.

9.   A. Dufour, « Fédéralisme canadien et droit international », dans *Canadian Perspectives on International Law and Organization*, R. St. J. Macdonald, Gerald L. Morris et Douglas M. Johnston, éd., Toronto, University of Toronto Press, 1974, p. 72. Voir aussi Ronald G. Atkey, « The Role of the Provinces in International Affairs », *International Journal*, 26 (1970 – 71), pp. 249 – 273.

10.   Très caractéristique à cet égard est la conclusion du Comité sur la Constitution de l'Association du Barreau canadien (*Vers un Canada nouveau*, Montréal, Fondation du Barreau canadien, 1978, p. 137).

11.   Story, « Government — A 'Practical Thing' . . . », p. 124.

12.   Voir, à ce sujet, Canada, Secrétariat des Conférences intergouvernementales canadiennes, *Propositions constitutionnelles 1971 – 1978*, Ottawa, Le Secrétariat, 1978, p. 275.

13.   Ontario, Comité consultatif de la Confédération, *Le partage des pouvoirs entre les gouvernements fédéral et provinciaux : deuxième rapport du Comité consultatif de la Confédération*, Toronto, Le Comité, 1979. La mise de l'avant contenue dans le rapport de la Commission constitutionnelle du parti libéral du Québec (*Une nouvelle fédération canadienne*, Montréal, le parti libéral du Québec, 1980) se rapproche de cette position.

14.   Outre le rapport du Comité sur la Constitution de l'Association du Barreau canadien, *Vers un Canada nouveau*, voir Canada, Parlement, Le Comité spécial mixte du Sénat et de la Chambre des communes sur la Constitution du Canada, *Rapport final*, Ottawa, Information Canada, 1972; de même que le rapport du gouvernement de l'Alberta, *Harmony in Diversity: A New Federalism for Canada*, Edmonton, Queen's Printer, 1978.

15.   Voir, entre autres, Edward McWhinney, « Canadian Federalism, and the Foreign Affairs and Treaty Power. The Impact of Quebec's " Quiet Revolution " », *Annuaire canadien de droit international*, 7 (1969), pp. 3 – 32.

16.   Voir Bernier, *International Legal Aspects* . . ., pp. 152 – 171.

17.   *Ibid.*, pp. 107 – 114.

18.   Voir Jacomy-Millette, « Le rôle des provinces . . . », p. 308.

19.   Canada, Commission de l'unité canadienne, *Se retrouver : observations et recommandations*, Ottawa, ministre des Approvisionnements et Services Canada, 1979, pp. 92 – 93.

20.   *Entente entre le Gouvernement du Canada et le Gouvernement du Québec portant sur la collaboration en matière d'immigration et sur la sélection des ressortissants étrangers qui souhaitent s'établir au Québec à titre permanent ou temporaire*, signée à Montréal, le 20 février 1978.

21.   Secrétariat des Conférences intergouvernementales canadiennes, *Propositions constitutionnelles 1971 – 1978*; voir également Louis Sabourin, « L'action internationale du Québec », *Perspectives internationales* (mars-avril 1977), pp. 3 – 8.

22.   Voir « Un accord culturel reste lettre morte », *Le Soleil* (Québec), 9 février 1974. L'annonce de la création de la sous-commission culturelle Québec-Belgique se retrouve dans le communiqué n° 104 du ministère canadien des Affaires extérieures, en date du 29 octobre 1975.

23.   Colombie-Britannique, « The Distribution of Legislative Powers » (Paper No. 8), dans *British Columbia's Constitutional Proposals. Presented to the First Ministers Conference on the Constitution. October, 1978*, Victoria, Queen's Printer, 1978, p. 33.

24.   Voir Michael Bothe, « Regional Autonomy and Independence: The Consequences for the Legal Order of the Communities », *Common Market Law Review*, 15 (1978), pp. 393 – 414.

25.   Bernier, *International Legal Aspects . . .*, p. 40.

26.   *Ibid.*, p. 65.

27.   Voir, par exemple, Jacques Brossard, *L'accession à la souveraineté et le cas du Québec : conditions et modalités politico-juridiques*, Montréal, Les presses de l'université de Montréal, 1976, pp. 59−310, où cette distinction correspond à deux titres distincts.

28.   L'exercice du droit à l'autodétermination, par le biais d'un référendum ou autrement, pourrait aussi bien conduire au maintien pur et simple du lien existant. Ceci soulève la question de savoir si le droit à l'autodétermination, une fois exercé, ne se trouve pas par le fait même épuisé au regard du droit international. Sur le droit à l'autodétermination en rapport avec la question du Québec, voir John Claydon et John D. Whyte, « Legal Aspects of Quebec's Claim for Independence », dans *Must Canada Fail?*, Richard Simeon, éd., Montréal, McGill-Queen's University Press, 1977.

29.   Brossard, *L'accession à la souveraineté . . .*, pp. 250−256.

30.   *Dans l'affaire des questions soumises par le gouverneur en conseil sur la compétence législative du Parlement du Canada relativement à la Chambre haute, formulées dans le décret C.P. 1978−3581 en date du 23 novembre 1978*, (1980) 1 R.C.S. 54.

31.   Brossard, *L'accession à la souveraineté . . .*, pp. 275−281.

32.   J.-Maurice Arbour, « Secession and International Law — Some Economic Problems in Relation to State Succession », *Cahiers de droit*, 19 (1978), pp. 285−338.

33.   Ce qui fait, par exemple, que c'est la Commission des Communautés qui a participé aux récentes négociations GATT et non les États membres.

34.   Sauf en cas d'unanimité; voir l'article 149 du *Traité instituant la Communauté économique européenne*.

35.   L'article 6 du *Traité amendé instituant le Fonds monétaire international* oblige les membres, entre autres choses, « à collaborer avec le Fonds et avec les autres membres pour assurer le maintien de dispositions de change ordonnées et de promouvoir un système stable de taux de change ». Le Canada et le Québec séparément pourraient difficilement assumer une telle obligation.

36.   Voir Brossard, *L'accession à la souveraineté . . .*, pp. 429−463; Sir Arnold Duncan McNair, *The Law of Treaties*, Londres, Oxford University Press, 1961, p. 640.

37.   Brossard, *L'accession à la souveraineté . . .*, p. 432.

38.   Voir la *Loi de l'impôt provincial sur le revenu*, S.R.Q. 1964, chap. 69, art. 12.

39.   Voir *Moore and Others* c. *Attorney-General for the Irish Free State and Others*, (1935) A.C. 484.

40.   (1969) 1 A.C. 645.

41.   Pour les références pertinentes à la doctrine, voir Brossard, *L'accession à la souveraineté . . .*, p. 398.

42.   Cette opinion est également partagée par Gerald L. Morris, « Quebec and Sovereignty: The Interface Between Constitutional and International Law », dans *The Constitution and the Future of Canada*, Special Lectures of the Law Society of Upper Canada, Toronto, Richard De Boo, 1978, pp. 47−65.

L'auteur

YVAN BERNIER est doyen de la Faculté de droit de l'université Laval. Diplômé de cette même université en 1964, il a reçu un doctorat de l'université de Western Ontario en 1969. Il est également professeur à la Faculté de droit, son enseignement portant sur le droit constitutionnel et le droit international public. Ses publications récentes ont porté, entre autres, sur les lois et pratiques relatives à la libre circulation des marchandises, des personnes, des services et des capitaux au Canada, et sur la survie des entreprises en difficulté au regard du droit international économique.

External Economic Relations
and Constitutional Change

CAROLINE PESTIEAU
C.D. Howe Institute, Montreal

Contents

External Economic Relations
and Constitutional Change

Introduction

A country's external economic relations are basically shaped by
three sets of factors: world demand, or the evolution of
economic forces outside the country; domestic supply, or the
country's response to world demand, given its resources endowments and economic potential; and domestic policies, or the
series of on-going and discretionary measures the country takes
that influence its role in the world economy.[1]

The object of this paper is to survey the probable effects on
Canada's and Quebec's international economic relations of each
of four constitutional options. The first set of factors determining these relations, referred to as 'world demand', remains the
same under the different options. But the other two, 'domestic
supply' and 'domestic policies' (particularly the latter), are likely
to be affected by the option chosen. In the following pages I
shall summarize very briefly some of the principal forces
currently acting on world demand and then consider international economic relations from a Canadian perspective. I shall
discuss the manner in which Canada and Quebec participate in
the world economy and identify some of the major economic-
policy concerns that relate to their respective international roles.
Finally, I shall consider the ways in which the choice of different
constitutional options — classical federalism, special status for

223

one or more provinces, an independent Quebec, and
sovereignty-association — would affect the external relations of
the two economies.

There are three obstacles to the successful pursuit of this
objective. First, the four options are imprecise and mean
different things to different people. Secondly, although this
paper does not discuss the domestic economy, yet external
economic relations are strongly influenced by domestic trends
and policies. Moreover there is a very large element of
uncertainty involved in any survey of constitutional options.
This uncertainty arises from both behavioural assumptions (Will
people behave in the rational manner hypothesized?) and the
so-called 'transitional problem'. Although we might assume that
under certain conditions a particular equilibrium would be
attained in the long run, changes occurring in the meantime
may prevent society from reaching that equilibrium even if
events verify the assumptions. For these reasons I cannot
forecast in this paper precisely what circumstances might evolve
under any of the constitutional options that might be adopted.

Selected Factors Influencing World Demand

Canada's external relations are influenced by the multifarious
factors making up the world market and constantly modifying
its character. It is posited that constitutional change within the
Canadian economic space is unlikely to affect world demand
significantly. On the other hand, since the economics of both
Canada and Quebec are very open, conditions in the international market provide the framework within which different
constitutional options can be exercised. For this reason we shall
look at some of the most important factors currently influencing
world trade before we turn to an examination of Canada's place
in this trade.

The Changed Energy-Supply Picture

Despite the current oil glut on world markets, the oil and gas
shortages of 1973–74 and 1978–79 have had long-term effects
on the international economic landscape. Those most relevant to
our theme include the prospects of slower economic growth and
the changes in the ranking of claims on funds available for
investment.

Hydrocarbon price hikes and shortages in the 1970s led to a large-scale transfer of purchasing power from oil importers to oil exporters. The fact that the exporters did not use up their new purchasing power to buy goods and services from the oil-importing countries, plus the uncertainties created by the oil crises, led to a slow-down in economic growth in the United States, Europe, and Japan. The slow-down, which has been characterized by high unemployment and inflation, is continuing into the 1980s, bringing with it a climate of extreme prudence among investors and of looking inward among governments.

As a result of this prudence and of the need to absorb higher energy costs, investments that appeared attractive in the early 1970s are now less so. This change affects Canada's attractiveness to foreign investors. In the early 1970s Canada held trump cards. Widespread fears of impending exhaustion of raw materials, particularly minerals, as well as the realization of the limits to growth imposed by a finite environment and the resulting concern about the level of pollution in the smaller industrialized countries seemed to give a resource-rich, sparsely populated territory a leading edge in attracting capital. But these advantages have been overshadowed, at least temporarily, by shorter-term anxiety about stagflation and medium-term concern to reduce energy consumption. As a result Canada is not perceived as such an attractive location for investment today as it was ten years ago, except by those industries dependent on large supplies of electricity or natural gas.

The Post—Tokyo Round Trading Environment

The conclusion of the six-year multilateral trade negotiations (MTNs) in 1979 signalled the consolidation of the three major trading blocks: the United States, the European Community (EC), and Japan. Canada was not able to pursue its own strategy as a medium-sized power in these negotiations as it had done in the Kennedy Round. One could almost say that medium-sized powers had been absorbed or reduced to marginal status in the General Agreement on Tariffs and Trade (GATT) negotiations over the intervening years. This leaves Canada in a highly exposed position, with little option but to rely on the United States for support *vis-à-vis* the other two trading blocs. However, although they share many concerns, Canada and the United States do not have identical trade objectives. The new power structure, therefore, tends to make Canada more dependent on the United States and hence more vulnerable than it was previously.[2]

Another result of the Tokyo Round negotiations is that tariff rates have become much less important in many industrial sectors.[3] Non-tariff barriers (NTBs) have consequently assumed greater importance. This means that to be worthwhile, any trade agreements that Canada or Quebec may wish to conclude with other countries will have to be based on mutually satisfactory reduction in NTBs, including access to government purchasing and freedom from countervailing action against industrial development-incentive programs.

However, all the active participants in world trade are now acutely aware of the potential impact of NTBs on their respective industrial strategies. The Codes of Conduct negotiated in Geneva are being closely scrutinized to determine their implications for domestic economic policy. Each country is likely to apply them as defensively as possible while taking maximum advantage of any loopholes. The post–Tokyo Round environment will, therefore, be one of competitive, even if controlled, protectionism with little scope for 'free riding' or for individual initiatives by small countries.[4]

The United States in the 1980s

Although trends in the American economy are of major importance to Canada, they cannot all be reviewed here. Among the most significant is the long-term slow-down in the rate of growth — particularly that of productivity growth — that was apparent even before the oil crisis.[5] This trend, combined with the inability to overcome stagflation, is likely to accentuate still further the post-1970s switch by the United States from a generally liberal trading stance to an increasingly inward-looking and defensive one. In such a climate, protectionist pressure groups tend to rally more support power than those that promote trade liberalization, and despite the market orientation of the Reagan administration, they may be able to block Canadian and Quebec industrial transformation strategies by insisting on a strict and legalistic interpretation of the recently negotiated Codes of Conduct.[6] This means that successful penetration of the American market will require that the private sector work more closely with the different levels of government to make the best use of existing opportunities.

Meanwhile, within the United States, there is no sign of a slackening in the shift of economic activity to the Southwest. The significant depreciation of the American dollar over the past ten years has made investment at home relatively much more attractive to Americans than it was in the 1950s and 1960s. These two factors, along with the reduction in tariff barriers, mean that new investment or the expansion of existing facilities in Canada by American firms will have to satisfy much more stringent profitability criteria than they had to satisfy in the past.

The Emergence of the Newly Industrializing Countries

The newly industrializing countries, which include the fast-growing countries of Southeast Asia and some of the major Latin American nations, offer important market opportunities for Canada in the short run. During the down-turn in world trade in the mid-1970s, their imports were of major importance in sustaining export levels in the industrialized countries.[7] Their demand structure is complementary to Canada's supply potential in a number of areas, but as yet Canadian exporters have left this market relatively untapped.[8]

In the long run, however, the newly industrializing countries may undercut Canadian production in both the labour-intensive sectors of the economy and in the export of resource-based products. With potentially large domestic markets and low wages, they are already able to benefit from economies of scale as well as from cheap labour and, in some countries, from a resource base comparable to Canada's.

Footloose Comparative Advantage

An important characteristic of international trade today is that exporters cannot count on continuing to sell traditionally successful products based on natural resources or long-established skills. A country's comparative advantage has to be continually re-established and maintained. With the exception of products based on a few very scarce natural resources, an increasingly large number of competing countries can produce virtually every type of goods or service. Cost competitiveness depends on factors such as technology breakthroughs, inflation rates, management skills, and access to capital that alter over time. Many countries are finding that the vulnerability of their export advantages requires them to establish quite sophisticated co-ordination mechanisms among business, labour, and government in order to sustain, develop, and promote potentially competitive exports.

Canada and Quebec: Examples of an Open Economy

International trade in goods and services is vital to the Canadian and Quebec economies. With sales outside the province equal to approximately 40 per cent of gross provincial product, Quebec is one of the most economically open societies in the world. Canada as a whole is among the most trade-dependent countries, with exports of goods and services valued at approximately 23 per cent of gross national product and imports at 27 per cent. Imports are of major importance in determining the cost of living in Canada: it has been estimated that a 1 per cent depreciation of the Canadian dollar or a 1 per cent increase in the price of all imported goods leads to a 0.5 per cent increase in the consumer price index. In this section we shall review features of Canada's international transactions and examine the way in which Canadians and their trading partners view the country's external economic relations.

Canadian and Quebec External Trade

Canada's foreign sales and purchases of goods follow a well established pattern that shows little sign of changing. About three quarters of both export and import transactions are concluded with the United States. Moreover intra-firm transactions are estimated to have accounted for approximately 60 per cent of Canadian sales to the United States in 1976.[9] Canada regularly incurs a very large deficit on trade in finished products in both the machinery and equipment and the consumer-goods sectors; this deficit has been traditionally balanced by a surplus on sales of raw materials and semi-processed and agricultural goods. In 1980, for example, a surplus of approximately $23 billion on commodities and industrial raw materials more than compensated for a deficit of $18 billion on finished products, giving Canada a surplus on its merchandise-trade account.[10]

When we look at Quebec, the concentration of exports by both composition and destination is even more striking. Foreign sales are largely concentrated in a small number of crude and semi-processed products destined for the Northeastern and North-Central regions of the United States. In the 1970s ore (17 per cent), non-ferrous metals (12 per cent), asbestos (6.5 per cent), and forest products (16 per cent), excluding pulp and paper, made up more than 41 per cent of Quebec's foreign sales, while more than 80 per cent of the province's exports to the United States in 1974 were destined for the Atlantic-Centre, North East-Centre, and New England States.[11] Very little diversification in either the destination or the composition of these foreign exports was observable from 1969 to 1976, a period during which Quebec's share of Canada's exports was falling.

Such a trade pattern clearly reveals a certain vulnerability in terms of dependence on one market and on raw and semi-processed goods. Since prices for raw materials, agricultural commodities, and industrial materials are generally set by world-market conditions, and their sale is often determined by long-standing contracts, Canadian policies have relatively little impact, at least in the short run, on export volumes. Traditionally Canada has run a surplus on its exports of goods, but this surplus tended to decline during the 1970s, and in the early 1980s was insufficient to compensate for the ever-growing deficit on the service account. The resulting deficit on the current account has to be financed by capital inflows.

Canada has always relied heavily on foreign capital, and from 1950 to 1978, just over 20 per cent of its total net investment came from foreign sources.[12] (This figure would be much higher if the re-investment of profits generated by foreign-owned companies were included.) Although there are signs of some diversification, most of the money needed is raised in the United States. The very close linkages between the Canadian and American capital markets are well known; in fact the New York market is used as a financial intermediary by Canadian lenders who wish to hold liquid assets and by Canadian borrowers who need long-term loans. Turning to Quebec, we see a similar reliance on foreign capital. Quebec governments have established a tradition of raising a larger share of their capital needs outside the country than do other provincial governments. In the mid-1970s, 45 per cent of Quebec's provincial and hydro debt was in foreign bonds, and borrowings in yen and Euro-currencies are continuing this policy into the 1980s.

Dependence on foreign capital is likely to continue well into the future. There is no likelihood in the near term that Canada will generate a large enough trade surplus to compensate for the deficit on the service account. This means that Canadian interest rates must be attractive enough to prevent short-term money from flowing out of the country. The balance-of-payments deficit thus limits Canada's monetary-policy options. At the same time very large amounts of equity or long-term debt financing will be required in the 1980s for 'lumpy' energy projects such as oil-sands development and the exploitation and transportation of frontier oil and gas. Moreover multinational corporations will continue to play a major role in Canadian capital formation, usually in terms of their reinvestment of locally generated profits. Canada, therefore, also has to maintain a relatively attractive climate for new and already established investors.

Reliance on multinational corporations for investment and job creation is a well known aspect of Canada's economic openness to the outside world. More recently the importance of parent companies' foreign-located product-design and engineering capacity has been demonstrated.[13] Not only industrial invention and innovation, but also product development and adaptation, which are more important commercially, usually take place abroad. The results of what is, in fact, 'on-going invention' tend to be transferred 'ready made' to Canadian subsidiaries. Consequently the latter are not equipped to undertake their own product development, yet can under-sell independent Canadian producers who have to carry the costs of product engineering.

Foreign-owned firms control a smaller share of Quebec's industry than of Ontario's, but many of them ship their output from Quebec in crude or semi-processed form. The level of their activity thus depends entirely on external demand, and they probably generate relatively fewer local purchasing and subcontracting jobs than do foreign-owned firms in Ontario. However, even if more local processing took place in Quebec, that province's economy would still depend heavily on international demand for forest products, asbestos and aluminum products, iron ore, steel, and other resource-based goods.

With their continued dependence on foreign loans (often denominated in the lenders' currencies), on multinational corporations, and on a limited range of export commodities and markets, Canada and Quebec are clearly very vulnerable to changes in the world economy. Some of the trends in the early 1980s suggest that Quebec, or perhaps even Canada as a whole, is in danger of 'peripheralization'. The consolidation of the three big trading blocs, the pressure of oil prices on Japanese and European trade balances, and the shift of demand in the United States to the southwestern regions of the country, all suggest that sales of Canadian — particularly Eastern Canadian — goods will require ever greater efforts.

Perceptions of Canada's and Quebec's Roles in the World Economy

The preceding paragraphs have painted a pessimistic picture. Yet Canada and Quebec undoubtedly enjoy enormous potential advantages in terms of future world demand for both goods and services. One reason for the apparent contradiction between Canada's and Quebec's extreme vulnerability to changes in external economic conditions and the fact that both regions are well endowed to take advantage of such changes, is that Canadians, as well as foreigners, perceive Canada's role in the international economy in restricted terms.

There are two sides to this question: foreign and domestic perceptions. Although each could be the subject of a separate study, we shall simply review very briefly, first, foreigners' perceptions of Canada and Quebec, and secondly Canadians' and Quebecers' own perceptions.

At present Quebec and the rest of Canada offer only moderate attractions to foreign corporations looking for investment opportunities in the manufacturing sector. Canadian and Quebec domestic markets are small and in danger of being 'balkanized' by interprovincial trade barriers such as provincial governments' preferential purchasing policies. Wages and overheads are relatively higher than in other comparable locations. In fact, in most manufacturing sectors, Quebec and Canada are badly placed in the so-called 'product life cycle'.

Fortunately we can qualify this discouraging picture in two ways. First, in the natural resource area, investment in Canadian hydro-electric development is still considered both safe and profitable. Other energy sources, such as frontier oil and gas, and uranium, attract considerable foreign interest despite the high risks involved. Secondly Quebec and Canada are potentially attractive investment locations as a gateway to the American market. Japanese and European investors, and even investors from newly industrializing countries who believe that the Canadian market is easier to penetrate than the American market, may well be attracted to the Canadian locations by the various incentive programs offered by both levels of government. This factor may be important in outweighing the declining attractiveness of Canada for American manufacturing firms.

Canada still enjoys a 'good' international reputation, but its partners in the United States, as well as in the EC, are somewhat disillusioned, although for different reasons, with Canada's attempts to secure special deals in its international economic affairs. Many Canadians hope for another sectoral trade arrangement with the United States on the lines of the auto pact. Such an arrangement would bring Canadians the efficiency gains of international specialization without exposing them to American domination. But influential groups in the United States are far from satisfied with the results of the auto pact, particularly with the way Canadians have interpreted the safeguard clauses, and it seems most unlikely that any other limited sectoral-trade packages would rally the support of the American government.

In 1976 Canada negotiated a 'contractual link', or framework agreement, with the EC. The Community generally concludes special institutional agreements only with developing countries, principally former colonies of EC-member countries, or with neighbouring Mediterranean countries likely either to join the Community later on or to suffer from its preferential trade arrangements. The agreement with Canada was thus in the nature of a special favour, and its 'granting' was, of course, influenced by Canada's resource potential; but it has borne little fruit to date, and some Community officials think that nothing has been gained by such an initiative, while an unwelcome precedent has been set for other developed countries to request special contractual links with the EC.

Although Japan and newly industrializing countries in Asia are also clearly interested in Canada's energy and environmental advantages, Canadians have so far been unable to establish their country as a preferred investment location for Japanese firms. At the same time Canada's protective stance toward manufactured exports of newly industrializing Asian countries does not endear it to many of these nations.

Foreign businesses and governments seem to show much the same attitudes toward Quebec as toward Canada as a whole. It is clear, however, that there is no obvious economic advantage for any major power in negotiating a formal trading agreement with an independent Quebec unless the latter is assured free entry into markets in the rest of Canada and, preferably, into American markets as well.[14]

When we turn to consider Canadians' and Quebecers' awareness of economic opportunities abroad, it appears that, by and large, decision makers in the private sector continue to focus on the American market almost all the attention they can spare from domestic preoccupations. A combination of realism and inertia has made these people little inclined to invest in developing markets in Europe and the newly industrializing countries. As a result the efforts of the federal government under successive Liberal administrations to stimulate diversification of Canadian trade and develop the Third Option, which included closer links with the EC, have gone largely unnoticed.[15]

Furthermore, in the early 1980s, there seems to be much less hostility in English Canada than there was in the early 1970s towards the idea of negotiating some form of general bilateral trade agreement with the United States. The complex evolution of public opinion that underlies this assertion cannot be analysed here. It is merely advanced to support the hypothesis that Canadian policy makers are likely to continue to turn first to other North Americans for help in solving the economic issues of the 1980s rather than to search actively for ways to reduce their dependence on their southern neighbour.

The Government of Quebec has taken a series of steps away from almost exclusive dependence on traditional English-speaking partners in order to diversify its trade and economic relations. But these initiatives will take a long time to bear fruit. On the other hand, an economic association among Quebec, the rest of Canada, and the United States could be a very attractive long-term goal for Quebec nationalists since it would offer access to American technology and economies of scale while safeguarding apparent political sovereignty and assuring Canadian support in negotiating special phased integration of Quebec manufacturing into the American market. Political circumstances, however, prevent any active support for such a long-term strategy at this time.

It thus appears that there is scope for a widening of both Canadians' and foreigners' perceptions of Canada's potential contribution to world trade. While Canada is a valued and reliable trade partner, it is still considered almost exclusively as a supplier of raw or semi-processed goods. Many of its potential trade partners believe that it is already integrated into a *de facto* North American trade area, a belief Canadians themselves have not worked very hard to dispel. Constitutional options that may be chosen over the next few years will inevitably affect our trading partners' perceptions of Canada and of Quebec. They may also influence Canadians' and Quebecers' commercial policies.

Economic Policy and International Economic Relations

At the beginning of this paper, I stated that domestic policies are one of a series of factors that, together with world demand and domestic supply, shape a country's external economic relations. Given the context described above, it is clear that those responsible for economic policy making in Canada will be faced with difficult decisions in international fields during the 1980s. In addition measures in fields other than those usually associated with international trade and investment also affect a country's economic relations with the rest of the world. Policies relating to stabilization, redistribution, and development, at both the federal and provincial levels, can have a major impact on Canada's external transactions.

The choice of a particular constitutional arrangement will have repercussions on economic policy in all these fields, but it would be impossible to review the range of possible modifications in a paper of this kind. Instead, in this section we shall consider two interrelated areas of economic policy that are of concern to Canadians and Quebecers: the future competitiveness of economic activity in the Canadian economic space and the scope for implementing independent policies that the Canadian and Quebec governments can realistically hope to maintain or extend. Both areas will be affected by significant constitutional change, and both are at the heart of Canada's international economic relations in the 1980s.

International Competitiveness

Whether one looks at the short or the medium term, the international competitiveness of the Canadian and Quebec economies is in doubt. The depreciation of the Canadian dollar since the fourth quarter of 1976 has partly obscured the problem, but virtually all analysts are aware that our economies are badly posed to react to expected developments in the late twentieth century and that, despite our inherent strengths, we continually find ourselves negotiating from a position of weakness. Among the multitude of factors that have been advanced to explain or justify Canada's failure to establish broadly based competitive activities, the following seem most relevant to our theme:

- Traditional reliance on comparative advantage based solely on natural resources endowments.
- The cost burden accumulated by attempting to supply a small population spread over a very large and inhospitable territory, using as high a proportion of domestically produced goods as is politically acceptable. (This is another way of describing the National Policy.)
- An inefficient combination of production factors — particularly management — in manufacturing. Attention has been drawn to the inefficiency that results from excessive product diversification within Canadian plants, in contrast to the criticism often directed at Canadian companies that they suffer from an excessive number of plants.[16] This inefficient use of production factors in manufacturing has been attributed to the legacy of the National Policy, to the lack of aggressiveness of Canadian management, and to the constraints imposed by foreign ownership. An aspect of this third factor that is coming increasingly to the fore is multinational corporations' refusal to give their Canadian subsidiaries 'world product markets', that is, permission and encouragement to develop world-size capacity and expertise in certain lines. (The problem is that the ensuing export from Canada of those products would likely compete with exports or domestic shipments from the companies' other plants, including those in their home locations.)
- Uncompetitive costs for a labour force that is, on average, not as well educated as its American and Japanese counterparts and less mobile than the former. While wage parity with the United States had been reached in many sectors before the depreciation of the late 1970s, the labour-productivity gap is still significant.[17]
- Excessive government intervention in the economy, including regulation, counter-productive support programs, and balkanization of the Canadian common market by the creation of non-tariff barriers to interprovincial trade.
- The continuing attraction of the United States, which leads to the emigration of many of Canada's most dynamic and innovative economic agents.

There is now widespread awareness of the uncompetitive nature of much economic activity in Canada and of the country's vulnerability in its international relations, but the solutions to the problems remain elusive in the country as a whole and in Quebec. During the 1970s national and sectoral industrial strategies were proposed, and several attempts were made to develop structural policies to improve the competitiveness of Canadian industry.[18] Without entering into the specifics of the ensuing analysis, I suggest that there was general agreement on the need to improve both the quality and the productivity of labour, of management, and of capital inputs. Areas seen to require particular attention were skilled-labour training, including interprofessional mobility; investment in new plant and equipment; and the export performance of Canadian and Quebec firms. These are all areas on which constitutional change would impinge.[19]

Policy Independence

The scope for implementing independent economic policies has been narrowing in all countries, including the United States, since 1973. Growing interdependence is made apparent by the growth of the Euro-dollar and of Euro-bond markets, by repercussions of the international oil shortages, and by the vain attempts of various governments to shield their economies from the pervasive effects of stagflation. Since Canada and, *a fortiori*, Quebec, should it become a separate state, are relatively small units in the international economy, their policy independence will inevitably be limited unless they pursue an unlikely and extremely costly policy of autarky.

Nonetheless, Canada and Quebec can both choose to maximize their relative liberties in order to pursue their objectives consistently despite the ups and downs of the world market, and there is more likelihood of such a choice succeeding if the economy in question satisfies certain minimum conditions. In the Canadian and Quebec contexts, these minimum conditions would most probably include:

- Strength, in terms of sustained world competitiveness, in at least one industry in each of the major sectors: resources (for example grain, forest products), manufacturing (for example public transportation and telecommunications equipment), and services (for example communications, consulting engineering)

- A greater diversification of foreign sales of goods and services
- An operational consensus on economic objectives and on the means required to implement them among the major economic agents and decision makers. These include governments (at several levels, if necessary), multinational firms, domestically owned businesses, and a broadly based group of labour leaders.

These elements far from exhaust the list of means by which policy independence could be increased, but they are among the most important, and the impact of different constitutional options on each is of considerable interest to our theme.

Constitutional Options and International Economic Relations

Both Quebec and Canada as a whole are threatened with economic peripheralization. Both are exceptionally dependent on economic events and decisions outside their borders, and both need to take effective measures to strengthen their comparative advantages in their most successful export lines and to establish new economic activities in which they can compete in the world market. Both need to be able to rally general support behind consistent attempts to develop their potential advantages. How would the constitutional options envisaged affect the two societies' international economic relations?

As I have already stressed, this paper does not aim to present any formal modelling exercise to analyse the repercussions on Canada's and Quebec's external transactions of the different constitutional options under consideration. In the section that follows, I attempt to draw some general conclusions based on the preceding discussion. A summary definition of each of the options is provided to avoid misunderstanding.

Classical Federalism

This would be a revised version of the existing Canadian Confederation, characterized by an equal, or 'symmetrical', division of powers among the constituent provinces or regions. Hence each of the constituent parts would enjoy basically identical powers, at least in the economic sphere. The resulting federation could be more centralized, as centralized, or less

centralized than Confederation as we know it. We shall therefore consider the following:

- A federal system in which economic decision making is more
  centralized than it was at the time of the Quebec referendum
- A federal system in which all the provinces have approximately the same amount of control over economic decision
  making that they enjoyed in the late 1970s
- A less centralized federation in which a greater element of
  economic decision making devolves to all of the provinces in
  such areas as control over sales of natural resources, income
  security (including pensions), labour-force policy, and foreign
  investment review.

Classical federalism with greater centralization in economic decision making

Such an option appeared politically unfeasible throughout the
1970s and was therefore ignored by most commentators. The
early years of the 1980s have, however, seen a number of federal
moves that suggest that Ottawa is trying to recover ground lost
to the provinces in the 1960s and 1970s. Interprovincial trade,
health and welfare, education and manpower policy, regional
development, and natural resources are areas in which, to
varying degrees, the federal government has recently reaf-
firmed its concern and its presence. It remains to be seen
whether this effort will be sustained and, if so, whether it will
lead to a significant change in the sharing of decision making in
economic matters. The signs are numerous enough, however, to
warrant a brief discussion of increased centralization that would
have seemed unnecessary a few years ago.

Increased centralization in decision making would affect international economic matters differently from domestic
economic concerns. This is, therefore, an hypothesis in which
international issues have to be distinguished very clearly from
domestic ones, despite the fact that Canada's international
economic stance is, as we have seen, strongly influenced by
domestic decisions.

A more centralized federation would most probably be better
able than a decentralized one to promote the competitiveness of
Canadian output and sales. Strategies for investment, manpower training, and production could be adopted with greater
likelihood of their bearing fruit.[20] Greater policy independence
could also be obtained if there were one clearly accepted 'senior

government' with generally recognized responsibility for building a consensus between management and labour and for thinking through the country's export strategy. The Canadian position would be more visible, better articulated, and thus clearer to our partners. Canada would therefore stand a better chance of marshalling its strengths in the international economic community.

This appreciation naturally supposes that greater centralization is accepted by the provinces and that these do not combat it with offsetting measures in order to reassert their powers. The likelihood of their reacting favourably or unfavourably depends largely on the respective weights they give to achievement of economic goals on the international and on the domestic scenes. Considerations of individual welfare and regional identity may militate against centralization up until the moment when international competitiveness becomes an overriding consideration since, without it, interpersonal and interregional redistribution is impossible.

Classical federalism with the present degree of economic centralization

If such a régime were truly acceptable to the parties involved, that is, the ten provincial governments and the federal government, the former would cease trying to whittle away remaining federal constraints on their freedom of action. At the same time Ottawa would not attempt to obtain new, or to recover lost, powers as it has often done in the past. Under these circumstances we could expect a number of positive developments relevant to Canada's international economic relations.

First, there would be scope for improvement in the mechanisms of economic decision making as constitutional conflicts ceased to preoccupy or confuse decision makers in government and in the private sector. Improved decision making would have an effect on structural measures, as well as on measures to promote stabilization. There would be more likelihood of governments, management, and labour adopting a consistent series of industrial policies, including modernization of the manufacturing sector, coherent and efficient use of all forms of energy across the country as they became available, and joint government/private-sector export strategies.

Secondly there would be a halt to the balkanization of the Canadian common market, which would increase the attractiveness of Canadian locations for foreign investors and would encourage industrial specialization within existing firms. The combined effects of improvements in decision making and a guaranteed Canada-wide market would give Canadians an opportunity to combat the causes of poor international performance enumerated above and improve productivity and export structure.

Thirdly a confirmation of the Canadian government's current responsibilities in the economic sphere would assure a continued, unequivocal, Canadian presence in those international forums such as international grain- and law-of-the-sea negotiations in which the country carries some weight. It would also allow the federal government to negotiate with foreign partners, particularly the United States, on a firm basis, without fear of competition or obstruction from provincial administration.

These gains would not be insignificant, given the international context in the 1980s and the economic problems Canada faces. Thus this brief summary suggests that a *status quo* Confederation offers Canada opportunities for improving its competitiveness and making good use of its scope for economic decision making. However, an apparently painless solution of current constitutional problems could also yield negative results in these very same fields. If Canadians are persuaded that their present common market works efficiently enough to generate an acceptable level of economic return to its participants, they may choose to ignore the major outstanding problems arising from lack of international competitiveness and unnecessary dependence and, hence, vulnerability. In this case their external position is likely to deteriorate.

It must also be pointed out that while Quebec might benefit from opportunities to improve economic competitiveness under the proposed régime, it would not gain any greater scope for economic decision making, unless indirectly to the extent that major efficiency gains happened to take place in Quebec-controlled sectors and thus gave that province greater weight in Canada's international economic policy making.

Classical federalism with less centralization of economic decision making

This constitutional option could conceivably stimulate economic activity within the various provinces or regions and hence induce new enterprise and innovation. From the international point of view, however, its over-all effects promise to be negative since this option does not appear to offer any improvement in

Canadian productivity or to address the causes of Canada's failure to achieve international competitiveness. More specifically, with decreased centralization, circumstances would likely evolve as follows.

- There would be increased balkanization of an already small Canadian market, which would either deter new investment or encourage manufacturers to maintain a number of sub-optimal-sized plants to satisfy requirements for local content and employment.
- There would be increased difficulty in adopting Canada-wide economic policies in either the macroeconomic or the industrial development fields.
- Provincial governments would be encouraged to outbid one another to attract investment and to conclude special supply deals with foreign firms and foreign governments.
- Canada would face constant problems in maintaining a united front in international economic negotiations, and as a result these might well be conducted on an incremental rather than on an over-all basis, with the consequent danger of a sell-out of Canada's bargaining advantages.

From the point of view of a given province, decentralized symmetrical federalism may look more attractive. Each province would have greater opportunities for negotiating with foreign governments, establishing guide-lines for multinational corporations, and drawing up investment-incentive packages. It is far from certain, however, that the gains would outweigh the losses and lead to real increases in policy independence or in the diversification of provincial export patterns.

Special Status for One or More Provinces

This is basically an 'asymmetrical' federalism in which certain constituent parts of the federation enjoy special rights or powers. Given the relatively decentralized way in which Confederation now operates and the modest scope of the Quebec government's sovereignty-association proposal in the economic field, it is difficult to differentiate special status from sovereignty-association in terms of control over economic policy.[21] I shall therefore not discuss this option here.

Nonetheless, it should be remembered that in political and diplomatic terms, the distinction between these two options is of major importance. Foreign governments and investors might react in one way to a Canadian province enjoying special status and in another way to a 'sovereign Quebec associated with Canada', even if the Quebec government exercised very similar economic powers in both instances. I refer readers to other papers in this collection that deal with the political and diplomatic issues.

A Sovereign Independent Quebec

A sovereign independent Quebec would have no formal economic linkages with any other countries or with the former Canadian provinces, other than its obligations under the GATT, the International Monetary Fund (IMF), the World Bank, and any other international organizations such as the Inter-American Development Bank or the Organisation for Economic Co-operation and Development (OECD) that it chose to join. However, it could, of course, attempt to negotiate a form of economic association with one or more of its trading partners.

In the long run a sovereign Quebec with no formal trade association with the rest of Canada could undoubtedly improve its present level of international competitiveness and attain a degree of economic independence comparable to that enjoyed by other small industrialized countries. Sweden and Switzerland are examples frequently referred to. It is not implausible that the conditions mentioned above for improving competitiveness and optimizing national decision making would be better met, from Quebec's point of view, in a small unitary state than in a slow-moving balkanized federation. A smooth transition to independence would permit an improvement in the government/private-sector interface, a reduction in overhead costs arising from Confederation, and an opportunity to adopt better focused industrial policies. There would, however, be no quick way to diversify Quebec's export pattern, and separation from Canada would narrow even further the range of export goods on which Quebecers would have to depend to pay for their imports.

Furthermore, although accession to sovereign status would provide an opportunity to mobilize the energy and goodwill of diverse economic groups for a concerted industrial strategy, it could also lead to increased pressures within the new nation. A strong sense of national purpose and enterprise is a necessary, but not a sufficient, condition for a significant improvement in Quebec's international competitiveness. A major depreciation of the local currency would probably be needed also, while the required industrial transformation was taking place, to boost the competitiveness of Quebec products in world markets and thus compensate for the probable loss of sales to the rest of Canada. But such a measure, entailing at least a temporary fall in real incomes, would be difficult to implement both for political reasons and because of the very close linkages between capital markets across North America. Consequently a decision to create a national Quebec currency not pegged to an already established currency would probably entail devoting an unacceptably large share of national resources to maintaining confidence in the new money. This would hamper the pursuit of both industrial efficiency and policy independence.

An alternative strategy would be for Quebec to seek a new trading partner. The United States is the only plausible candidate. If such an association proved politically feasible and were negotiated, its effects would obviously be far reaching. While the cost competitiveness of economic activity in Quebec would very probably be improved through economies of scale and more immediate access to best-practice technology, the Government of Quebec would suffer a very severe loss of control over economic policy. The Quebec economy would also become increasingly peripheralized unless it could attract European and other foreign investors on the strength of its right of entry to the American market.

It is conceivable that Canada's nine remaining provinces could work together to improve their international competitiveness, but in the absence of any strong political or psychological catalyst, an over-all weakening of their joint bargaining power and level of economic efficiency seems a more probable sequence of events after the secession of Quebec.

Sovereignty-Association between Quebec and the Rest of Canada

Sovereignty-association as proposed by the Government of Quebec in 1979 entailed sharing a common market (with some exceptions) and a common currency with the rest of Canada. However, legislative powers within the two jurisdictions, including the right to tax, would be restricted to their respective governments.[22] If accepted and implemented in good faith by all parties, this régime could have a number of positive consequences in the areas that concern us.

There could be a catalysing effect on Quebec decision makers at all levels that would allow certain hard, but necessary, decisions to be taken as part of the response to the challenge of assuming self-determination. At the same time there would be scope for an improvement of economic decision making within Quebec. Freed from the wastage and irritation of overlapping jurisdictions and unable to continue to attribute the results of mistaken policies to another level of government, policy makers would be able to work to improve productivity and international competitiveness in selected industrial sectors. At the same time a treaty of association between Quebec and the rest of Canada would probably halt the erection of interprovincial non-tariff barriers. Many of these have taken root contrary to the spirit, but not to the letter, of the British North America Act. The new treaty would necessarily illuminate what is now a grey area. While it would inevitably introduce rigidities into relationships between the two partners, it would also, presumably, set up mechanisms for the policing of such barriers, and its example might even persuade governments in the rest of Canada to roll back some of their own interprovincial barriers.

Participation in a Canada-Quebec common market would allow Quebec to continue to benefit from a protected market for its own goods, but the need to diversify its exports would be more urgent than within Confederation since, in the absence of interprovincial redistribution mechanisms, Quebec would not share, as it does at present, in the benefits of strong demand for Canadian exports from the other nine provinces.

However, even if sovereignty-association were implemented in good faith by both partners, certain negative consequences for Quebec, as well as for the rest of Canada, could hardly be avoided. One would be an increasing peripheralization of Quebec as investors insured themselves against the risks of an unknown régime by investing in the 'Canadian' areas of the common market. Another would be the probability of a deterioration in both the process and the content of economic decision making north of the American border at the three main points, that is, at interprovincial, interassociational, and international levels.

At the interprovincial level Quebec's absence would not necessarily facilitate intergovernmental relations in the rest of Canada. While the process might be improved in the absence of the bilingual-bicultural constraint, there is no reason to suppose that the inherent conflicts of interests among province builders and between 'have' and 'have-not' regions would be attenuated.

An association of two equal sovereign states would likely lead to a series of impasses or to the economic domination of one by the other.

On the international scene Quebec-Canada's bargaining power would almost certainly be weaker than that enjoyed by Canada at present both because of the uncertainty about the stability of the association in the minds of its trading partners and because of the difficulty in maintaining a single negotiating position on a number of important issues.

A final consideration is that while Quebec would certainly gain some policy independence, the scope for implementing decisions significantly different from those taken in the other competing regions of North America would be narrower than many people realize. A common market and a common currency zone require a fairly high degree of harmonization of fiscal and industrial policies. For example, if goods can move freely from one region to another, and wages are the same in each, it may be counter-productive for one region to impose stricter controls on foreign investment or to require a higher level of local content in manufacturing than do the other regions.

Concluding Comments

It is obviously impossible to predict the outcome of any of the constitutional options in terms of Canada's or Quebec's international economic relations. All I have attempted are a survey of the different forces shaping the two societies' external economic relations and suggestions about ways in which constitutional changes would affect these forces.

Constitutional changes taking place in the Canadian economic space would have almost no impact on the first series of factors that we have called 'world demand'. The second series of factors, 'domestic supply', includes the various facets of Canada's and Quebec's existing international trading relationships. A pattern of resource-based exports, dependence on capital imports and multinational companies, and current perceptions of Canada's and Quebec's role in the world economy are major elements of the picture. While constitutional change would not alter resource endowments, it could modify control over natural resources. Probably more important would be its impact on attitudes toward Canada and Quebec among foreign clients and investors. It is widely believed that constitutional modifications tending to reduce the power of the federal Government of Canada or to create a second sovereign nation would be viewed negatively by the country's foreign trading and investment partners. While this is an over-simplification, there is considerable basis for such an argument.

If we turn to the third series of factors, that is, domestic economic policies, we can see that constitutional change could strongly influence the kinds of policies adopted within the Canadian economic space and the effectiveness with which they are implemented. Both a reaffirmation of current federalism and a shift to sovereignty-association could provide the catalyst for major improvements in the use of human resources for capital deepening and for export diversification.

The relative weight attributed to domestic and to external factors in determining Canada's international economic relations is thus of crucial importance. If the country's international relations are believed to be exclusively determined by factors outside Canadian and Quebec control, then the impact of significant constitutional change is likely to be judged as negative in the international field, and Canadians will have to bear its costs in terms of reduced confidence on the part of foreign partners. If, on the other hand, domestic factors such as improvements in decision making and in the quality and mobility of the labour force can have a significant influence on Canada's external relations, then constitutional changes may either strengthen or weaken the country's international position, depending on whether these factors have positive or negative effects on the key variables I have discussed.

Notes

1.   This is not to deny the obvious influence of political factors; for a discussion of these factors, readers are referred to other papers in this collection.

2.   Rodney de C. Grey, *Trade Policy in the 1980s: An Agenda for Canadian–U.S. Relations*, Policy Commentary No. 3 (Montreal: C.D. Howe Institute, 1981).

3.   Floating exchanges have also been important in bringing this about.

4.   This situation had already become apparent before the conclusion of the MTNs through the way in which small countries, such as Sweden and Canada, were singled out for reprobation by the Textile Surveillance Board (TSB), while more important offenders, such as EC members (France and Britain) and the United States, pursued similar protectionist measures unhampered by the TSB.

5.   Solomon Fabricant, *The Economic Growth of the United States: Perspective and Prospective*, Canada—U.S. Prospects Series (Montreal: C.D. Howe Institute, 1979).

6.   See Grey, *Trade Policy in the 1980s*.

7.   United Nations, GATT Secretariat, *Trade Liberalism, Protectionism and Interdependence*, GATT Studies in International Trade, No. 5 (Geneva, 1977).

8.   Wendy Dobson, *Exports to Developing Countries: An Opportunity for Canada*, Observation No. 20 (Montreal: C.D. Howe Institute, 1979).

9.   Pierre-Paul Proulx, *et al.*, *Étude des relations commerciales Québec—U.S.A., Québec—Canada; options et impacts; contraintes et potentiels* (Québec: Éditeur officiel, 1978).

10.   Canada, Statistics Canada, External Trade Division, *Summary of External Trade* (Ottawa, 1981 and *Current Economic Analysis*, October 1981).

11.   Carmine Nappi, *Structure of Quebec's Exports* (Montreal: C.D. Howe Institute, 1978).

12.   Robert M. Dunn Jr., *The Canada—U.S. Capital Market: Intermediation, Integration, and Policy Independence*, Canada—U.S. Prospects Series (Montreal: C.D. Howe Institute, 1978).

13.   Pierre Bourgault and Harold Crookell, "Commercial Innovation in Secondary Industry," in *Business Quarterly* 44 (Autumn 1979): 56—64.

14.   See, for example, Kimon Valaskakis, « *L'option Europe* »: *Analyse de la plausibilité d'une association Québec/Canada/Europe* (Québec: Éditeur officiel, 1978).

15.   The Third Option was formulated in the Department of External Affairs paper, *Canada—United States: Options for the Future*, in 1972 as an alternative either to closer integration with the United States or to a continuation of the *status quo*. While the federal government has had little encouragement for its contractual link with the EC from the private sector, it has itself alienated goodwill in EC circles by apparently refusing to consider seriously the competitive bids European tenderers submitted for military aircraft in the late 1970s.

16.   Donald J. Daly, "Canada's Comparative Advantage," Discussion Paper No. 135 (Ottawa: Economic Council of Canada, 1979).

17.   *Ibid*.

18.   For a discussion of attempts to conceptualize and implement industrial strategy in the 1970s, see Richard D. French, *How Ottawa Decides Planning and Industrial Policy-Making, 1968—1980* (Ottawa: James Lorimer for Canadian Institute for Economic Policy, 1980).

19.   An example of the way in which constitutional considerations impinge on economic policies is provided by the provinces' reaction to the federal government's National Training Program announced in late 1981, to improve skilled-manpower training. Education and hence training are provincial responsibilities, but information on future needs and resources for programs may only be available country wide.

20.   At present it is extremely difficult to draw up and implement any extensive industrial strategy for Canada. There is even doubt if it is constitutionally possible to do so. See Richard Simeon, "Federalism and the Politics of an Industrial Strategy," in Science Council of Canada, *The Politics of an Industrial Strategy: A Seminar* (Ottawa: Minister of Supply and Services Canada, 1979), pp. 5—43, and Michael Jenkin, "The Prospects for a New National Policy," *Journal of Canadian Studies* 14 (Fall 1979): 126—41.

21.   This does not imply that the two constitutional options would yield the same economic results. There are, of course, very significant differences, particularly from a distributional point of view, but these do not necessarily affect external economic relations.

22.   Québec, Conseil exécutif, *Québec–Canada: A New Deal* (Quebec: Éditeur officiel, 1979).

The Author

CAROLINE PESTIEAU is head of the Montreal office of the C.D. Howe Institute. She was project manager of that Institute's Accent Québec Program, under which the Institute published fourteen papers between 1977 and 1980 on the Quebec economy and the economics of the Canadian Confederation. She was co-author, with Judith Maxwell, of the Program's final report, *Economic Realities of Contemporary Confederation*. Many of Caroline Pestieau's other professional responsibilities have been in the fields of international trade, commercial policy and industrial adjustment.

Appendix

CANADA

THE CONSTITUTION ACT, 1982

LA LOI CONSTITUTIONNELLE DE

1982

CONSTITUTION ACT, 1982

LOI CONSTITUTIONNELLE DE 1982

PART I

PARTIE I

CANADIAN CHARTER OF RIGHTS AND FREEDOMS

CHARTE CANADIENNE DES DROITS ET LIBERTÉS

Whereas Canada is founded upon principles that recognize the supremacy of God and the rule of law:

Attendu que le Canada est fondé sur des principes qui reconnaissent la suprématie de Dieu et la primauté du droit :

Guarantee of Rights and Freedoms

Garantie des droits et libertés

Rights and freedoms in Canada

1. The *Canadian Charter of Rights and Freedoms* guarantees the rights and freedoms set out in it subject only to such reasonable limits prescribed by law as can be demonstrably justified in a free and democratic society.

1. La *Charte canadienne des droits et libertés* garantit les droits et libertés qui y sont énoncés. Ils ne peuvent être restreints que par une règle de droit, dans des limites qui soient raisonnables et dont la justification puisse se démontrer dans le cadre d'une société libre et démocratique.

Droits et libertés au Canada

Fundamental Freedoms

Libertés fondamentales

Fundamental freedoms

2. Everyone has the following fundamental freedoms:

(*a*) freedom of conscience and religion;

(*b*) freedom of thought, belief, opinion and expression, including freedom of the press and other media of communication;

(*c*) freedom of peaceful assembly; and

(*d*) freedom of association.

2. Chacun a les libertés fondamentales suivantes :

a) liberté de conscience et de religion;

b) liberté de pensée, de croyance, d'opinion et d'expression, y compris la liberté de la presse et des autres moyens de communication;

c) liberté de réunion pacifique;

d) liberté d'association.

Libertés fondamentales

Democratic Rights

Droits démocratiques

Democratic rights of citizens

3. Every citizen of Canada has the right to vote in an election of members of the House of Commons or of a legislative assembly and to be qualified for membership therein.

3. Tout citoyen canadien a le droit de vote et est éligible aux élections législatives fédérales ou provinciales.

Droits démocratiques des citoyens

Maximum duration of legislative bodies

4. (1) No House of Commons and no legislative assembly shall continue for longer than five years from the date fixed for the return of the writs at a general election of its members.

4. (1) Le mandat maximal de la Chambre des communes et des assemblées législatives est de cinq ans à compter de la date fixée pour le retour des brefs relatifs aux élections générales correspondantes.

Mandat maximal des assemblées

Continuation in special circumstances

(2) In time of real or apprehended war, invasion or insurrection, a House of Commons may be continued by Parliament and a legisla-

(2) Le mandat de la Chambre des communes ou celui d'une assemblée législative peut être prolongé respectivement par le Parlement ou par la

Prolongations spéciales

tive assembly may be continued by the legislature beyond five years if such continuation is not opposed by the votes of more than one-third of the members of the House of Commons or the legislative assembly, as the case may be.

législature en question au-delà de cinq ans en cas de guerre, d'invasion ou d'insurrection, réelles ou appréhendées, pourvu que cette prolongation ne fasse pas l'objet d'une opposition exprimée par les voix de plus du tiers des députés de la Chambre des communes ou de l'assemblée législative.

Annual sitting of legislative bodies

5. There shall be a sitting of Parliament and of each legislature at least once every twelve months.

5. Le Parlement èt les législatures tiennent une séance au moins une fois tous les douze mois.

Séance annuelle

Mobility Rights

Liberté de circulation et d'établissement

Mobility of citizens

6. (1) Every citizen of Canada has the right to enter, remain in and leave Canada.

6. (1) Tout citoyen canadien a le droit de demeurer au Canada, d'y entrer ou d'en sortir.

Liberté de circulation

Rights to move and gain livelihood

(2) Every citizen of Canada and every person who has the status of a permanent resident of Canada has the right

(*a*) to move to and take up residence in any province; and

(*b*) to pursue the gaining of a livelihood in any province.

(2) Tout citoyen canadien et toute personne ayant le statut de résident permanent au Canada ont le droit :

a) de se déplacer dans tout le pays et d'établir leur résidence dans toute province;

b) de gagner leur vie dans toute province.

Liberté d'établissement

Limitation

(3) The rights specified in subsection (2) are subject to

(*a*) any laws or practices of general application in force in a province other than those that discriminate among persons primarily on the basis of province of present or previous residence; and

(*b*) any laws providing for reasonable residency requirements as a qualification for the receipt of publicly provided social services.

(3) Les droits mentionnés au paragraphe (2) sont subordonnés :

a) aux lois et usages d'application générale en vigueur dans une province donnée, s'ils n'établissent entre les personnes aucune distinction fondée principalement sur la province de résidence antérieure ou actuelle;

b) aux lois prévoyant de justes conditions de résidence en vue de l'obtention des services sociaux publics.

Restriction

Affirmative action programs

(4) Subsections (2) and (3) do not preclude any law, program or activity that has as its object the amelioration in a province of conditions of individuals in that province who are socially or economically disadvantaged if the rate of employment in that province is below the rate of employment in Canada.

(4) Les paragraphes (2) et (3) n'ont pas pour objet d'interdire les lois, programmes ou activités destinés à améliorer, dans une province, la situation d'individus défavorisés socialement ou économiquement, si le taux d'emploi dans la province est inférieur à la moyenne nationale.

Programmes de promotion sociale

Legal Rights

Garanties juridiques

Life, liberty and security of person

7. Everyone has the right to life, liberty and security of the person and the right not to be deprived thereof

7. Chacun a droit à la vie, à la liberté et à la sécurité de sa personne; il ne peut être porté atteinte à ce

Vie, liberté et sécurité

except in accordance with the principles of fundamental justice.

droit qu'en conformité avec les principes de justice fondamentale.

Search or seizure

8. Everyone has the right to be secure against unreasonable search or seizure.

8. Chacun a droit à la protection contre les fouilles, les perquisitions ou les saisies abusives.

Fouilles, perquisitions ou saisies

Detention or imprisonment

9. Everyone has the right not to be arbitrarily detained or imprisoned.

9. Chacun a droit à la protection contre la détention ou l'emprisonnement arbitraires.

Détention ou emprisonnement

Arrest or detention

10. Everyone has the right on arrest or detention

(*a*) to be informed promptly of the reasons therefor;

(*b*) to retain and instruct counsel without delay and to be informed of that right; and

(*c*) to have the validity of the detention determined by way of *habeas corpus* and to be released if the detention is not lawful.

10. Chacun a le droit, en cas d'arrestation ou de détention :

a) d'être informé dans les plus brefs délais des motifs de son arrestation ou de sa détention;

b) d'avoir recours sans délai à l'assistance d'un avocat et d'être informé de ce droit;

c) de faire contrôler, par *habeas corpus,* la légalité de sa détention et d'obtenir, le cas échéant, sa libération.

Arrestation ou détention

Proceedings in criminal and penal matters

11. Any person charged with an offence has the right

(*a*) to be informed without unreasonable delay of the specific offence;

(*b*) to be tried within a reasonable time;

(*c*) not to be compelled to be a witness in proceedings against that person in respect of the offence;

(*d*) to be presumed innocent until proven guilty according to law in a fair and public hearing by an independent and impartial tribunal;

(*e*) not to be denied reasonable bail without just cause;

(*f*) except in the case of an offence under military law tried before a military tribunal, to the benefit of trial by jury where the maximum punishment for the offence is imprisonment for five years or a more severe punishment;

(*g*) not to be found guilty on account of any act or omission unless, at the time of the act or omission, it constituted an offence under Canadian or international law or was criminal according to the general principles of law recognized by the community of nations;

11. Tout inculpé a le droit :

a) d'être informé sans délai anormal de l'infraction précise qu'on lui reproche;

b) d'être jugé dans un délai raisonnable;

c) de ne pas être contraint de témoigner contre lui-même dans toute poursuite intentée contre lui pour l'infraction qu'on lui reproche;

d) d'être présumé innocent tant qu'il n'est pas déclaré coupable, conformément à la loi, par un tribunal indépendant et impartial à l'issue d'un procès public et équitable;

e) de ne pas être privé sans juste cause d'une mise en liberté assortie d'un cautionnement raisonnable;

f) sauf s'il s'agit d'une infraction relevant de la justice militaire, de bénéficier d'un procès avec jury lorsque la peine maximale prévue pour l'infraction dont il est accusé est un emprisonnement de cinq ans ou une peine plus grave;

g) de ne pas être déclaré coupable en raison d'une action ou d'une omission qui, au moment où elle est survenue, ne constituait pas une infraction d'après le droit interne

Affaires criminelles et pénales

(*h*) if finally acquitted of the offence, not to be tried for it again and, if finally found guilty and punished for the offence, not to be tried or punished for it again; and

(*i*) if found guilty of the offence and if the punishment for the offence has been varied between the time of commission and the time of sentencing, to the benefit of the lesser punishment.

du Canada ou le droit international et n'avait pas de caractère criminel d'après les principes généraux de droit reconnus par l'ensemble des nations;

h) d'une part de ne pas être jugé de nouveau pour une infraction dont il a été définitivement acquitté, d'autre part de ne pas être jugé ni puni de nouveau pour une infraction dont il a été définitivement déclaré coupable et puni;

i) de bénéficier de la peine la moins sévère, lorsque la peine qui sanctionne l'infraction dont il est déclaré coupable est modifiée entre le moment de la perpétration de l'infraction et celui de la sentence.

Treatment or punishment

12. Everyone has the right not to be subjected to any cruel and unusual treatment or punishment.

12. Chacun a droit à la protection contre tous traitements ou peines cruels et inusités. **Cruauté**

Self-crimination

13. A witness who testifies in any proceedings has the right not to have any incriminating evidence so given used to incriminate that witness in any other proceedings, except in a prosecution for perjury or for the giving of contradictory evidence.

13. Chacun a droit à ce qu'aucun témoignage incriminant qu'il donne ne soit utilisé pour l'incriminer dans d'autres procédures, sauf lors de poursuites pour parjure ou pour témoignages contradictoires. **Témoignage incriminant**

Interpreter

14. A party or witness in any proceedings who does not understand or speak the language in which the proceedings are conducted or who is deaf has the right to the assistance of an interpreter.

14. La partie ou le témoin qui ne peuvent suivre les procédures, soit parce qu'ils ne comprennent pas ou ne parlent pas la langue employée, soit parce qu'ils sont atteints de surdité, ont droit à l'assistance d'un interprète. **Interprète**

Equality Rights

Droits à l'égalité

Equality before and under law and equal protection and benefit of law

15. (1) Every individual is equal before and under the law and has the right to the equal protection and equal benefit of the law without discrimination and, in particular, without discrimination based on race, national or ethnic origin, colour, religion, sex, age or mental or physical disability.

15. (1) La loi ne fait acception de personne et s'applique également à tous, et tous ont droit à la même protection et au même bénéfice de la loi, indépendamment de toute discrimination, notamment des discriminations fondées sur la race, l'origine nationale ou ethnique, la couleur, la religion, le sexe, l'âge ou les déficiences mentales ou physiques. **Égalité devant la loi, égalité de bénéfice et protection égale de la loi**

Affirmative action programs

(2) Subsection (1) does not preclude any law, program or activity that has as its object the amelioration of conditions of disadvantaged individuals or groups including those that are disadvantaged because of

(2) Le paragraphe (1) n'a pas pour effet d'interdire les lois, programmes ou activités destinés à améliorer la situation d'individus ou de groupes défavorisés, notamment du fait de leur race, de leur origine nationale ou **Programmes de promotion sociale**

race, national or ethnic origin, colour, religion, sex, age or mental or physical disability.

ethnique, de leur couleur, de leur religion, de leur sexe, de leur âge ou de leurs déficiences mentales ou physiques.

Official Languages of Canada

Langues officielles du Canada

Official languages of Canada

16. (1) English and French are the official languages of Canada and have equality of status and equal rights and privileges as to their use in all institutions of the Parliament and government of Canada.

16. (1) Le français et l'anglais sont les langues officielles du Canada; ils ont un statut et des droits et privilèges égaux quant à leur usage dans les institutions du Parlement et du gouvernement du Canada.

Langues officielles du Canada

Official languages of New Brunswick

(2) English and French are the official languages of New Brunswick and have equality of status and equal rights and privileges as to their use in all institutions of the legislature and government of New Brunswick.

(2) Le français et l'anglais sont les langues officielles du Nouveau-Brunswick; ils ont un statut et des droits et privilèges égaux quant à leur usage dans les institutions de la Législature et du gouvernement du Nouveau-Brunswick.

Langues officielles du Nouveau-Brunswick

Advancement of status and use

(3) Nothing in this Charter limits the authority of Parliament or a legislature to advance the equality of status or use of English and French.

(3) La présente charte ne limite pas le pouvoir du Parlement et des législatures de favoriser la progression vers l'égalité de statut ou d'usage du français et de l'anglais.

Progression vers l'égalité

Proceedings of Parliament

17. (1) Everyone has the right to use English or French in any debates and other proceedings of Parliament.

17. (1) Chacun a le droit d'employer le français ou l'anglais dans les débats et travaux du Parlement.

Travaux du Parlement

Proceedings of New Brunswick legislature

(2) Everyone has the right to use English or French in any debates and other proceedings of the legislature of New Brunswick.

(2) Chacun a le droit d'employer le français ou l'anglais dans les débats et travaux de la Législature du Nouveau-Brunswick.

Travaux de la Législature du Nouveau-Brunswick

Parliamentary statutes and records

18. (1) The statutes, records and journals of Parliament shall be printed and published in English and French and both language versions are equally authoritative.

18. (1) Les lois, les archives, les comptes rendus et les procès-verbaux du Parlement sont imprimés et publiés en français et en anglais, les deux versions des lois ayant également force de loi et celles des autres documents ayant même valeur.

Documents parlementaires

New Brunswick statutes and records

(2) The statutes, records and journals of the legislature of New Brunswick shall be printed and published in English and French and both language versions are equally authoritative.

(2) Les lois, les archives, les comptes rendus et les procès-verbaux de la Législature du Nouveau-Brunswick sont imprimés et publiés en français et en anglais, les deux versions des lois ayant également force de loi et celles des autres documents ayant même valeur.

Documents de la Législature du Nouveau-Brunswick

Proceedings in courts established by Parliament

19. (1) Either English or French may be used by any person in, or in any pleading in or process issuing from, any court established by Parliament.

19. (1) Chacun a le droit d'employer le français ou l'anglais dans toutes les affaires dont sont saisis les tribunaux établis par le Parlement et dans tous les actes de procédure qui en découlent.

Procédures devant les tribunaux établis par le Parlement

Proceedings in New Brunswick courts

(2) Either English or French may be used by any person in, or in any pleading in or process issuing from, any court of New Brunswick.

(2) Chacun a le droit d'employer le français ou l'anglais dans toutes les affaires dont sont saisis les tribunaux du Nouveau-Brunswick et dans tous les actes de procédure qui en découlent.

Procédures devant les tribunaux du Nouveau-Brunswick

Communications by public with federal institutions

20. (1) Any member of the public in Canada has the right to communicate with, and to receive available services from, any head or central office of an institution of the Parliament or government of Canada in English or French, and has the same right with respect to any other office of any such institution where

(*a*) there is a significant demand for communications with and services from that office in such language; or

(*b*) due to the nature of the office, it is reasonable that communications with and services from that office be available in both English and French.

20. (1) Le public a, au Canada, droit à l'emploi du français ou de l'anglais pour communiquer avec le siège ou l'administration centrale des institutions du Parlement ou du gouvernement du Canada ou pour en recevoir les services; il a le même droit à l'égard de tout autre bureau de ces institutions là où, selon le cas :

a) l'emploi du français ou de l'anglais fait l'objet d'une demande importante;

b) l'emploi du français et de l'anglais se justifie par la vocation du bureau.

Communications entre les administrés et les institutions fédérales

Communications by public with New Brunswick institutions

(2) Any member of the public in New Brunswick has the right to communicate with, and to receive available services from, any office of an institution of the legislature or government of New Brunswick in English or French.

(2) Le public a, au Nouveau-Brunswick, droit à l'emploi du français ou de l'anglais pour communiquer avec tout bureau des institutions de la législature ou du gouvernement ou pour en recevoir les services.

Communications entre les administrés et les institutions du Nouveau-Brunswick

Continuation of existing constitutional provisions

21. Nothing in sections 16 to 20 abrogates or derogates from any right, privilege or obligation with respect to the English and French languages, or either of them, that exists or is continued by virtue of any other provision of the Constitution of Canada.

21. Les articles 16 à 20 n'ont pas pour effet, en ce qui a trait à la langue française ou anglaise ou à ces deux langues, de porter atteinte aux droits, privilèges ou obligations qui existent ou sont maintenus aux termes d'une autre disposition de la Constitution du Canada.

Maintien en vigueur de certaines dispositions

Rights and privileges preserved

22. Nothing in sections 16 to 20 abrogates or derogates from any legal or customary right or privilege acquired or enjoyed either before or after the coming into force of this Charter with respect to any language that is not English or French.

22. Les articles 16 à 20 n'ont pas pour effet de porter atteinte aux droits et privilèges, antérieurs ou postérieurs à l'entrée en vigueur de la présente charte et découlant de la loi ou de la coutume, des langues autres que le français ou l'anglais.

Droits préservés

Minority Language Educational Rights

Droits à l'instruction dans la langue de la minorité

Language of instruction

23. (1) Citizens of Canada

(*a*) whose first language learned and still understood is that of the English or French linguistic

23. (1) Les citoyens canadiens :

a) dont la première langue apprise et encore comprise est celle de la minorité francophone ou anglo-

Langue d'instruction

minority population of the province in which they reside, or

(*b*) who have received their primary school instruction in Canada in English or French and reside in a province where the language in which they received that instruction is the language of the English or French linguistic minority population of the province,

have the right to have their children receive primary and secondary school instruction in that language in that province.

Continuity of language instruction

(2) Citizens of Canada of whom any child has received or is receiving primary or secondary school instruction in English or French in Canada, have the right to have all their children receive primary and secondary school instruction in the same language.

Application where numbers warrant

(3) The right of citizens of Canada under subsections (1) and (2) to have their children receive primary and secondary school instruction in the language of the English or French linguistic minority population of a province

(*a*) applies wherever in the province the number of children of citizens who have such a right is sufficient to warrant the provision to them out of public funds of minority language instruction; and

(*b*) includes, where the number of those children so warrants, the right to have them receive that instruction in minority language educational facilities provided out of public funds.

Enforcement

Enforcement of guaranteed rights and freedoms

24. (1) Anyone whose rights or freedoms, as guaranteed by this Charter, have been infringed or denied may apply to a court of competent jurisdiction to obtain such remedy as the court considers appropriate and just in the circumstances.

Exclusion of evidence bringing administration of justice into disrepute

(2) Where, in proceedings under subsection (1), a court concludes that evidence was obtained in a manner

phone de la province où ils résident,

b) qui ont reçu leur instruction, au niveau primaire, en français ou en anglais au Canada et qui résident dans une province où la langue dans laquelle ils ont reçu cette instruction est celle de la minorité francophone ou anglophone de la province,

ont, dans l'un ou l'autre cas, le droit d'y faire instruire leurs enfants, aux niveaux primaire et secondaire, dans cette langue.

(2) Les citoyens canadiens dont un enfant a reçu ou reçoit son instruction, au niveau primaire ou secondaire, en français ou en anglais au Canada ont le droit de faire instruire tous leurs enfants, aux niveaux primaire et secondaire, dans la langue de cette instruction.

Continuité d'emploi de la langue d'instruction

(3) Le droit reconnu aux citoyens canadiens par les paragraphes (1) et (2) de faire instruire leurs enfants, aux niveaux primaire et secondaire, dans la langue de la minorité francophone ou anglophone d'une province :

a) s'exerce partout dans la province où le nombre des enfants des citoyens qui ont ce droit est suffisant pour justifier à leur endroit la prestation, sur les fonds publics, de l'instruction dans la langue de la minorité;

b) comprend, lorsque le nombre de ces enfants le justifie, le droit de les faire instruire dans des établissements d'enseignement de la minorité linguistique financés sur les fonds publics.

Justification par le nombre

Recours

24. (1) Toute personne, victime de violation ou de négation des droits ou libertés qui lui sont garantis par la présente charte, peut s'adresser à un tribunal compétent pour obtenir la réparation que le tribunal estime convenable et juste eu égard aux circonstances.

Recours en cas d'atteinte aux droits et libertés

(2) Lorsque, dans une instance visée au paragraphe (1), le tribunal a conclu que des éléments de preuve

Irrecevabilité d'éléments de preuve qui risqueraient de déconsidérer l'administration de la justice

that infringed or denied any rights or freedoms guaranteed by this Charter, the evidence shall be excluded if it is established that, having regard to all the circumstances, the admission of it in the proceedings would bring the administration of justice into disrepute.

ont été obtenus dans des conditions qui portent atteinte aux droits ou libertés garantis par la présente charte, ces éléments de preuve sont écartés s'il est établi, eu égard aux circonstances, que leur utilisation est susceptible de déconsidérer l'administration de la justice.

General

Dispositions générales

Aboriginal rights and freedoms not affected by Charter

25. The guarantee in this Charter of certain rights and freedoms shall not be construed so as to abrogate or derogate from any aboriginal, treaty or other rights or freedoms that pertain to the aboriginal peoples of Canada including

(*a*) any rights or freedoms that have been recognized by the Royal Proclamation of October 7, 1763; and

(*b*) any rights or freedoms that may be acquired by the aboriginal peoples of Canada by way of land claims settlement.

25. Le fait que la présente charte garantit certains droits et libertés ne porte pas atteinte aux droits ou libertés — ancestraux, issus de traités ou autres — des peuples autochtones du Canada, notamment :

a) aux droits ou libertés reconnus par la Proclamation royale du 7 octobre 1763;

b) aux droits ou libertés acquis par règlement de revendications territoriales.

Maintien des droits et libertés des autochtones

Other rights and freedoms not affected by Charter

26. The guarantee in this Charter of certain rights and freedoms shall not be construed as denying the existence of any other rights or freedoms that exist in Canada.

26. Le fait que la présente charte garantit certains droits et libertés ne constitue pas une négation des autres droits ou libertés qui existent au Canada.

Maintien des autres droits et libertés

Multicultural heritage

27. This Charter shall be interpreted in a manner consistent with the preservation and enhancement of the multicultural heritage of Canadians.

27. Toute interprétation de la présente charte doit concorder avec l'objectif de promouvoir le maintien et la valorisation du patrimoine multiculturel des Canadiens.

Maintien du patrimoine culturel

Rights guaranteed equally to both sexes

28. Notwithstanding anything in this Charter, the rights and freedoms referred to in it are guaranteed equally to male and female persons.

28. Indépendamment des autres dispositions de la présente charte, les droits et libertés qui y sont mentionnés sont garantis également aux personnes des deux sexes.

Égalité de garantie des droits pour les deux sexes

Rights respecting certain schools preserved

29. Nothing in this Charter abrogates or derogates from any rights or privileges guaranteed by or under the Constitution of Canada in respect of denominational, separate or dissentient schools.

29. Les dispositions de la présente charte ne portent pas atteinte aux droits ou privilèges garantis en vertu de la Constitution du Canada concernant les écoles séparées et autres écoles confessionnelles.

Maintien des droits relatifs à certaines écoles

Application to territories and territorial authorities

30. A reference in this Charter to a province or to the legislative assembly or legislature of a province shall be deemed to include a reference to the Yukon Territory and the Northwest Territories, or to the

30. Dans la présente charte, les dispositions qui visent les provinces, leur législature ou leur assemblée législative visent également le territoire du Yukon, les territoires du Nord-Ouest ou leurs autorités législatives compétentes.

Application aux territoires

appropriate legislative authority
thereof, as the case may be.

Legislative powers not extended

31. Nothing in this Charter
extends the legislative powers of any
body or authority.

31. La présente charte n'élargit
pas les compétences législatives de
quelque organisme ou autorité que ce
soit. *Non-élargissement des compétences législatives*

Application of Charter

Application de la charte

Application of Charter

32. (1) This Charter applies
(*a*) to the Parliament and government of Canada in respect of all
matters within the authority of
Parliament including all matters
relating to the Yukon Territory
and Northwest Territories; and
(*b*) to the legislature and government of each province in respect of
all matters within the authority of
the legislature of each province.

32. (1) La présente charte s'applique :
a) au Parlement et au gouvernement du Canada, pour tous les
domaines relevant du Parlement, y
compris ceux qui concernent le territoire du Yukon et les territoires
du Nord-Ouest;
b) à la législature et au gouvernement de chaque province, pour tous
les domaines relevant de cette
législature. *Application de la charte*

Exception

(2) Notwithstanding subsection
(1), section 15 shall not have effect
until three years after this section
comes into force.

(2) Par dérogation au paragraphe
(1), l'article 15 n'a d'effet que trois
ans après l'entrée en vigueur du présent article. *Restriction*

Exception where express declaration

33. (1) Parliament or the legislature of a province may expressly
declare in an Act of Parliament or of
the legislature, as the case may be,
that the Act or a provision thereof
shall operate notwithstanding a provision included in section 2 or sections
7 to 15 of this Charter.

33. (1) Le Parlement ou la législature d'une province peut adopter une
loi où il est expressément déclaré que
celle-ci ou une de ses dispositions a
effet indépendamment d'une disposition donnée de l'article 2 ou des articles 7 à 15 de la présente charte. *Dérogation par déclaration expresse*

Operation of exception

(2) An Act or a provision of an Act
in respect of which a declaration is
made under this section is in effect
shall have such operation as it would
have but for the provision of this
Charter referred to in the declaration.

(2) La loi ou la disposition qui fait
l'objet d'une déclaration conforme au
présent article et en vigueur a l'effet
qu'elle aurait sauf la disposition en
cause de la charte. *Effet de la dérogation*

Five year limitation

(3) A declaration made under subsection (1) shall cease to have effect
five years after it comes into force or
on such earlier date as may be specified in the declaration.

(3) La déclaration visée au paragraphe (1) cesse d'avoir effet à la
date qui y est précisée ou, au plus
tard, cinq ans après son entrée en
vigueur. *Durée de validité*

Re-enactment

(4) Parliament or the legislature of
a province may re-enact a declaration
made under subsection (1).

(4) Le Parlement ou une législature peut adopter de nouveau une
déclaration visée au paragraphe (1). *Nouvelle adoption*

Five year limitation

(5) Subsection (3) applies in
respect of a re-enactment made under
subsection (4).

(5) Le paragraphe (3) s'applique à
toute déclaration adoptée sous le
régime du paragraphe (4). *Durée de validité*

Citation

Citation

34. This Part may be cited as the *Canadian Charter of Rights and Freedoms.*

PART II

RIGHTS OF THE ABORIGINAL
PEOPLES OF CANADA

Recognition of existing aboriginal and treaty rights

35. (1) The existing aboriginal and treaty rights of the aboriginal peoples of Canada are hereby recognized and affirmed.

Definition of "aboriginal peoples of Canada"

(2) In this Act, "aboriginal peoples of Canada" includes the Indian, Inuit and Métis peoples of Canada.

PART III

EQUALIZATION AND REGIONAL
DISPARITIES

Commitment to promote equal opportunities

36. (1) Without altering the legislative authority of Parliament or of the provincial legislatures, or the rights of any of them with respect to the exercise of their legislative authority, Parliament and the legislatures, together with the government of Canada and the provincial governments, are committed to

(*a*) promoting equal opportunities for the well-being of Canadians;

(*b*) furthering economic development to reduce disparity in opportunities; and

(*c*) providing essential public services of reasonable quality to all Canadians.

Commitment respecting public services

(2) Parliament and the government of Canada are committed to the principle of making equalization payments to ensure that provincial governments have sufficient revenues to provide reasonably comparable levels of public services at reasonably comparable levels of taxation.

Titre

34. Titre de la présente partie : *Charte canadienne des droits et libertés.* Titre

PARTIE II

DROITS DES PEUPLES AUTOCHTONES
DU CANADA

35. (1) Les droits existants — ancestraux ou issus de traités — des peuples autochtones du Canada sont reconnus et confirmés. Confirmation des droits existants des peuples autochtones

(2) Dans la présente loi, «peuples autochtones du Canada» s'entend notamment des Indiens, des Inuit et des Métis du Canada. Définition de «peuples autochtones du Canada»

PARTIE III

PÉRÉQUATION ET INÉGALITÉS
RÉGIONALES

36. (1) Sous réserve des compétences législatives du Parlement et des législatures et de leur droit de les exercer, le Parlement et les législatures, ainsi que les gouvernements fédéral et provinciaux, s'engagent à : Engagements relatifs à l'égalité des chances

a) promouvoir l'égalité des chances de tous les Canadiens dans la recherche de leur bien-être;

b) favoriser le développement économique pour réduire l'inégalité des chances;

c) fournir à tous les Canadiens, à un niveau de qualité acceptable, les services publics essentiels.

(2) Le Parlement et le gouvernement du Canada prennent l'engagement de principe de faire des paiements de péréquation propres à donner aux gouvernements provinciaux des revenus suffisants pour les mettre en mesure d'assurer les services publics à un niveau de qualité et de fiscalité sensiblement comparables. Engagement relatif aux services publics

PART IV

CONSTITUTIONAL CONFERENCE

PARTIE IV

CONFÉRENCE CONSTITUTIONNELLE

Constitutional conference

37. (1) A constitutional conference composed of the Prime Minister of Canada and the first ministers of the provinces shall be convened by the Prime Minister of Canada within one year after this Part comes into force.

37. (1) Dans l'année suivant l'entrée en vigueur de la présente partie, le premier ministre du Canada convoque une conférence constitutionnelle réunissant les premiers ministres provinciaux et lui-même.

Conférence constitution-nelle

Participation of aboriginal peoples

(2) The conference convened under subsection (1) shall have included in its agenda an item respecting constitutional matters that directly affect the aboriginal peoples of Canada, including the identification and definition of the rights of those peoples to be included in the Constitution of Canada, and the Prime Minister of Canada shall invite representatives of those peoples to participate in the discussions on that item.

(2) Sont placées à l'ordre du jour de la conférence visée au paragraphe (1) les questions constitutionnelles qui intéressent directement les peuples autochtones du Canada, notamment la détermination et la définition des droits de ces peuples à inscrire dans la Constitution du Canada. Le premier ministre du Canada invite leurs représentants à participer aux travaux relatifs à ces questions.

Participation des peuples autochtones

Participation of territories

(3) The Prime Minister of Canada shall invite elected representatives of the governments of the Yukon Territory and the Northwest Territories to participate in the discussions on any item on the agenda of the conference convened under subsection (1) that, in the opinion of the Prime Minister, directly affects the Yukon Territory and the Northwest Territories.

(3) Le premier ministre du Canada invite des représentants élus des gouvernements du territoire du Yukon et des territoires du Nord-Ouest à participer aux travaux relatifs à toute question placée à l'ordre du jour de la conférence visée au paragraphe (1) et qui, selon lui, intéresse directement le territoire du Yukon et les territoires du Nord-Ouest.

Participation des territoires

PART V

PROCEDURE FOR AMENDING CONSTITUTION OF CANADA

PARTIE V

PROCÉDURE DE MODIFICATION DE LA CONSTITUTION DU CANADA

General procedure for amending Constitution of Canada

38. (1) An amendment to the Constitution of Canada may be made by proclamation issued by the Governor General under the Great Seal of Canada where so authorized by

(*a*) resolutions of the Senate and House of Commons; and

(*b*) resolutions of the legislative assemblies of at least two-thirds of the provinces that have, in the aggregate, according to the then latest general census, at least fifty per cent of the population of all the provinces.

38. (1) La Constitution du Canada peut être modifiée par proclamation du gouverneur général sous le grand sceau du Canada, autorisée à la fois :

a) par des résolutions du Sénat et de la Chambre des communes;

b) par des résolutions des assemblées législatives d'au moins deux tiers des provinces dont la population confondue représente, selon le recensement général le plus récent à l'époque, au moins cinquante pour cent de la population de toutes les provinces.

Procédure normale de modification

Majority of members

(2) An amendment made under subsection (1) that derogates from the legislative powers, the proprietary rights or any other rights or privileges

(2) Une modification faite conformément au paragraphe (1) mais dérogatoire à la compétence législative, aux droits de propriété ou à tous

Majorité simple

of the legislature or government of a province shall require a resolution supported by a majority of the members of each of the Senate, the House of Commons and the legislative assemblies required under subsection (1).

autres droits ou privilèges d'une législature ou d'un gouvernement provincial exige une résolution adoptée à la majorité des sénateurs, des députés fédéraux et des députés de chacune des assemblées législatives du nombre requis de provinces.

Expression of dissent

(3) An amendment referred to in subsection (2) shall not have effect in a province the legislative assembly of which has expressed its dissent thereto by resolution supported by a majority of its members prior to the issue of the proclamation to which the amendment relates unless that legislative assembly, subsequently, by resolution supported by a majority of its members, revokes its dissent and authorizes the amendment.

(3) La modification visée au paragraphe (2) est sans effet dans une province dont l'assemblée législative a, avant la prise de la proclamation, exprimé son désaccord par une résolution adoptée à la majorité des députés, sauf si cette assemblée, par résolution également adoptée à la majorité, revient sur son désaccord et autorise la modification.

Désaccord

Revocation of dissent

(4) A resolution of dissent made for the purposes of subsection (3) may be revoked at any time before or after the issue of the proclamation to which it relates.

(4) La résolution de désaccord visée au paragraphe (3) peut être révoquée à tout moment, indépendamment de la date de la proclamation à laquelle elle se rapporte.

Levée du désaccord

Restriction on proclamation

39. (1) A proclamation shall not be issued under subsection 38(1) before the expiration of one year from the adoption of the resolution initiating the amendment procedure thereunder, unless the legislative assembly of each province has previously adopted a resolution of assent or dissent.

39. (1) La proclamation visée au paragraphe 38(1) ne peut être prise dans l'année suivant l'adoption de la résolution à l'origine de la procédure de modification que si l'assemblée législative de chaque province a préalablement adopté une résolution d'agrément ou de désaccord.

Restriction

Idem

(2) A proclamation shall not be issued under subsection 38(1) after the expiration of three years from the adoption of the resolution initiating the amendment procedure thereunder.

(2) La proclamation visée au paragraphe 38(1) ne peut être prise que dans les trois ans suivant l'adoption de la résolution à l'origine de la procédure de modification.

Idem

Compensation

40. Where an amendment is made under subsection 38(1) that transfers provincial legislative powers relating to education or other cultural matters from provincial legislatures to Parliament, Canada shall provide reasonable compensation to any province to which the amendment does not apply.

40. Le Canada fournit une juste compensation aux provinces auxquelles ne s'applique pas une modification faite conformément au paragraphe 38(1) et relative, en matière d'éducation ou dans d'autres domaines culturels, à un transfert de compétences législatives provinciales au Parlement.

Compensation

Amendment by unanimous consent

41. An amendment to the Constitution of Canada in relation to the following matters may be made by proclamation issued by the Governor General under the Great Seal of

41. Toute modification de la Constitution du Canada portant sur les questions suivantes se fait par proclamation du gouverneur général sous le grand sceau du Canada, autorisée par

Consentement unanime

Canada only where authorized by resolutions of the Senate and House of Commons and of the legislative assembly of each province:

    (*a*) the office of the Queen, the Governor General and the Lieutenant Governor of a province;

    (*b*) the right of a province to a number of members in the House of Commons not less than the number of Senators by which the province is entitled to be represented at the time this Part comes into force;

    (*c*) subject to section 43, the use of the English or the French language;

    (*d*) the composition of the Supreme Court of Canada; and

    (*e*) an amendment to this Part.

Amendment by general procedure

42. (1) An amendment to the Constitution of Canada in relation to the following matters may be made only in accordance with subsection 38(1) :

    (*a*) the principle of proportionate representation of the provinces in the House of Commons prescribed by the Constitution of Canada;

    (*b*) the powers of the Senate and the method of selecting Senators;

    (*c*) the number of members by which a province is entitled to be represented in the Senate and the residence qualifications of Senators;

    (*d*) subject to paragraph 41(*d*), the Supreme Court of Canada;

    (*e*) the extension of existing provinces into the territories; and

    (*f*) notwithstanding any other law or practice, the establishment of new provinces.

Exception

(2) Subsections 38(2) to (4) do not apply in respect of amendments in relation to matters referred to in subsection (1).

Amendment of provisions relating to some but not all provinces

43. An amendment to the Constitution of Canada in relation to any provision that applies to one or more, but not all, provinces, including

    (*a*) any alteration to boundaries between provinces, and

des résolutions du Sénat, de la Chambre des communes et de l'assemblée législative de chaque province :

    a) la charge de Reine, celle de gouverneur général et celle de lieutenant-gouverneur;

    b) le droit d'une province d'avoir à la Chambre des communes un nombre de députés au moins égal à celui des sénateurs par lesquels elle est habilitée à être représentée lors de l'entrée en vigueur de la présente partie;

    c) sous réserve de l'article 43, l'usage du français ou de l'anglais;

    d) la composition de la Cour suprême du Canada;

    e) la modification de la présente partie.

42. (1) Toute modification de la Constitution du Canada portant sur les questions suivantes se fait conformément au paragraphe 38(1) :

    a) le principe de la représentation proportionnelle des provinces à la Chambre des communes prévu par la Constitution du Canada;

    b) les pouvoirs du Sénat et le mode de sélection des sénateurs;

    c) le nombre des sénateurs par lesquels une province est habilitée à être représentée et les conditions de résidence qu'ils doivent remplir;

    d) sous réserve de l'alinéa 41*d*), la Cour suprême du Canada;

    e) le rattachement aux provinces existantes de tout ou partie des territoires;

    f) par dérogation à toute autre loi ou usage, la création de provinces.

Procédure normale de modification

(2) Les paragraphes 38(2) à (4) ne s'appliquent pas aux questions mentionnées au paragraphe (1).

Exception

43. Les dispositions de la Constitution du Canada applicables à certaines provinces seulement ne peuvent être modifiées que par proclamation du gouverneur général sous le grand sceau du Canada, autorisée par des résolutions du Sénat, de la Chambre

Modification à l'égard de certaines provinces

(*b*) any amendment to any provision that relates to the use of the English or the French language within a province,

may be made by proclamation issued by the Governor General under the Great Seal of Canada only where so authorized by resolutions of the Senate and House of Commons and of the legislative assembly of each province to which the amendment applies.

des communes et de l'assemblée législative de chaque province concernée. Le présent article s'applique notamment :

a) aux changements du tracé des frontières interprovinciales;

b) aux modifications des dispositions relatives à l'usage du français ou de l'anglais dans une province.

Amendments by Parliament

44. Subject to sections 41 and 42, Parliament may exclusively make laws amending the Constitution of Canada in relation to the executive government of Canada or the Senate and House of Commons.

44. Sous réserve des articles 41 et 42, le Parlement a compétence exclusive pour modifier les dispositions de la Constitution du Canada relatives au pouvoir exécutif fédéral, au Sénat ou à la Chambre des communes.

Modification par le Parlement

Amendments by provincial legislatures

45. Subject to section 41, the legislature of each province may exclusively make laws amending the constitution of the province.

45. Sous réserve de l'article 41, une législature a compétence exclusive pour modifier la constitution de sa province.

Modification par les législatures

Initiation of amendment procedures

46. (1) The procedures for amendment under sections 38, 41, 42 and 43 may be initiated either by the Senate or the House of Commons or by the legislative assembly of a province.

46. (1) L'initiative des procédures de modification visées aux articles 38, 41, 42 et 43 appartient au Sénat, à la Chambre des communes ou à une assemblée législative.

Initiative des procédures

Revocation of authorization

(2) A resolution of assent made for the purposes of this Part may be revoked at any time before the issue of a proclamation authorized by it.

(2) Une résolution d'agrément adoptée dans le cadre de la présente partie peut être révoquée à tout moment avant la date de la proclamation qu'elle autorise.

Possibilité de révocation

Amendments without Senate resolution

47. (1) An amendment to the Constitution of Canada made by proclamation under section 38, 41, 42 or 43 may be made without a resolution of the Senate authorizing the issue of the proclamation if, within one hundred and eighty days after the adoption by the House of Commons of a resolution authorizing its issue, the Senate has not adopted such a resolution and if, at any time after the expiration of that period, the House of Commons again adopts the resolution.

47. (1) Dans les cas visés à l'article 38, 41, 42 ou 43, il peut être passé outre au défaut d'autorisation du Sénat si celui-ci n'a pas adopté de résolution dans un délai de cent quatre-vingts jours suivant l'adoption de celle de la Chambre des communes et si cette dernière, après l'expiration du délai, adopte une nouvelle résolution dans le même sens.

Modification sans résolution du Sénat

Computation of period

(2) Any period when Parliament is prorogued or dissolved shall not be counted in computing the one hundred and eighty day period referred to in subsection (1).

(2) Dans la computation du délai visé au paragraphe (1), ne sont pas comptées les périodes pendant lesquelles le Parlement est prorogé ou dissous.

Computation du délai

Advice to issue proclamation

48. The Queen's Privy Council for Canada shall advise the Governor General to issue a proclamation under this Part forthwith on the adoption of the resolutions required for an amendment made by proclamation under this Part.

48. Le Conseil privé de la Reine pour le Canada demande au gouverneur général de prendre, conformément à la présente partie, une proclamation dès l'adoption des résolutions prévues par cette partie pour une modification par proclamation.

Demande de proclamation

Constitutional conference

49. A constitutional conference composed of the Prime Minister of Canada and the first ministers of the provinces shall be convened by the Prime Minister of Canada within fifteen years after this Part comes into force to review the provisions of this Part.

49. Dans les quinze ans suivant l'entrée en vigueur de la présente partie, le premier ministre du Canada convoque une conférence constitutionnelle réunissant les premiers ministres provinciaux et lui-même, en vue du réexamen des dispositions de cette partie.

Conférence constitutionnelle

PART VI

AMENDMENT TO THE CONSTITUTION ACT, 1867

PARTIE VI

MODIFICATION DE LA LOI CONSTITUTIONNELLE DE 1867

Amendment to *Constitution Act, 1867*

50. The *Constitution Act, 1867* (formerly named the *British North America Act, 1867*) is amended by adding thereto, immediately after section 92 thereof, the following heading and section:

50. La *Loi constitutionnelle de 1867* (antérieurement désignée sous le titre : *Acte de l'Amérique du Nord britannique, 1867*) est modifiée par insertion, après l'article 92, de la rubrique et de l'article suivants :

Modification de la *Loi constitutionnelle de 1867*

"Non-Renewable Natural Resources, Forestry Resources and Electrical Energy

«Ressources naturelles non renouvelables, ressources forestières et énergie électrique

Laws respecting non-renewable natural resources, forestry resources and electrical energy

92A. (1) In each province, the legislature may exclusively make laws in relation to

(*a*) exploration for non-renewable natural resources in the province;

(*b*) development, conservation and management of non-renewable natural resources and forestry resources in the province, including laws in relation to the rate of primary production therefrom; and

(*c*) development, conservation and management of sites and facilities in the province for the generation and production of electrical energy.

92A. (1) La législature de chaque province a compétence exclusive pour légiférer dans les domaines suivants :

a) prospection des ressources naturelles non renouvelables de la province;

b) exploitation, conservation et gestion des ressources naturelles non renouvelables et des ressources forestières de la province, y compris leur rythme de production primaire;

c) aménagement, conservation et gestion des emplacements et des installations de la province destinés à la production d'énergie électrique.

Compétence provinciale

Export from provinces of resources

(2) In each province, the legislature may make laws in relation to the export from the province to another part of Canada of the primary production from non-renewable natural resources and forestry

(2) La législature de chaque province a compétence pour légiférer en ce qui concerne l'exportation, hors de la province, à destination d'une autre partie du Canada, de la production primaire tirée des

Exportation hors des provinces

resources in the province and the production from facilities in the province for the generation of electrical energy, but such laws may not authorize or provide for discrimination in prices or in supplies exported to another part of Canada.

Authority of Parliament

(3) Nothing in subsection (2) derogates from the authority of Parliament to enact laws in relation to the matters referred to in that subsection and, where such a law of Parliament and a law of a province conflict, the law of Parliament prevails to the extent of the conflict.

Taxation of resources

(4) In each province, the legislature may make laws in relation to the raising of money by any mode or system of taxation in respect of

(a) non-renewable natural resources and forestry resources in the province and the primary production therefrom, and

(b) sites and facilities in the province for the generation of electrical energy and the production therefrom,

whether or not such production is exported in whole or in part from the province, but such laws may not authorize or provide for taxation that differentiates between production exported to another part of Canada and production not exported from the province.

"Primary production"

(5) The expression "primary production" has the meaning assigned by the Sixth Schedule.

Existing powers or rights

(6) Nothing in subsections (1) to (5) derogates from any powers or rights that a legislature or government of a province had immediately before the coming into force of this section."

ressources naturelles non renouvelables et des ressources forestières de la province, ainsi que de la production d'énergie électrique de la province, sous réserve de ne pas adopter de lois autorisant ou prévoyant des disparités de prix ou des disparités dans les exportations destinées à une autre partie du Canada.

Pouvoir du Parlement

(3) Le paragraphe (2) ne porte pas atteinte au pouvoir du Parlement de légiférer dans les domaines visés à ce paragraphe, les dispositions d'une loi du Parlement adoptée dans ces domaines l'emportant sur les dispositions incompatibles d'une loi provinciale.

Taxation des ressources

(4) La législature de chaque province a compétence pour prélever des sommes d'argent par tout mode ou système de taxation :

a) des ressources naturelles non renouvelables et des ressources forestières de la province, ainsi que de la production primaire qui en est tirée;

b) des emplacements et des installations de la province destinés à la production d'énergie électrique, ainsi que de cette production même.

Cette compétence peut s'exercer indépendamment du fait que la production en cause soit ou non, en totalité ou en partie, exportée hors de la province, mais les lois adoptées dans ces domaines ne peuvent autoriser ou prévoir une taxation qui établisse une distinction entre la production exportée à destination d'une autre partie du Canada et la production non exportée hors de la province.

«Production primaire»

(5) L'expression «production primaire» a le sens qui lui est donné dans la sixième annexe.

Pouvoirs ou droits existants

(6) Les paragraphes (1) à (5) ne portent pas atteinte aux pouvoirs ou droits détenus par la législature ou le gouvernement d'une province lors de l'entrée en vigueur du présent article.»

Idem
51. The said Act is further amended by adding thereto the following Schedule:

51. Ladite loi est en outre modifiée Idem par adjonction de l'annexe suivante :

"THE SIXTH SCHEDULE

Primary Production from Non-Renewable Natural Resources and Forestry Resources

1. For the purposes of section 92A of this Act,

(*a*) production from a non-renewable natural resource is primary production therefrom if

(i) it is in the form in which it exists upon its recovery or severance from its natural state, or

(ii) it is a product resulting from processing or refining the resource, and is not a manufactured product or a product resulting from refining crude oil, refining upgraded heavy crude oil, refining gases or liquids derived from coal or refining a synthetic equivalent of crude oil; and

(*b*) production from a forestry resource is primary production therefrom if it consists of sawlogs, poles, lumber, wood chips, sawdust or any other primary wood product, or wood pulp, and is not a product manufactured from wood."

«SIXIÈME ANNEXE

Production primaire tirée des ressources naturelles non renouvelables et des ressources forestières

1. Pour l'application de l'article 92A :

a) on entend par production primaire tirée d'une ressource naturelle non renouvelable :

(i) soit le produit qui se présente sous la même forme que lors de son extraction du milieu naturel,

(ii) soit le produit non manufacturé de la transformation, du raffinage ou de l'affinage d'une ressource, à l'exception du produit du raffinage du pétrole brut, du raffinage du pétrole brut lourd amélioré, du raffinage des gaz ou des liquides dérivés du charbon ou du raffinage d'un équivalent synthétique du pétrole brut;

b) on entend par production primaire tirée d'une ressource forestière la production constituée de billots, de poteaux, de bois d'œuvre, de copeaux, de sciure ou d'autre produit primaire du bois, ou de pâte de bois, à l'exception d'un produit manufacturé en bois.»

PART VII

GENERAL

PARTIE VII

DISPOSITIONS GÉNÉRALES

Primacy of Constitution of Canada

52. (1) The Constitution of Canada is the supreme law of Canada, and any law that is inconsistent with the provisions of the Constitution is, to the extent of the inconsistency, of no force or effect.

52. (1) La Constitution du Canada est la loi suprême du Canada; elle rend inopérantes les dispositions incompatibles de toute autre règle de droit.

Primauté de la Constitution du Canada

Constitution of Canada

(2) The Constitution of Canada includes

(*a*) the *Canada Act 1982*, including this Act;

(*b*) the Acts and orders referred to in the schedule; and

(2) La Constitution du Canada comprend :

a) la *Loi de 1982 sur le Canada*, y compris la présente loi;

b) les textes législatifs et les décrets figurant à l'annexe;

Constitution du Canada

(*c*) any amendment to any Act or order referred to in paragraph (*a*) or (*b*).

c) les modifications des textes législatifs et des décrets mentionnés aux alinéas *a*) ou *b*).

Amendments to Constitution of Canada (3) Amendments to the Constitution of Canada shall be made only in accordance with the authority contained in the Constitution of Canada.

(3) La Constitution du Canada ne peut être modifiée que conformément aux pouvoirs conférés par elle. **Modification**

Repeals and new names **53.** (1) The enactments referred to in Column I of the schedule are hereby repealed or amended to the extent indicated in Column II thereof and, unless repealed, shall continue as law in Canada under the names set out in Column III thereof.

53. (1) Les textes législatifs et les décrets énumérés à la colonne I de l'annexe sont abrogés ou modifiés dans la mesure indiquée à la colonne II. Sauf abrogation, ils restent en vigueur en tant que lois du Canada sous les titres mentionnés à la colonne III. **Abrogation et nouveaux titres**

Consequential amendments (2) Every enactment, except the *Canada Act 1982*, that refers to an enactment referred to in the schedule by the name in Column I thereof is hereby amended by substituting for that name the corresponding name in Column III thereof, and any British North America Act not referred to in the schedule may be cited as the *Constitution Act* followed by the year and number, if any, of its enactment.

(2) Tout texte législatif ou réglementaire, sauf la *Loi de 1982 sur le Canada,* qui fait mention d'un texte législatif ou décret figurant à l'annexe par le titre indiqué à la colonne I est modifié par substitution à ce titre du titre correspondant mentionné à la colonne III; tout Acte de l'Amérique du Nord britannique non mentionné à l'annexe peut être cité sous le titre de *Loi constitutionnelle* suivi de l'indication de l'année de son adoption et éventuellement de son numéro. **Modifications corrélatives**

Repeal and consequential amendments **54.** Part IV is repealed on the day that is one year after this Part comes into force and this section may be repealed and this Act renumbered, consequentially upon the repeal of Part IV and this section, by proclamation issued by the Governor General under the Great Seal of Canada.

54. La partie IV est abrogée un an après l'entrée en vigueur de la présente partie et le gouverneur général peut, par proclamation sous le grand sceau du Canada, abroger le présent article et apporter en conséquence de cette double abrogation les aménagements qui s'imposent à la présente loi. **Abrogation et modifications qui en découlent**

French version of Constitution of Canada **55.** A French version of the portions of the Constitution of Canada referred to in the schedule shall be prepared by the Minister of Justice of Canada as expeditiously as possible and, when any portion thereof sufficient to warrant action being taken has been so prepared, it shall be put forward for enactment by proclamation issued by the Governor General under the Great Seal of Canada pursuant to the procedure then applicable to an amendment of the same provisions of the Constitution of Canada.

55. Le ministre de la Justice du Canada est chargé de rédiger, dans les meilleurs délais, la version française des parties de la Constitution du Canada qui figurent à l'annexe; toute partie suffisamment importante est, dès qu'elle est prête, déposée pour adoption par proclamation du gouverneur général sous le grand sceau du Canada, conformément à la procédure applicable à l'époque à la modification des dispositions constitutionnelles qu'elle contient. **Version française de certains textes constitutionnels**

English and French versions of certain constitutional texts

56. Where any portion of the Constitution of Canada has been or is enacted in English and French or where a French version of any portion of the Constitution is enacted pursuant to section 55, the English and French versions of that portion of the Constitution are equally authoritative.

56. Les versions française et anglaise des parties de la Constitution du Canada adoptées dans ces deux langues ont également force de loi. En outre, ont également force de loi, dès l'adoption, dans le cadre de l'article 55, d'une partie de la version française de la Constitution, cette partie et la version anglaise correspondante.

Versions française et anglaise de certains textes constitutionnels

English and French versions of this Act

57. The English and French versions of this Act are equally authoritative.

57. Les versions française et anglaise de la présente loi ont également force de loi.

Versions française et anglaise de la présente loi

Commencement

58. Subject to section 59, this Act shall come into force on a day to be fixed by proclamation issued by the Queen or the Governor General under the Great Seal of Canada.

58. Sous réserve de l'article 59, la présente loi entre en vigueur à la date fixée par proclamation de la Reine ou du gouverneur général sous le grand sceau du Canada.

Entrée en vigueur

Commencement of paragraph 23(1)(*a*) in respect of Quebec

59. (1) Paragraph 23(1)(*a*) shall come into force in respect of Quebec on a day to be fixed by proclamation issued by the Queen or the Governor General under the Great Seal of Canada.

59. (1) L'alinéa 23(1)*a*) entre en vigueur pour le Québec à la date fixée par proclamation de la Reine ou du gouverneur général sous le grand sceau du Canada.

Entrée en vigueur de l'alinéa 23(1)*a*) pour le Québec

Authorization of Quebec

(2) A proclamation under subsection (1) shall be issued only where authorized by the legislative assembly or government of Quebec.

(2) La proclamation visée au paragraphe (1) ne peut être prise qu'après autorisation de l'assemblée législative ou du gouvernement du Québec.

Autorisation du Québec

Repeal of this section

(3) This section may be repealed on the day paragraph 23(1)(*a*) comes into force in respect of Quebec and this Act amended and renumbered, consequentially upon the repeal of this section, by proclamation issued by the Queen or the Governor General under the Great Seal of Canada.

(3) Le présent article peut être abrogé à la date d'entrée en vigueur de l'alinéa 23(1)*a*) pour le Québec, et la présente loi faire l'objet, dès cette abrogation, des modifications et changements de numérotation qui en découlent, par proclamation de la Reine ou du gouverneur général sous le grand sceau du Canada.

Abrogation du présent article

Short title and citations

60. This Act may be cited as the *Constitution Act, 1982*, and the Constitution Acts 1867 to 1975 (No. 2) and this Act may be cited together as the *Constitution Acts, 1867 to 1982*.

60. Titre abrégé de la présente annexe : *Loi constitutionnelle de 1982*; titre commun des lois constitutionnelles de 1867 à 1975 (n° 2) et de la présente loi : *Lois constitutionnelles de 1867 à 1982*.

Titres

SCHEDULE

to the

CONSTITUTION ACT, 1982

MODERNIZATION OF THE CONSTITUTION

Item	Column I Act Affected	Column II Amendment	Column III New Name
1.	British North America Act, 1867, 30-31 Vict., c. 3 (U.K.)	(1) Section 1 is repealed and the following substituted therefor: "1. This Act may be cited as the *Constitution Act, 1867.*" (2) Section 20 is repealed. (3) Class 1 of section 91 is repealed. (4) Class 1 of section 92 is repealed.	Constitution Act, 1867
2.	An Act to amend and continue the Act 32-33 Victoria chapter 3; and to establish and provide for the Government of the Province of Manitoba, 1870, 33 Vict., c. 3 (Can.)	(1) The long title is repealed and the following substituted therefor: "*Manitoba Act, 1870.*" (2) Section 20 is repealed.	Manitoba Act, 1870
3.	Order of Her Majesty in Council admitting Rupert's Land and the North-Western Territory into the union, dated the 23rd day of June, 1870		Rupert's Land and North-Western Territory Order
4.	Order of Her Majesty in Council admitting British Columbia into the Union, dated the 16th day of May, 1871		British Columbia Terms of Union
5.	British North America Act, 1871, 34-35 Vict., c. 28 (U.K.)	Section 1 is repealed and the following substituted therefor: "1. This Act may be cited as the *Constitution Act, 1871.*"	Constitution Act, 1871
6.	Order of Her Majesty in Council admitting Prince Edward Island into the Union, dated the 26th day of June, 1873		Prince Edward Island Terms of Union
7.	Parliament of Canada Act, 1875, 38-39 Vict., c. 38 (U.K.)		Parliament of Canada Act, 1875
8.	Order of Her Majesty in Council admitting all British possessions and Territories in North America and islands adjacent thereto into the Union, dated the 31st day of July, 1880		Adjacent Territories Order

ANNEXE

LOI CONSTITUTIONNELLE DE 1982

ACTUALISATION DE LA CONSTITUTION

Colonne I Loi visée	Colonne II Modification	Colonne III Nouveau titre
1. Acte de l'Amérique du Nord britannique, 1867, 30-31 Vict., c. 3 (R.-U.)	(1) L'article 1 est abrogé et remplacé par ce qui suit : «1. Titre abrégé : *Loi constitutionnelle de 1867.*» (2) L'article 20 est abrogé. (3) La catégorie 1 de l'article 91 est abrogée. (4) La catégorie 1 de l'article 92 est abrogée.	Loi constitutionnelle de 1867
2. Acte pour amender et continuer l'acte trente-deux et trente-trois Victoria, chapitre trois, et pour établir et constituer le gouvernement de la province de Manitoba, 1870, 33 Vict., c. 3 (Canada)	(1) Le titre complet est abrogé et remplacé par ce qui suit : *«Loi de 1870 sur le Manitoba.»* (2) L'article 20 est abrogé.	Loi de 1870 sur le Manitoba
3. Arrêté en conseil de Sa Majesté admettant la Terre de Rupert et le Territoire du Nord-Ouest, en date du 23 juin 1870		Décret en conseil sur la terre de Rupert et le territoire du Nord-Ouest
4. Arrêté en conseil de Sa Majesté admettant la Colombie-Britannique, en date du 16 mai 1871		Conditions de l'adhésion de la Colombie-Britannique
5. Acte de l'Amérique du Nord britannique, 1871, 34-35 Vict., c. 28 (R.-U.)	L'article 1 est abrogé et remplacé par ce qui suit : «1. Titre abrégé : *Loi constitutionnelle de 1871.*»	Loi constitutionnelle de 1871
6. Arrêté en conseil de Sa Majesté admettant l'Île-du-Prince-Édouard, en date du 26 juin 1873		Conditions de l'adhésion de l'Île-du-Prince-Édouard
7. Acte du Parlement du Canada, 1875, 38-39 Vict., c. 38 (R.-U.)		Loi de 1875 sur le Parlement du Canada
8. Arrêté en conseil de Sa Majesté admettant dans l'Union tous les territoires et possessions britanniques dans l'Amérique du Nord, et les îles adjacentes à ces territoires et possessions, en date du 31 juillet 1880		Décret en conseil sur les territoires adjacents

SCHEDULE

to the

CONSTITUTION ACT, 1982—*Continued*

Item	Column I Act Affected	Column II Amendment	Column III New Name
9.	British North America Act, 1886, 49-50 Vict., c. 35 (U.K.)	Section 3 is repealed and the following substituted therefor: "3. This Act may be cited as the *Constitution Act, 1886.*"	Constitution Act, 1886
10.	Canada (Ontario Boundary) Act, 1889, 52-53 Vict., c. 28 (U.K.)		Canada (Ontario Boundary) Act, 1889
11.	Canadian Speaker (Appointment of Deputy) Act, 1895, 2nd Sess., 59 Vict., c. 3 (U.K.)	The Act is repealed.	
12.	The Alberta Act, 1905, 4-5 Edw. VII, c. 3 (Can.)		Alberta Act
13.	The Saskatchewan Act, 1905, 4-5 Edw. VII, c. 42 (Can.)		Saskatchewan Act
14.	British North America Act, 1907, 7 Edw. VII, c. 11 (U.K.)	Section 2 is repealed and the following substituted therefor: "2. This Act may be cited as the *Constitution Act, 1907.*"	Constitution Act, 1907
15.	British North America Act, 1915, 5-6 Geo. V, c. 45 (U.K.)	Section 3 is repealed and the following substituted therefor: "3. This Act may be cited as the *Constitution Act, 1915.*"	Constitution Act, 1915
16.	British North America Act, 1930, 20-21 Geo. V, c. 26 (U.K.)	Section 3 is repealed and the following substituted therefor: "3. This Act may be cited as the *Constitution Act, 1930.*"	Constitution Act, 1930
17.	Statute of Westminster, 1931, 22 Geo. V, c. 4 (U.K.)	In so far as they apply to Canada, (*a*) section 4 is repealed; and (*b*) subsection 7(1) is repealed.	Statute of Westminster, 1931

ANNEXE (*suite*)

LOI CONSTITUTIONNELLE DE 1982

Colonne I Loi visée	Colonne II Modification	Colonne III Nouveau titre
9. Acte de l'Amérique du Nord britannique, 1886, 49-50 Vict., c. 35 (R.-U.)	L'article 3 est abrogé et remplacé par ce qui suit : «3. Titre abrégé : *Loi constitutionnelle de 1886.*»	Loi constitutionnelle de 1886
10. Acte du Canada (limites d'Ontario) 1889, 52-53 Vict., c. 28 (R.-U.)		Loi de 1889 sur le Canada (frontières de l'Ontario)
11. Acte concernant l'Orateur canadien (nomination d'un suppléant) 1895, 2ᵉ session, 59 Vict., c. 3 (R.-U.)	La loi est abrogée.	
12. Acte de l'Alberta, 1905, 4-5 Ed. VII, c. 3 (Canada)		Loi sur l'Alberta
13. Acte de la Saskatchewan, 1905, 4-5 Ed. VII, c. 42 (Canada)		Loi sur la Saskatchewan
14. Acte de l'Amérique du Nord britannique, 1907, 7 Ed. VII, c. 11 (R.-U.)	L'article 2 est abrogé et remplacé par ce qui suit : «2. Titre abrégé : *Loi constitutionnelle de 1907.*»	Loi constitutionnelle de 1907
15. Acte de l'Amérique du Nord britannique, 1915, 5-6 Geo. V, c. 45 (R.-U.)	L'article 3 est abrogé et remplacé par ce qui suit : «3. Titre abrégé : *Loi constitutionnelle de 1915.*»	Loi constitutionnelle de 1915
16. Acte de l'Amérique du Nord britannique, 1930, 20-21 Geo. V, c. 26 (R.-U.)	L'article 3 est abrogé et remplacé par ce qui suit : «3. Titre abrégé : *Loi constitutionnelle de 1930.*»	Loi constitutionnelle de 1930
Statut de Westminster, 1931, 22 Geo. V, c. 4 (R.-U.)	Dans la mesure où ils s'appliquent au Canada : *a*) l'article 4 est abrogé; *b*) le paragraphe 7(1) est abrogé.	Statut de Westminster de 1931

SCHEDULE

to the

CONSTITUTION ACT, 1982—*Continued*

Item	Column I Act Affected	Column II Amendment	Column III New Name
18.	British North America Act, 1940, 3-4 Geo. VI, c. 36 (U.K.)	Section 2 is repealed and the following substituted therefor: "2. This Act may be cited as the *Constitution Act, 1940*."	Constitution Act, 1940
19.	British North America Act, 1943, 6-7 Geo. VI, c. 30 (U.K.)	The Act is repealed.	
20.	British North America Act, 1946, 9-10 Geo. VI, c. 63 (U.K.)	The Act is repealed.	
21.	British North America Act, 1949, 12-13 Geo. VI, c. 22 (U.K.)	Section 3 is repealed and the following substituted therefor: "3. This Act may be cited as the *Newfoundland Act*."	Newfoundland Act
22.	British North America (No. 2) Act, 1949, 13 Geo. VI, c. 81 (U.K.)	The Act is repealed.	
23.	British North America Act, 1951, 14-15 Geo. VI, c. 32 (U.K.)	The Act is repealed.	
24.	British North America Act, 1952, 1 Eliz. II, c. 15 (Can.)	The Act is repealed.	
25.	British North America Act, 1960, 9 Eliz. II, c. 2 (U.K.)	Section 2 is repealed and the following substituted therefor: "2. This Act may be cited as the *Constitution Act, 1960*."	Constitution Act, 1960
26.	British North America Act, 1964, 12-13 Eliz. II, c. 73 (U.K.)	Section 2 is repealed and the following substituted therefor: "2. This Act may be cited as the *Constitution Act, 1964*."	Constitution Act, 1964

ANNEXE (*suite*)

LOI CONSTITUTIONNELLE DE 1982

Colonne I Loi visée	Colonne II Modification	Colonne III Nouveau titre
18. Acte de l'Amérique du Nord britannique, 1940, 3-4 Geo. VI, c. 36 (R.-U.)	L'article 2 est abrogé et remplacé par ce qui suit : «2. Titre abrégé : *Loi constitutionnelle de 1940*.»	Loi constitutionnelle de 1940
19. Acte de l'Amérique du Nord britannique, 1943, 6-7 Geo. VI, c. 30 (R.-U.)	La loi est abrogée.	
20. Acte de l'Amérique du Nord britannique, 1946, 9-10 Geo. VI, c. 63 (R.-U.)	La loi est abrogée.	
21. Acte de l'Amérique du Nord britannique, 1949, 12-13 Geo. VI, c. 22 (R.-U.)	L'article 3 est abrogé et remplacé par ce qui suit : «3. Titre abrégé : *Loi sur Terre-Neuve*.»	Loi sur Terre-Neuve
22. Acte de l'Amérique du Nord britannique (N° 2), 1949, 13 Geo. VI, c. 81 (R.-U.)	La loi est abrogée.	
23. Acte de l'Amérique du Nord britannique, 1951, 14-15 Geo. VI, c. 32 (R.-U.)	La loi est abrogée.	
24. Acte de l'Amérique du Nord britannique, 1952, 1 Eliz. II, c. 15 (Canada)	La loi est abrogée.	
25. Acte de l'Amérique du Nord britannique, 1960, 9 Eliz. II, c. 2 (R.-U.)	L'article 2 est abrogé et remplacé par ce qui suit : «2. Titre abrégé : *Loi constitutionnelle de 1960*.»	Loi constitutionnelle de 1960
26. Acte de l'Amérique du Nord britannique, 1964, 12-13 Eliz. II, c. 73 (R.-U.)	L'article 2 est abrogé et remplacé par ce qui suit : «2. Titre abrégé : *Loi constitutionnelle de 1964*.»	Loi constitutionnelle de 1964

SCHEDULE

to the

CONSTITUTION ACT, 1982— *Concluded*

Item	Column I Act Affected	Column II Amendment	Column III New Name
27.	British North America Act, 1965, 14 Eliz. II, c. 4, Part I (Can.)	Section 2 is repealed and the following substituted therefor: "2. This Part may be cited as the *Constitution Act, 1965*."	Constitution Act, 1965
28.	British North America Act, 1974, 23 Eliz. II, c. 13, Part I (Can.)	Section 3, as amended by 25-26 Eliz. II, c. 28, s. 38(1) (Can.), is repealed and the following substituted therefor: "3. This Part may be cited as the *Constitution Act, 1974*."	Constitution Act, 1974
29.	British North America Act, 1975, 23-24 Eliz. II, c. 28, Part I (Can.)	Section 3, as amended by 25-26 Eliz. II, c. 28, s. 31 (Can.), is repealed and the following substituted therefor: "3. This Part may be cited as the *Constitution Act (No. 1), 1975*."	Constitution Act (No. 1), 1975
30.	British North America Act (No. 2), 1975, 23-24 Eliz. II, c. 53 (Can.)	Section 3 is repealed and the following substituted therefor: "3. This Act may be cited as the *Constitution Act (No. 2), 1975*."	Constitution Act (No. 2), 1975

ANNEXE *(fin)*

LOI CONSTITUTIONNELLE DE 1982

Colonne I Loi visée	Colonne II Modification	Colonne III Nouveau titre
27. Acte de l'Amérique du Nord britannique, 1965, 14 Eliz. II, c. 4, Partie I (Canada)	L'article 2 est abrogé et remplacé par ce qui suit : «2. Titre abrégé de la présente partie : *Loi constitutionnelle de 1965.*»	Loi constitutionnelle de 1965
28. Acte de l'Amérique du Nord britannique, 1974, 23 Eliz. II, c. 13, Partie I (Canada)	L'article 3, modifié par le paragraphe 38(1) de la loi 25-26 Elizabeth II, c. 28 (Canada), est abrogé et remplacé par ce qui suit : «3. Titre abrégé de la présente partie : *Loi constitutionnelle de 1974.*»	Loi constitutionnelle de 1974
29. Acte de l'Amérique du Nord britannique, 1975, 23-24 Eliz. II, c. 28, Partie I (Canada)	L'article 3, modifié par l'article 31 de la loi 25-26 Elizabeth II, c. 28 (Canada), est abrogé et remplacé par ce qui suit : «3. Titre abrégé de la présente partie : *Loi constitutionnelle n° 1 de 1975.*»	Loi constitutionnelle n° 1 de 1975
30. Acte de l'Amérique du Nord britannique n° 2, 1975, 23-24 Eliz. II, c. 53 (Canada)	L'article 3 est abrogé et remplacé par ce qui suit : «3. Titre abrégé : *Loi constitutionnelle n° 2 de 1975.*»	Loi constitutionnelle n° 2 de 1975

QUEEN'S PRINTER FOR CANADA © IMPRIMEUR DE LA REINE POUR LE CANADA
OTTAWA, 1982.

The Members' of the Institute

Dr. Marie-Andrée Bertrand
School of Criminology, University of
Montreal
Dr. Roger Blais, P.Eng.
Director, Centre d'innovation industrielle
(Montréal)
Dr. D. Owen Carrigan
Representing the Canada Council, Halifax
George Cooper
McInnes, Cooper & Robertson, Halifax
James S. Cowan, Q.C.
Stewart, MacKeen & Covert, Halifax
Marc Eliesen
Deputy Minister, Manitoba Energy &
Mines, Winnipeg
Emery Fanjoy
Secretary, Council of Maritime Premiers,
Halifax
Allan Gillmore
Executive Director, Association of
Universities and Colleges of Canada,
Ottawa
Dr. Donald Glendenning
President, Holland College, Charlottetown
Richard W. Johnston
President, Spencer Stuart & Associates,
Toronto
Dr. Leon Katz, O.C.
Department of Physics, University of
Saskatchewan, Saskatoon
Tom Kierans
President, McLeod, Young, Weir Ltd.,
Toronto
Dr. Leo Kristjanson
President, University of Saskatchewan,
Saskatoon
R. Terrence Mactaggart
President, Niagara Institute,
Niagara-on-the-Lake
Dr. John S. McCallum
Faculty of Administrative Studies,
University of Manitoba, Winnipeg
Professor Claude Morin
École nationale d'administration publique,
Montreal
Professor William A.W. Neilson
Faculty of Law, University of Victoria
Roderick C. Nolan, P. Eng.
Vice-President & General Manager, Neill
& Gunter Ltd., Fredericton
Robert Olivero
President, Management House Ltd.,
St. John's
Maureen O'Neil
Co-ordinator, Status of Women Canada,
Ottawa
Garnet T. Page
Chairman, Coal Research Management
Committee of Alberta, Calgary
Professor Gilles Paquet
Dean, Faculty of Management, University
of Ottawa
Dr. K. George Pedersen
President, Simon Fraser University,
Burnaby

Professor Marilyn L. Pilkington
Osgoode Hall Law School, Downsview
Dr. David W. Slater
Chairman, Economic Council of Canada,
Ottawa
Dr. Stuart Smith
President, Science Council of Canada,
Ottawa
Eldon D. Thompson
President, Telesat Canada, Vanier
Professor Marc-Adélard Tremblay
Department of Anthropology, University
of Laval, Quebec
Dr. Israel Unger
Department of Chemistry, University of
New Brunswick, Fredericton
Philip Vineberg, O.C., Q.C.
Phillips, Vineberg, and Associates,
Montreal
Dr. Norman Wagner
President, University of Calgary
Ida Wasacase, C.M.
Director, Saskatchewan Indian Federated
College, University of Regina
Dr. R. Sherman Weaver
Executive Director, Alberta
Environmental Research Centre,
Vegreville
Professor Paul Weiler
Mackenzie King Professor,
Harvard University Law School,
Cambridge
Dr. John Tuzo Wilson, C.C., O.B.E.
Director General, Ontario Science Centre,
Don Mills
Right Rev. Dr. Lois M. Wilson
United Church of Canada, Kingston

Institute Management

Gordon Robertson	President
Louis Vagianos	Executive Director
John M. Curtis	Director, International Economics Program
Gérald d'Amboise	Director, Small and Medium-sized Business Program
Barbara L. Hodgins	Director, Western Resources Program
Barry Lesser	Director, Regional Employment Opportunities Program
Zavis P. Zeman	Director, Technology and Society Program
W.T. Stanbury	Senior Program Adviser
Donald Wilson	Director, Conferences and Seminars Program
Gail Grant	Associate Director, Conferences and Seminars Program
Dana Phillip Doiron	Director, Communications Services
Ann C. McCoomb	Associate Director, Communications Services
Tom Kent	Editor, *Policy Options Politiques*

The Institute for Research on Public Policy

Publications Available*
January 1983

Books

Leroy O. Stone & Claude Marceau	*Canadian Population Trends and Public Policy Through the 1980s.* 1977 $4.00
Raymond Breton	*The Canadian Condition: A Guide to Research in Public Policy.* 1977 $2.95
Raymond Breton	*Une orientation de la recherche politique dans le contexte canadien.* 1977 $2.95
J.W. Rowley & W.T. Stanbury, eds.	*Competition Policy in Canada: Stage II, Bill C-13.* 1978 $12.95
C.F. Smart & W.T. Stanbury, eds.	*Studies on Crisis Management.* 1978 $9.95
W.T. Stanbury, ed.	*Studies on Regulation in Canada.* 1978 $9.95
Michael Hudson	*Canada in the New Monetary Order: Borrow? Devalue? Restructure!* 1978 $6.95
David K. Foot, ed.	*Public Employment and Compensation in Canada: Myths and Realities.* 1978 $10.95
W.E. Cundiff & Mado Reid, eds.	*Issues in Canadian/U.S. Transborder Computer Data Flows.* 1979 $6.50
David K. Foot, ed.	*Public Employment in Canada: Statistical Series.* 1979 $15.00
Meyer W. Bucovetsky, ed.	*Studies in Public Employment and Compensation in Canada.* 1979 $14.95
Richard French & André Béliveau	*The RCMP and the Management of National Security.* 1979 $6.95
Richard French & André Béliveau	*La GRC et la gestion de la sécurité nationale.* 1979 $6.95

---

* Order Address: The Institute for Research on Public Policy
                   P.O. Box 9300, Station A
                   TORONTO, Ontario
                   M5W 2C7

Leroy O. Stone &
Michael J. MacLean

Future Income Prospects for Canada's Senior Citizens. 1979 $7.95

Richard M. Bird

The Growth of Public Employment in Canada. 1979 $12.95

G. Bruce Doern &
Allan M. Maslove, eds.

The Public Evaluation of Government Spending. 1979 $10.95

Richard Price, ed.

The Spirit of the Alberta Indian Treaties. 1979 $8.95

Richard J. Schultz

Federalism and the Regulatory Process. 1979 $1.50

Richard J. Schultz

Le fédéralisme et le processus de réglementation. 1979 $1.50

Lionel D. Feldman &
Katherine A. Graham

Bargaining for Cities. Municipalities and Intergovernmental Relations: An Assessment. 1979 $10.95

Elliot J. Feldman &
Neil Nevitte, eds.

The Future of North America: Canada, the United States, and Quebec Nationalism. 1979 $7.95

Maximo Halty-Carrere

Technological Development Strategies for Developing Countries: A Review for Policy Makers. 1979 $12.95

G.B. Reschenthaler

Occupational Health and Safety in Canada: The Economics and Three Case Studies. 1979 $5.00

David R. Protheroe

Imports and Politics: Trade Decision Making in Canada, 1968–1979. 1980 $8.95

G. Bruce Doern

Government Intervention in the Canadian Nuclear Industry. 1980 $8.95

G. Bruce Doern &
Robert W. Morrison, eds.

Canadian Nuclear Policies. 1980 $14.95

Yoshi Tsurumi with
Rebecca R. Tsurumi

Sogoshosha: Engines of Export-Based Growth. 1980 $8.95

Allan M. Maslove &
Gene Swimmer

Wage Controls in Canada, 1975–78: A Study of Public Decision Making. 1980 $11.95

T. Gregory Kane

Consumers and the Regulators: Intervention in the Federal Regulatory Process. 1980 $10.95

Albert Breton &
Anthony Scott

The Design of Federations. 1980 $6.95

A.R. Bailey & D.G. Hull	*The Way Out: A More Revenue-Dependent Public Sector and How It Might Revitalize the Process of Governing.* 1980 $6.95
Réjean Lachapelle & Jacques Henripin	*La situation démolinguistique au Canada : évolution passée et prospective.* 1980 $24.95
Raymond Breton, Jeffrey G. Reitz & Victor F. Valentine	*Cultural Boundaries and the Cohesion of Canada.* 1980 $18.95
David R. Harvey	*Christmas Turkey or Prairie Vulture? An Economic Analysis of the Crow's Nest Pass Grain Rates.* 1980 $10.95
Richard M. Bird	*Taxing Corporations.* 1980 $6.95
Albert Breton & Raymond Breton	*Why Disunity? An Analysis of Linguistic and Regional Cleavages in Canada.* 1980 $6.95
Leroy O. Stone & Susan Fletcher	*A Profile of Canada's Older Population.* 1980 $7.95
Peter N. Nemetz, ed.	*Resource Policy: International Perspectives.* 1980 $18.95
Keith A.J. Hay, ed.	*Canadian Perspectives on Economic Relations With Japan.* 1980 $18.95
Raymond Breton & Gail Grant	*La langue de travail au Québec : synthèse de la recherche sur la rencontre de deux langues.* 1981 $10.95
Diane Vanasse	*L'évolution de la population scolaire du Québec.* 1981 $12.95
Raymond Breton, Jeffrey G. Reitz & Victor F. Valentine	*Les frontières culturelles et la cohésion du Canada.* 1981 $18.95
H.V. Kroeker, ed.	*Sovereign People or Sovereign Governments.* 1981 $12.95
Peter Aucoin, ed.	*The Politics and Management of Restraint in Government.* 1981 $17.95
David M. Cameron, ed.	*Regionalism and Supranationalism: Challenges and Alternatives to the Nation-State in Canada and Europe.* 1981 $9.95
Heather Menzies	*Women and the Chip: Case Studies of the Effects of Informatics on Employment in Canada.* 1981 $6.95

Nicole S. Morgan	*Nowhere to Go? Possible Consequences of the Demographic Imbalance in Decision-Making Groups of the Federal Public Service.* 1981 $8.95
Nicole S. Morgan	*Où aller? Les conséquences prévisibles des déséquilibres démographiques chez les groupes de décision de la fonction publique fédérale.* 1981 $8.95
Peter N. Nemetz, ed.	*Energy Crisis: Policy Response.* 1981 $10.95
Allan Tupper & G. Bruce Doern, eds.	*Public Corporations and Public Policy in Canada.* 1981 $16.95
James Gillies	*Where Business Fails.* 1981 $9.95
Réjean Lachapelle & Jacques Henripin	*The Demolinguistic Situation in Canada: Past Trends and Future Prospects.* 1982 $24.95
Ian McAllister	*Regional Development and the European Community: A Canadian Perspective.* 1982 $13.95
Robert J. Buchan, C. Christopher Johnston, T. Gregory Kane, Barry Lesser, Richard J. Schultz & W.T. Stanbury	*Telecommunications Regulation and the Constitution.* 1982 $18.95
W.T. Stanbury & Fred Thompson	*Regulatory Reform in Canada.* 1982 $7.95
Rodney de C. Grey	*United States Trade Policy Legislation: A Canadian View.* 1982 $7.95
John Quinn & Philip Slayton, eds.	*Non-Tariff Barriers After the Tokyo Round.* 1982 $17.95
R. Brian Woodrow & Kenneth B. Woodside, eds.	*The Introduction of Pay-TV in Canada: Issues and Implications.* 1982 $14.95
Stanley M. Beck & Ivan Bernier, eds.	*Canada and the New Constitution: The Unfinished Agenda.* 2 vols. 1983 $10.95

Occasional Papers

W.E. Cundiff (No. 1)	*Nodule Shock? Seabed Mining and the Future of the Canadian Nickel Industry.* 1978 $3.00
Robert A. Russel (No. 3)	*The Electronic Briefcase: The Office of the Future.* 1978 $3.00

C.C. Gotlieb (No. 4)	*Computers in the Home: What They Can Do for Us—And to Us.* 1978 $3.00
Raymond Breton & Gail Grant Akian (No. 5)	*Urban Institutions and People of Indian Ancestry: Suggestions for Research.* 1979 $3.00
K.A.J. Hay (No. 6)	*Friends or Acquaintances? Canada and Japan's Other Trading Partners in the Early 1980s.* 1979 $3.00
Thomas H. Atkinson (No. 7)	*Trends in Life Satisfaction Among Canadians, 1968 –1977.* 1979 $3.00
Fred Thompson & W.T. Stanbury (No. 9)	*The Political Economy of Interest Groups in the Legislative Process in Canada.* 1979 $3.00
Pierre Sormany (No. 11)	*Les micro-esclaves : vers une bio-industrie canadienne.* 1979 $3.00
Zavis P. Zeman & David Hoffman, eds. (No. 13)	*The Dynamics of the Technological Leadership of the World.* 1980 $3.00
Russell Wilkins (No. 13*a*)	*Health Status in Canada, 1926 –1976.* 1980 $3.00
Russell Wilkins (No. 13*b*)	*L'état de santé au Canada, 1926 –1976.* 1980 $3.00
P. Pergler (No. 14)	*The Automated Citizen: Social and Political Impact of Interactive Broadcasting.* 1980 $4.95
Donald G. Cartwright (No. 16)	*Official Language Populations in Canada: Patterns and Contacts.* 1980 $4.95

Reports

Dhiru Patel	*Dealing With Interracial Conflict: Policy Alternatives.* 1980 $5.95
Robert A. Russel	*Office Automation: Key to the Information Society.* 1981 $3.00
Irving Brecher	*Canada's Competition Policy Revisited: Some New Thoughts on an Old Story.* 1982 $3.00
Donald J. Daly	*Canada in an Uncertain World Economic Environment.* 1982 $3.00

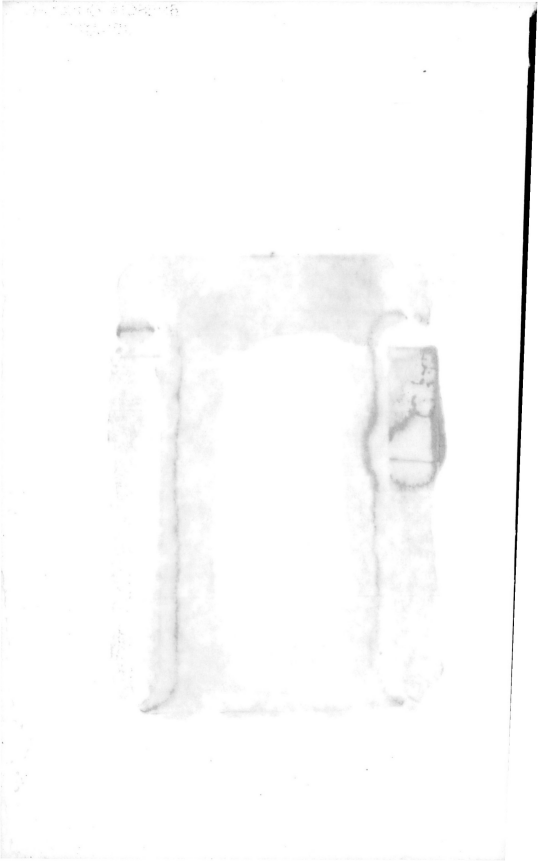